CLIMBING SELF-RESCUE

Essential Skills, Technical Tips & Improvised Solutions

CLIMBING SELF-RESCUE

Essential Skills, Technical Tips & Improvised Solutions

Ian Nicholson

To editor Mary Metz, honoring her 37 years of service at Mountaineers Books

MOUNTAINEERS BOOKS is dedicated to the exploration, preservation, and enjoyment of outdoor and wilderness areas.

1001 SW Klickitat Way, Suite 201, Seattle, WA 98134
800-553-4453, www.mountaineersbooks.org

Printed in China
Distributed in the United Kingdom by Cordee, www.cordee.co.uk
First edition, 2024

Design and layout: McKenzie Long
Illustrations: John McMullen unless credited otherwise
All photographs by the author unless credited otherwise
Cover photograph: *Tino Villanueva practices a counter-balance rappel on Mount Erie in Anacortes, Washington.*
Back cover photograph: *Climber on* Crossfire *in Smith Rock State Park, Oregon* (Photo by Graham Zimmerman)
Frontispiece: *Ian Nicholson climbing* Ragged Edge *on Vesper Creek in Washington's Glacier Peak Wilderness* (Photo by Jonathan Spitzer)

Library of Congress Cataloging-in-Publication data is on file for this title at https://lccn.loc.gov/2023025241. A record for the ebook edition is available at https://lccn.loc.gov/2023025242.

Mountaineers Books titles may be purchased for corporate, educational, or other promotional sales, and our authors are available for a wide range of events. For information on special discounts or booking an author, contact our customer service at 800-553-4453 or mbooks@mountaineersbooks.org.

Printed on FSC®-certified materials

ISBN (paperback): 978-1-68051-620-3
ISBN (ebook): 978-1-68051-621-0

An independent nonprofit publisher since 1960

Contents

Opposite: *Kate Rutherford (leading) and Madaleine Sorkin (belaying) while free climbing El Capitan in Yosemite National Park, California* (Photo by Mikey Schaefer)

Introduction: Getting Started with Self-Rescue

If you climb technical mountains or multi-pitch rock routes, odds are that you've already had to deal with something unexpected—a stuck or damaged rope, a dropped belay device, a rappel that was too long for your rope, or some other unforeseen circumstance. If you have been climbing a long time (or have had an unlucky day), you might have dealt with a more serious situation. Maybe it was something life-threatening or something that could have become life-threatening if you hadn't been able to solve or deal with certain problems.

Every climber will eventually have to deal with an unforeseen issue or circumstance, and the more familiar you are with the various techniques that can be adapted to a given set of circumstances, the better your chances of handling the situation deftly. Sure, you need the strength and technical skill to ascend the route itself, but equally important to successfully completing the climb—to keeping your day going safely and smoothly—is having the skills to deal with any issues that may arise.

Along the near-infinite spectrum of problems that you could find yourself facing lies the goal of this book: to provide a wide range of repeatable techniques, tips, and tricks to help climbers get out of jams so that they avoid *the need to be rescued*, as well as the skills to execute a technical rescue should the situation arise. The key is *repeatable*—both in the techniques themselves and in the ability to apply them successfully to a wide range of potential problems. To a lot of people, the number of possible scenarios—and techniques with which to deal with them—seems limitless. While that might not be totally true, the number is certainly overwhelming. This book provides a core set of repeatable techniques that work well in a wide range of situations.

The technical systems described in this book follow a pattern, providing the means to solve an array of common problems that climbers and mountaineers encounter. Each tool and technique can be applied in a number of ways to assist in solving this wide range of problems. Generally considered to be "best practices" for improvised rescue, these systems are also the most current and the most widely adopted. As with many things in life, though, it takes practice to build proficiency. To that end, chapter 12 describes 10 situations to stretch the cognitive side of rescue by

Opposite: *Graham Zimmerman leads the third pitch of* Davis-Holland/Lovin' Arms *on the Upper Town Wall, Index, Washington.*

helping you to think about what you would do and how you would solve the problem, and chapter 13 describes the techniques that are most useful to practice.

THIS IS NOT AN INTRODUCTORY CLIMBING MANUAL

This book is written for people who already have a basic working knowledge of climbing techniques for multipitch routes—it is not an introductory climbing manual. It assumes that the reader is familiar with common belay, rappel, and anchor-construction techniques and does not discuss the placement of rock protection. It also does not cover traveling on glaciers and crevasse rescue, a broad topic beyond the scope of this book.

This is also not a first-aid manual. While many of the circumstances described here are likely to require both technical rope skills and first-aid skills, medical training is an equally, if not more, involved set of skills beyond the scope of this book. If you are interested in learning more about the medical side, consider taking a wilderness-oriented first-aid course or an 80-hour wilderness first responder course. Also see Suggested Reading at the back of this book for some recommended first-aid books.

This book also assumes that readers already have basic outdoor skills and know the most common basic items to bring on a multipitch rock climb or technical alpine climb. The goal of this book is to teach climbers how to perform rescues and deal with potentially hazardous situations with the gear they are already carrying on the climb; this knowledge, which is much more lightweight than the lightest gear, will increase a party's margin of safety, their confidence, and their self-sufficiency.

A few chapters include descriptions of gear to be used in specific rescue techniques, but the items needed for 90 percent of rescues will already be on most climbers' harnesses. The section on gear considerations comes near the end of the book (see "What Should You Bring?" in chapter 13) because, by that point, readers will know more about how rescue systems work and will understand which items could be most useful for them.

DECISION MAKING

Dealing with unforeseen circumstances and keeping a bad situation from becoming worse largely come down to decision making. Most people are aware that the majority of accidents are the result of an accumulation of poor decisions rather than just one bad decision. Sure, in some incidents people were simply in the wrong place at the wrong time, but it's worth noting that these incidents are in the minority, not the majority.

While it sounds basic, attempting to make the best possible decision rather than just the easiest, simplest, or fastest one will at least set you up for success when it comes to keeping a bad situation from getting worse. In a lot of these incidents, having the skills to deal with small setbacks, to stop and fix the problem rather than just push through, is often what turns a sketchy or even dangerous situation into only a minor hiccup.

Climbing a multipitch route in the alpine requires solid decision making. Here, Sara Vavra follows the fifth pitch of the Tooth Fairy, *Snoqualmie Pass, Washington.*

PREPARING FOR STRESSFUL SITUATIONS

If you are forced to deal with a problematic situation such as a stuck rope, the need to ascend that rope—or to execute another rarely (or never- before) performed task—is often stressful. If you see someone who is hurt, severely injured, and/or potentially unresponsive, you will unquestionably feel a lot of adrenaline and emotion pumping through you. While this is normal, it is rarely helpful when it comes to orchestrating and executing a technical rescue system.

This book gives extensive advice on easy and repeatable techniques to help set you up for success because, as countless studies have shown, stressed-out individuals don't always rise to the occasion when forced to deal with an accident, injury, or otherwise dangerous situation. There are many small things you can do that require essentially no gear and just a little bit of knowledge to vastly increase your

KNOWLEDGE IS LIGHT

BY ROBERT SMITH

Over the last 20 years, I have used loads of different self-rescue techniques with varying levels of success. Some of the methods I used were proper techniques that I learned from being a mountain guide and from books like this, and some of them were desperate and improvised because there simply were no other options, or at least I didn't know of any. Rather than diving into some war story from a previous alpine climbing event, here I speak about what I have learned from all of these self-rescue situations, both small and large.

The common theme for me with self-rescue in the mountains and the need to self-rescue is bad decision making. From being caught in a large slab avalanche in the Alps to falling into a crevasse in Alaska or getting my ropes horribly stuck in a Patagonian windstorm, leaving me only 45 meters of rope to rappel 1,000 meters (3,280 feet) of very steep terrain, these events, in hindsight, were all very much avoidable had I made better decisions earlier.

My desire to try to climb big and remote routes, often setting out in only the smallest of weather windows, has gotten me into a lot of scary situations. I personally believe careful decision making and continually trying to make the best decision are the biggest tools that can be used throughout any difficult situation, not just at the start of it. Being able to think on your feet and make decisions in a timely manner, often in very stressful situations, are essential skills for any climber or alpinist.

Being able to do a lot with a little is everything, whether you are on a high mountain or a long rock climb. While you might not have much gear, knowledge is light and you can carry a lot of it. To some extent, knowledge will just come with experience, which will come only with time. It can take years or decades to build the confidence to pull off a difficult self-rescue situation under extreme circumstances, but practice and seeking education will unquestionably expedite the process.

In the moment, staying calm and using good judgment are equally if not more important than your knowledge of and ability to use lots of rope tricks. Remember, the best form of self-rescue is to make good decisions and, when things start to go wrong, to keep making the best decisions to hopefully not find yourself in a scary and sometimes desperate situation.

For people new to long routes or high mountains, a great first step is to spend a few days with a mentor, like I did with Ian Nicholson, and try to get a baseline set of skills to build from for different types of rescue scenarios.

Robert Smith, a.k.a. Uncle Rob, is an International Federation of Mountain Guides Associations mountain guide based in Chamonix, France, who has made first ascents and clocked blisteringly fast times on routes from Alaska to Patagonia, including an 18-hour ascent of Mount Foraker's *Infinite Spur* and a 17-hour ascent of Denali's *Slovak Direct*.

Weigh all of your options and consider potential consequences prior to committing, as Kris Irwin does here on the North Buttress of Mount Hunter, a 4,000-foot technical route in the Alaska Range with a lot of challenging terrain requiring good decision making. (Photo by Robert Smith)

margin of safety, even in a stressful situation. For example, see the section below on guesstimating remaining hours of daylight.

ASSESSING REMAINING DAYLIGHT WITH YOUR HAND

Ever forget to look at the forecasted time for sunset and wonder how much longer you have until the sun sinks below the horizon? At some point every climber, backpacker, or mountaineer has asked, "How long until dark?" Luckily, there is an easy and accurate way to gauge how much daylight you have using nothing more than an extended arm and your hand:

Face the sun, extend your arm out in front of you, and turn your wrist so that it is at 90 degrees to your arm, with the back of your hand flatly facing the sun and thumb folded in (fig. I-1). Each whole hand width equals around one hour, so you can estimate the sun's distance from the horizon. To fine-tune this technique, each finger width in the horizontal position described represents about 15 minutes. So if the sun is one whole hand plus your pinky and ring fingers from the horizon, you have roughly one and a half hours until it sets.

BRING A HEADLAMP

A basic and essential piece of advice is to bring a headlamp; there are so many bright, tiny headlamps available now. If you climb multipitch rock routes long enough, there will come a day when you will misjudge the time it takes to ascend and descend the route. It could be a mistake on your part, such as a routefinding error, or it could be a slower team in front of you, but at some point you will be in technical terrain when it gets dark—even hiking in the dark can be hard. Ask around; if you know very many climbers, you know

"Catastrophe" knots: a couple of overhand knots behind a belay device back it up, allowing the belayer to troubleshoot without compromising the safety of the two climbers below. (Photo by Dale Remsberg)

Figure I-1. Estimating the amount of time until dark: **a**, *face the sun and extend your arm in front of you with your palm facing you, wrist bent 90 degrees and fingers parallel to the horizon;* **b**, *position your index finger just below the sun and your little finger parallel to the horizon—each finger ascending from the horizon represents about 15 minutes until the sun sets, and the whole hand (four fingers) represents about one hour.*

someone who has rappelled in the dark at some point without a headlamp. There are many quality headlamps on the market that weigh less than an ounce; buy one and bring it with you—throw it in the bottom of your multipitch pack or your chalk bag. You might even thank me someday for recommending that you buy and bring the tiny headlamp that is going to help you find the next rappel station or stay on the trail on the way out.

THE UNQUESTIONABLE IMPORTANCE OF PRACTICE

Many studies on humans' response to stress in sports or performance-focused or life-threatening situations have shown that very few people actually elevate to a previously unknown skill level, but the majority of people can still rise to the level that they've practiced. The percentage of people who excel or thrive

IFMGA/AMGA mountain guide Geoff Unger goes over foundational rescue skills in the Shawangunks (a.k.a. the Gunks), New York. (Photo by Silas Rossi)

Rebecca Schroeder belays Ryan O'Connell on Outer Space, *Snow Creek Wall, North Cascades, Washington.*

under stressful situations in which someone is severely injured, particularly if the injured person is someone they know, is quite small.

Fortunately, most people can perform to the level they have trained to, even under immense stress, exemplifying the importance of practice. While you are unlikely to spontaneously think of a new way to solve a problem or to perform a complex but unpracticed technical system when suddenly faced with a stressful situation, your brain will likely remember what you've learned so you'll be able to apply those earlier lessons, provided you've practiced them sufficiently.

The truth is, most people need to channel their nervous energy into focus rather than let it overwhelm them. I have been part of several rescues that have involved very injured people, several of whom were unresponsive and in at least one case not even breathing. Regardless of how much practice you've done, there is always a strong emotional response. You feel for the person who is hurt; you think, "What will happen to them? How will this affect them?"

While that is well and good, in this sort of situation you need to harness that energy (or block it out) and focus on the task at hand. Try to think critically about what needs to happen in a big-picture sense, then zero in on the tasks that will get you there. There is no sure way to do this, but recognize that if you are ever in this kind of situation you will very likely feel a strong emotion: fear, dread, regret, et cetera.

There aren't an endless number of hard skills that need to be practiced—in all reality, learning just a handful from each chapter can prepare you for a lot of potential situations. However,in rock and alpine climbing, there is a *very* great variety of situations you could be faced with. The better you can execute the techniques in this book in a comfortable environment and the more familiar you become with their possible applications and limitations, the better you will be able to apply them to myriad of situations.

PROBLEM-SOLVING

The goal of this book is to give you the tools to assess a given situation, then think critically about the best way to solve the problem. Avoid cutting corners, as the sketchy option might be logistically similar to a better option but is rarely truly faster since odds are you will be forced to slow down anyway, to avoid getting seriously hurt or dying yourself. Plus repeatedly taking unnecessary risks will only increase the odds that one day those "low-risk" simple solutions might catch up with you in a catastrophic way.

Equally important as learning technical rescue skills is figuring out when they are best

Jason Antin keeps his ropes in check, avoiding several potential issues on a problematic descent around the upper gendarme on the East Ridge of Dorado Needle, North Cascades, Washington.

Climbing a big wall in Alaska requires a well-developed ability to cope with stress. Here, David Allfrey leads on the first ascent of the 3,000-foot big wall route Pace of Comfort *on Kichatna Spire, Alaska Range.* (Photo by Graham Zimmerman)

employed. This book focuses on the application of different techniques as well as how to execute them. The bigger the day or the more complex the objective, the more likely it is that something will arise; the larger your repertoire for dealing with a situation, the more likely you'll be able to handle it smoothly and prevent it from becoming an issue.

While applying a technical solution to a problem or during a rescue, continue to think critically about your decisions and the techniques you have used. Are they working well? Would something else be better? Always consider all of your options and avoid getting too married to one idea. It is nearly always better to stop and fix something that isn't working than to see it through to its end for no other reason than it was the first option you chose.

HOW TO USE THIS BOOK

This book is divided into thirteen chapters, with the first nine focused on various aspects of climbing (rappelling, ascending, hauling, et cetera), followed by one chapter on improvised litters and harnesses and another on the specifics of calling for outside help; the final two chapters review how to solve some common problem scenarios and what to practice. Each chapter starts with more-basic techniques and works up to bigger problems, and as readers will discover, a number of repeated techniques are interchangeable between applications. For those interested in learning more, there is a list of recommended reading at the back of the book.

Several experienced climbers and guides have contributed first-person anecdotes illustrating a chapter's primary area of focus. The multiple perspectives in these sidebars give an idea of the range not only of problems encountered on climbs but also of strategies for solving them in the field. Short "Tips" are also scattered throughout the text. And throughout the chapters, you'll find plenty of photos illustrating step-by-step instructions for techniques described in the text. Here's a summary of what each chapter covers:

Chapter 1 reviews all the knots, bends, and hitches discussed in this book. Remember, this book isn't a beginning knot-tying guide. This chapter helps climbers who may be familiar with a large number of knots but aren't familiar with a specific knot's best application for the rescue scenarios discussed in this book.

Chapter 2 provides an in-depth look at options for belay devices as well as a range of belay techniques and basic anchors.

Chapter 3 discusses escaping the belay or tying off the belay device and transferring the load of the climber onto an anchor. This chapter describes a foundational skill for the majority of more serious self-rescue situations: escaping the belay for the leader and the follower.

Chapter 4 dives into complex situations such as rappelling with an unconscious climber. This chapter also covers managing the rope(s) on descent, escaping the rappel, tandem rappels, counterbalanced rappels, and transitioning from rappelling to ascending.

Chapter 5 focuses on techniques associated with lowering a climber directly off an

Munter-mule-overhand: among the most useful and most commonly used hitches for rock rescue, the munter-mule (tied on the striped yellow rope) can be tied off to create a load-releasable system—and it can be released even under tension. (Photo by Jim Meyers)

Ian Nicholson demonstrates an in-line knot pass, the most efficient technique for passing a knot in steep terrain, though it requires the system to be set up in advance before the lower begins. Thus, the person passing the knot must know a knot is coming rather than finding an unanticipated knot or damaged section of rope as they are performing the lower. (Photo by Jim Meyers)

anchor. While this skill might seem basic, a lot of climbers are not as familiar with this less-used tactic, and knowing a few ways to smoothly lower someone or something directly off the anchor has a number of applications.

Chapter 6 covers various techniques for passing knots in the rope while lowering and rappelling. These knots could be tied in the rope by mistake or tied to isolate a damaged section of rope or to lower someone the distance of two or more ropes tied together. This chapter also discusses strategies for dealing with a stuck rope.

Chapter 7 focuses on improvised ascending techniques utilizing a variety of tools for single- and double-rope ascension. You might need to ascend a rope to free a stuck line, to assist an injured leader, or for any number of other reasons. This chapter covers using traditional as well as improvised ascenders and tips for using aid-climbing techniques in a rescue situation.

Chapter 8 focuses on rescuing the leader, which is among the most complex forms of technical rescue. The chapter discusses a number of tactics and techniques, from lowering and climbing counterbalanced to self-belay, as well as their best uses for a variety of conditions, depending on whether the leader is mildly or seriously injured or unconscious.

Chapter 9 reviews the principles of mechanical advantage and then provides a number of hauling techniques, from simple hauls to helping your partner get through a tricky section to more-complex hauling systems that provide greater pulling potential for longer or heavier loads.

Chapter 10 provides a selection of useful rescue techniques ranging from how to build a litter out of a climbing rope to carrying an injured climber out in any of several types of improvised litters. Other rescue techniques covered in this chapter include the dulfersitz rappel.

Chapter 11 discusses considerations for and information about calling for outside help—when to do it, how to do it, what you should expect, and things to do to set yourself up for interacting with outside help (including helicopters) should the situation arise.

Chapter 12 includes 10 scenarios based on real-world stories that represent and deal with some of the most common problems that climbers encounter. The idea is, you get to exercise your brain about what you would do in any of these scenarios, with direct feedback in the solution and considerations sections that weigh possible options for each scenario.

Chapter 13 illustrates the most useful techniques to practice and some gear options to consider. While it would be wonderful to have a working knowledge of every technique in this book, this chapter helps you zero in on a few of the most used and most versatile systems, which ideally will set you up for success in dealing with some of the most common problems climbers face. The chapter also includes considerations about gear that is most useful in a rescue situation.

Sometimes you need to call for outside help. Here, Yosemite Search and Rescue (YOSAR) performs a technical rescue with a helicopter in Yosemite National Park, California. (Photo by Tom Healy, National Park Service)

My hope is that this book will be a resource for both at-home practice and in-the-field climbs, regardless of whether you ever have to apply these techniques for self-rescue in a real-world scenario.

A NOTE ABOUT SAFETY

Safety is an important concern in all outdoor activities. No book can alert you to every hazard or anticipate the limitations of every reader. The descriptions of techniques and procedures in this book are intended to provide general information. This is not a complete text on self-rescue technique. Nothing substitutes for formal instruction, routine practice, and plenty of experience. When you follow any of the procedures described here, you assume responsibility for your own safety. Use this book as a general guide to further information. Under normal conditions, excursions into the backcountry require attention to traffic, road and trail conditions, weather, terrain, the capabilities of your party, and other factors. Keeping informed on current conditions and exercising common sense are the keys to a safe, enjoyable outing.

—Mountaineers Books

Opposite: *Peter Webb ascends the East Ridge of Ingalls Peak, Stuart Range, Washington.*

CHAPTER 1

Knots, Bends, and Hitches

This chapter assumes that readers are already familiar with the most common knots and hitches used while rock climbing; the primary focus is on how these knots and hitches are used in rescue situations.

FOUNDATIONAL TERMINOLOGY AND CONCEPTS

Knowing a few foundational terms and concepts is extremely helpful in understanding how technical climbing systems are constructed.

LOAD STRAND VERSUS BRAKE STRAND

Understanding the difference between the climbing rope's load strand and brake strand is critical to understanding technical systems that relate to belaying. The load strand is the side of the belay system (generally secured with a belay device or munter hitch) that goes from the climber, or *load,* to the belay system; if the climber weights the rope, this strand becomes taut (fig. 1-1a). The brake strand (fig. 1-1b) is exactly what it sounds like: the side of the belay system where friction is added to slow (in the case of lowering or rappelling) or stop the climber on the load strand.

BIGHTS AND LOOPS

Commonly used terms regarding ropes and knots are *bight* and *loop*. A bight is like a "mouth" or a V or C shape in the rope where the rope strands do not cross (fig. 1-2a). A loop is created by making a circle with the rope in which the strands cross once to complete the loop (fig. 1-2b).

APPLICATIONS OF A VARIETY OF KNOTS, BENDS, AND HITCHES

There are a nearly infinite number of knots and hitches, but this section focuses on the application of knots, bends, and hitches commonly used in climbing and rescue that should be in every climber's repertoire. This section breaks down the differences between knots, bends, and hitches and gives a few tips on tying them as well as their pros and cons for various applications. Practice these knots, bends, and hitches to the point where you can tie them correctly the first time, every time, and can remember how to create them under the duress of a real-life rescue scenario.

This book assumes that readers are already familiar with basic knots, bends, and hitches used in rock and alpine climbing—the

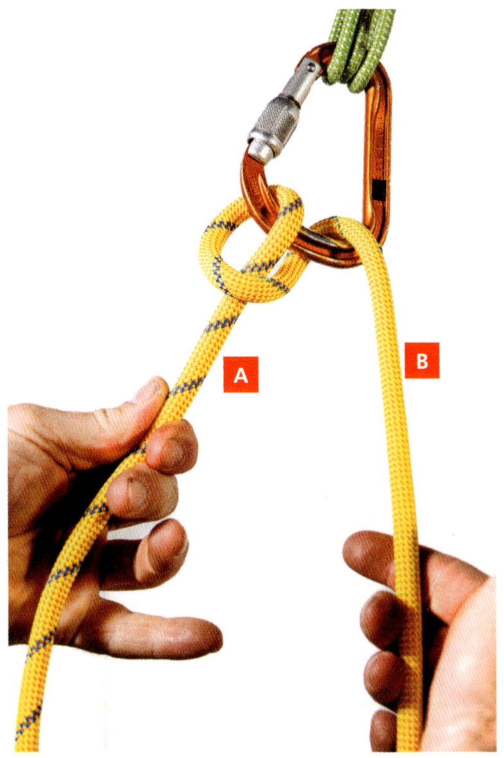

Figure 1-1. The climbing rope hitched to a carabiner to create a belay system: **a,** *the brake strand comes out of the "back" of the carabiner where the belayer holds tension and adjusts friction with their braking hand, whether they're using a belay device or, as shown here, a friction hitch;* **b,** *the load strand goes from the carabiner toward the load—often the climber being belayed or hanging on the rope.*

overhand knot, fisherman's bend, figure-eight bend, girth hitch, and overhand slip knot—and so does not cover how to tie these knots. Knot-tying details are provided in this section only for specialized knots. For some

Figure 1-2. Rope terms: **a,** *a bight is an open "bend" in the rope where the strands do not cross;* **b,** *a loop is created when the rope is bent to form a circle in which the strands cross once.*

recommended books for learning more about basic knots, see Suggested Reading.

USEFUL KNOTS AND BENDS

A *knot* is tied within one rope, whereas a *bend* is used to connect two ropes. In the climbing world, if a knot can be used for either purpose, we still call it a knot, whereas knots that are *exclusively* used to join ropes, like a Flemish bend or a double fisherman's bend, are bends.

Rewoven Figure Eight

The rewoven figure eight, also known as the figure eight follow-through or figure eight retrace (fig. 1-3), is one of the most important knots in climbing, commonly used by a climber to tie in to the rope, an anchor, et cetera. This is far and away the most commonly tied knot for climbers the world over, and with good reason: It is easy to tie, easy to check whether it is tied correctly, won't come untied on its own, and is one of the

Figure 1-3. The rewoven figure eight, the most commonly used knot by climbers, is among the strongest knots and is easy to check visually, striking an excellent balance between being secure but not too difficult to untie. (Photo by Truc Allen)

strongest knots. It maintains around 75–80 percent of the strength of the material with which it is tied due to its shallow bends, and it is even around 5–10 percent stronger than a bowline. Also, unlike a bowline, a rewoven figure eight does not need a backup knot: it is plenty strong enough with a fist's worth of tail (around 3–4 inches).

Figure Eight on a Bight

A figure eight on a bight has the same characteristics as a rewoven figure eight, offering the same strength and being easy to check. It has the additional advantage of being tieable

Figure 1-4. The figure eight on a bight looks exactly like a rewoven figure eight except that it is tied at a point along the rope, not at one of the ends.

Tip: Sometimes people struggle to untie their figure eight if it becomes weighted. A good technique to make it *far* easier to untie is to make sure the figure eight is well tightened and well dressed, meaning no overlaps. Take the extra five or ten seconds to push the overlaps around so you end up with all five "pairs" of ropes running parallel and not crossing over each other, then cinch them down. Surprisingly, a well-cinched knot is far easier to untie.

at any point along the rope rather than only at one of the ends (fig. 1-4). However, the disadvantage is that it has to be clipped, rather than

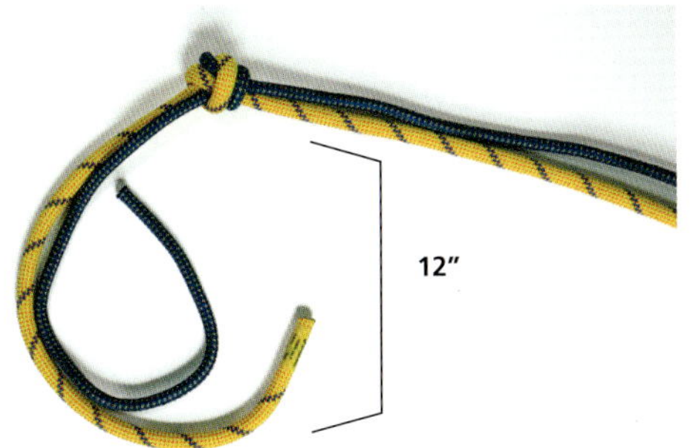

Figure 1-5. The flat overhand is the most common knot for joining two ropes for rappelling, especially two ropes of different diameters. This knot is very strong as long as it is dressed correctly, with each strand tightened independently and is tied with plenty of tail—about 1 foot. (Photo by Truc Allen)

tied directly, to whatever it is being attached to (generally a carabiner). For example, you cannot reasonably attach the climbing rope to your harness with a figure eight on a bight without carabiners or some other attachment mechanism.

Flat Overhand

The flat overhand, also called an offset overhand, is the most common knot for joining two ropes together for rappelling. Despite its ominous old nickname—the European Death Knot (EDK)—this knot is, despite its relatively small size and simplicity, quite strong, offering more than enough strength for joining two ropes of different diameters for rappelling (fig. 1-5).

The key to making the flat overhand strong is to individually tighten all four strands of of the knot (fig. 1-6)—avoid tightening them two at a time—and leave around 1 foot of tail. Making the tails too long increases the chance of them catching when the rope is being pulled. Also, climbers have had accidents after mistakenly threading overlong tails instead of the main strands of rope into their belay device.

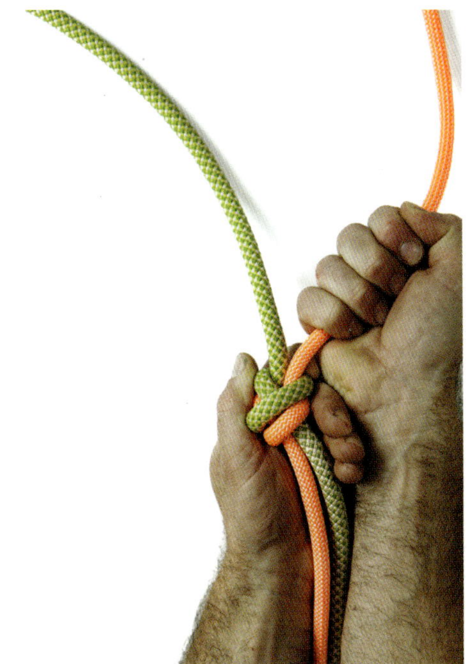

Figure 1-6. Pull each strand of the flat overhand independently to tighten the knot, and aim to have around 1 foot of tail.

Tip: After extensive testing, labs have reported that when two ropes of different diameters—up to 4 millimeters in difference—are tied together, they can even be stronger than two ropes of the same diameter tied together, provided that smaller-diameter strand is positioned such that it could not pass over the larger-diameter rope if the knot were to invert.

Contrary to popular belief, it is okay to rappel with a flat overhand using ropes of different diameters—up to around 4 millimeters of difference. Here, Ian Nicholson rappels off a 5-millimeter rope tied to a 9.5-millimeter rope in the French Valley, Torres del Paine, Chile. (Photo by Graham Zimmerman)

Reasons to use the flat overhand over a double fisherman's bend or Flemish bend include that the flat overhand is easier to tie, *far* easier to untie, and much lower-profile—meaning it is less likely to get stuck in cracks, flakes, or pieces of protection. It has the tendency to "stand up," allowing the bulk of the knot to stand above the rock rather than dragging along the surface, which further reduces the likelihood of it getting stuck.

Tip: *Do not use a flat figure eight* to tie two ropes together (fig. 1-7): it is not as strong and can fail with less than 2 kilonewtons (under 500 pounds) of force. There have been fatalities due to using the flat figure eight to tie two ropes together.

Flemish Bend

The Flemish bend is a bulkier knot, but it is easier to tie than a double fisherman's bend; it is used to join two ropes into one line for top-roping. While the Flemish bend is more than adequate for rappelling, its bulk makes it less desirable than the flat overhand. The advantage of a Flemish bend is that if you are familiar with a rewoven figure eight, the Flemish bend is just a variation on that. Make your figure-eight skeleton on one rope in the same way you would as if you were going to tie in, but then run the second rope through it

Figure 1-7. Do not use a flat figure eight (shown here) to tie two ropes together for a rappel: while this configuration might look more familiar and even appear strong, it isn't. Instead, use a flat overhand or, for extended top-roping with ropes of drastically different diameters (more than 4 millimeters), use a Flemish bend.

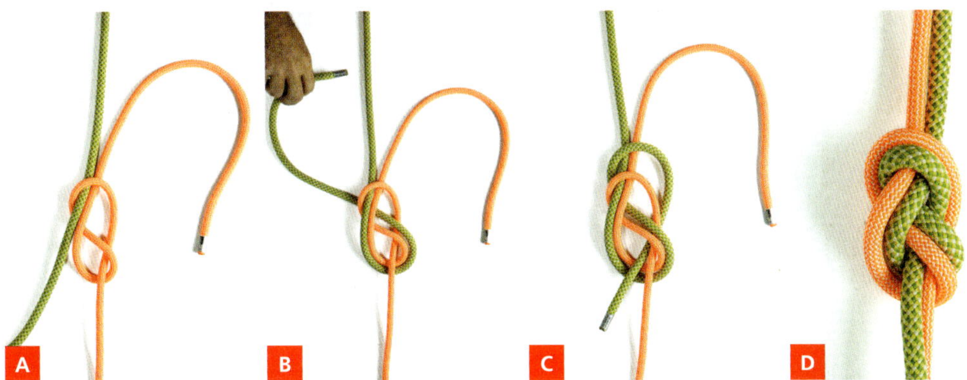

Figure 1-8. Using a Flemish bend to join two ropes: **a**, *tie a figure-eight skeleton on one rope exactly as if you were about to tie in to your harness;* **b**, *feed the other rope into the figure eight from the opposite side, as if you were tying a rewoven figure eight;* **c**, *continue to retrace the figure eight;* **d**, *dress the knot.* (Photos by Truc Allen)

from the other side (fig. 1-8a and b), retracing the figure eight (fig. 1-8c) and dressing the knot (fig. 1-8d).

Tip: For the diameters of rope that climbers generally use (6–10 millimeters), it is okay to tie ropes of different diameters together. If you are using ropes of different diameters with a difference greater than 4 millimeters, consider a Flemish bend, double barrel knot, or double fisherman's bend, and if rappelling use a Reepschnur rappel with a "rap line" and a "pull line" (see chapter 4).

Double Fisherman's Bend

The double fisherman's bend is a very strong self-locking knot that can be difficult to untie when loaded. It is the preferred knot for joining two ends of cord that you don't intend to regularly untie or for long top ropes on routes where a single rope isn't long enough to top-rope from the ground. The double fisherman's bend is preferred over the flat overhand

Figure 1-9. A well-dressed double fisherman's bend: **a**, *all four "solid" strands should be on one side;* **b**, *both Xs should be on the other side.* (Photos by Truc Allen)

for top ropes because the knot is stronger when pulled in-line.

To dress the double fisherman's bend appropriately, all four "solid" strands should be on one side (fig. 1-9a), and both the Xs should be on the other side (fig. 1-9b). To get this outcome, reverse the directions of the loops created on the second fisherman's from those created on the first. The tails should be around two times as long as the length of the integral knot when it's tied. For a lot of smaller-diameter (6- to 7-millimeter) cords, that means the tails should be around 2 inches long; on a top rope with dynamic 9.2- to 9.7-millimeter ropes, the tails should be around 6 inches long.

Barrel Knots (a.k.a. Stopper Knots)

Barrel knots are sometimes called stopper knots or half fisherman's knots, as they are the same knot but tied with only one strand of rope. First, make a loop in the rope (fig. 1-10a), then bend the end of the rope back over itself to create a second loop and tuck the rope end through both loops (fig. 1-10b), then pull each side away from the knot to tighten it (fig. 1-10c).

A barrel knot is used is more frequently at the rope ends while rappelling to significantly reduce the chances of rappelling off the rope. Barrel knots are also used when lowering for the same purpose. Because it is bulky, the barrel knot will jam the belay device, completely halting its ability feed slack. Even the most reluctant climbers should tie stopper knots in the end of their ropes because statistically you are *far* more likely to die from rappelling off the end of your rope than from getting it stuck or forgetting to untie a knot.

Bowline

Along with the figure eight, the bowline is one of the stronger knots in the climbing world and has the distinct advantage of being far easier to untie than most other knots, such as the overhand knot, figure eight, and alpine butterfly, even after repeated heavy loading. A basic but

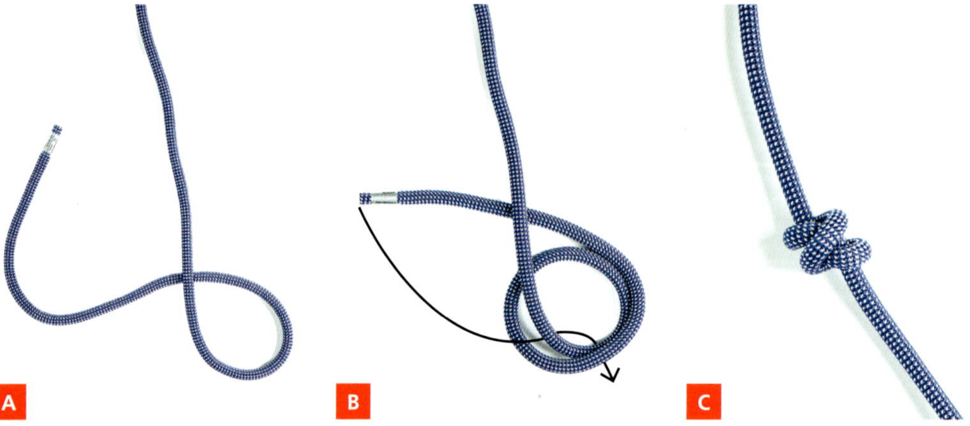

Figure 1-10. Barrel knot: **a**, *bend one end of the rope back over itself to create a loop;* **b**, *bend the end of the rope back over itself to make a second loop and feed the end of the rope though both loops;* **c**, *grip the knot and pull first one strand, then the other, in opposite directions from the knot to tighten it.* (Photos by Truc Allen)

Figure 1-11. A well-dressed single bowline with a barrel knot/half fisherman's knot backup.

effective adage for tying the bowline correctly is to make a loop that spirals up toward the short end of the rope then have the "rabbit" climb out of the hole, go around the "tree" (the "standing" leg of the rope), and then go back in the hole; but recognize that it also needs to be well dressed and backed up (fig. 1-11).

That distinct advantage of being easier to untie is also one of the bowline's biggest disadvantages and one of the major reasons that climbers prefer tying in with a figure eight, as there have been several incidents, including by some well-known climbers, of bowlines that came untied while the climbers were ascending. With that said, there isn't anything wrong with tying in with a well-dressed double bowline with a backup (fig. 1-12).

Regardless of the knot you choose to tie in with, the bowline has countless applications in climbing, from building anchors around trees or rocks to replacing rappel stations with single strands of cord connected to fixed pieces.

Figure 1-12. A well-dressed double bowline with a backup.

Alpine Butterfly Knot

The alpine butterfly knot, often shortened to just the "butterfly knot," is tied into the middle of the rope and can be loaded in-line better than a figure eight (fig. 1-13). Its main

Figure 1-13. Tighten the alpine butterfly knot by simultaneously pulling the two long ends of the rope away from each other.

application is in alpine climbing and glacier travel where people in the middle of a rope team use it to clip in because there is potential for them to experience a pull from the climbers both ahead of or behind them. The butterfly knot is also the preferred stopper knot for glacier teams to help arrest the group in the event of a crevasse fall.

USEFUL HITCHES

The difference between a hitch and a knot is that a knot "stands alone," whereas a hitch is tied around something. If that "something" is removed, the hitch falls apart.

Clove Hitch

Likely the most used hitch in all of climbing, the clove hitch is most commonly employed as a way for a climber to secure themself with a rope or to back up an anchor. This simple hitch is strong, and its primary advantage is that it's easy to adjust (fig. 1.14a), even after being loaded, before you pull on each strand to "lock it back down" (fig. 1-14b).

Munter Hitch

The munter hitch is named after famed Swiss mountain guide Werner Munter. It is also known as the Italian hitch due to the popularity it gained at least initially in Italy in the 1950s. Even today climbers may see "HMS" on some locking carabiners, which is short for *halbmastwurf sicherung*, a German phrase that means "half clove hitch belay."

The munter is an excellent hitch for belaying (fig. 1-15), as it is capable of providing a lot of friction and will work well to replace a traditional belay device, particularly when used on an anchor to belay a climber seconding a pitch. The munter can be very

Figure 1-14. Clove hitch: **a**, *tightened by pulling on each long end individually—not simultaneously;* **b**, *clipped to carabiner.*

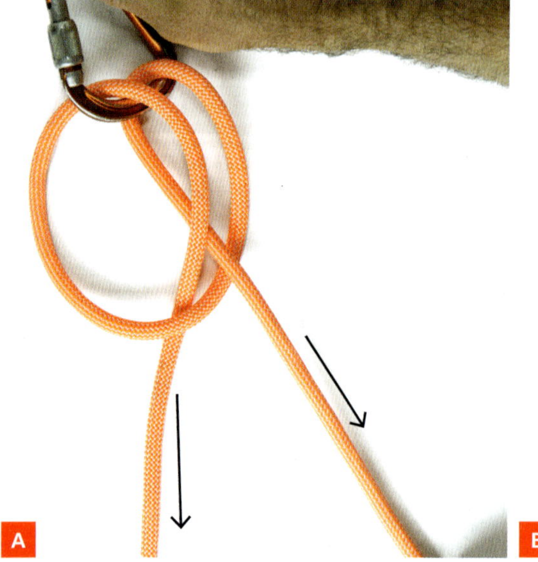

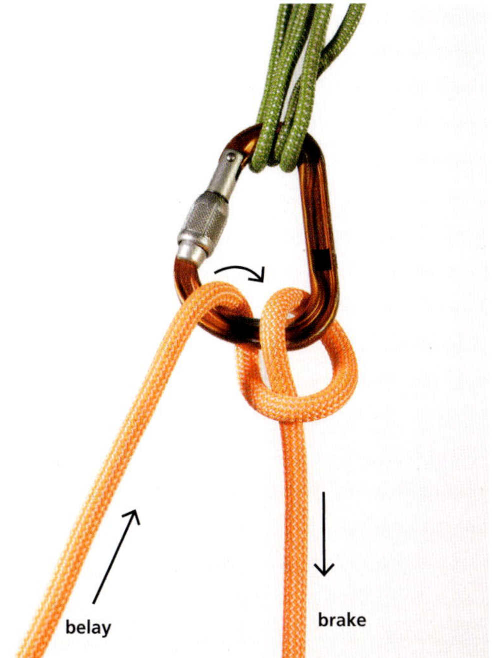

Figure 1-15. A munter hitch in the belay position on a locking carabiner on the anchor.

Figure 1-16. A munter hitch in the lowering position on a locking carabiner on the anchor.

effective for belaying a leader as far as the amount of friction it provides, but because its braking motion is an upward pull to lock the strands against each other (if it's clipped to the belay loop of your harness)—rather than the typical downward pull—extra care must be taken, due to the unusual opposite motion.

Because the munter hitch can be "flipped over" (fig. 1-16) and used in either direction, it is a very effective tool for lowering, but care must be taken to minimize twists in the rope as it passes through the hitch; do this by holding the brake and load strands as parallel as possible. It is possible to rappel with a munter as well, but twists are nearly unavoidable, so first consider other techniques for all but the shortest rappels.

Learning to tie the munter hitch in the lowering position isn't a requirement for its functionality, as it is a reversible hitch, but being able to do so provides a huge advantage in most rescue applications. This is because a munter hitch in the lowering position can be tied under tension, minimizing slack that might be accidentally worked into the system and eliminating the need to "flip" the munter from the belay position to the lowering position or to "milk" slack out.

Munter-Mule Hitch

The mule, also known as the trucker's hitch, presumably because truckers used this hitch to tie down tarps and goods before the advent of modern ratchet and tie-down

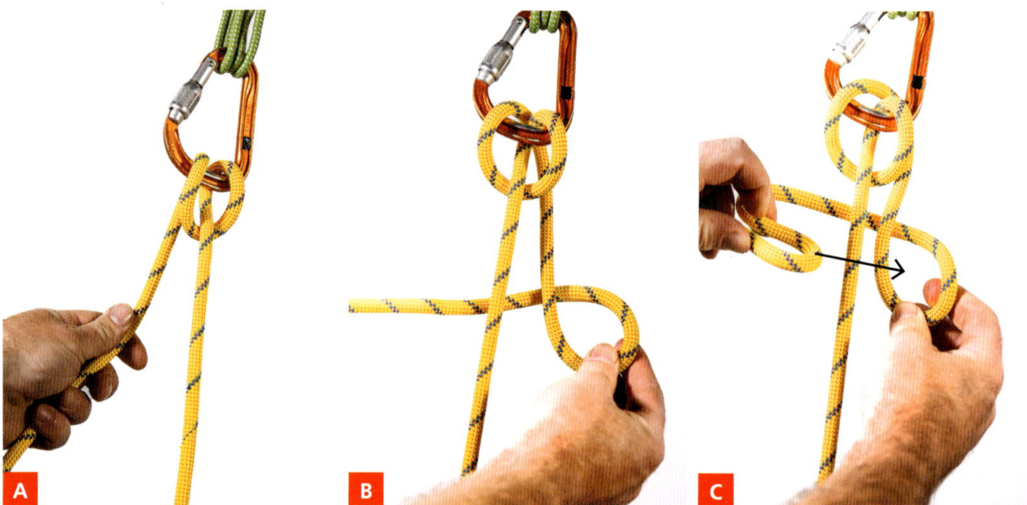

Figure 1-17. Munter-mule hitch: **a**, *pinch the brake and load strands together;* **b**, *fold the brake strand behind and past the load strand—not in between the brake strand and load strand—to create a loop;* **c**, *with the long end of the brake strand, create a bight on the opposite side of the load strand, then pass the bight through the loop, making sure the bight encircles the load strand.* (Photos by Truc Allen)

straps, is a blocking hitch that can be used for progress capture. The biggest advantage of the mule hitch is that it can be easily released even if it's been under tremendous load, because on a foundational level it is nothing more than a "blocking knot" created with a slip hitch.

The key to adding a mule hitch to a munter hitch is to pinch the brake and load strands together (fig. 1-17a) and fold the brake strand behind and past the load strand—not in between the brake strand and load strand—to make a loop that folds up and away from the two strands (fig. 1-17b), then create a bight with the brake strand on the opposite side of the load strand and pass the bight through the loop (fig. 1-17c). Pull enough of the bight through the loop that a backup knot can be tied with the bight (see the next knot).

Munter-Mule-Overhand

The munter-mule-overhand is a munter-mule with an overhand backup knot—and is the hitch most commonly used in rescue. With a foot or more of slack in the bight that finished the mule hitch (fig. 1-18a), pass the bight around the back of the load strand and then over it (fig. 1-18b), and then pass the bight up behind the load strand to create an overhand knot around the load strand; pull the overhand knot tight (fig. 1-18c).

The reason the munter-mule-overhand is the knot most commonly used in rescue is that you can readily belay or lower a person or other object and then "lock it off" with a mule hitch that is subsequently backed up by an overhand (fig. 1-19).

FRICTION HITCHES

Hitches that can "grab" another strand of rope but can be quickly adjusted are called friction

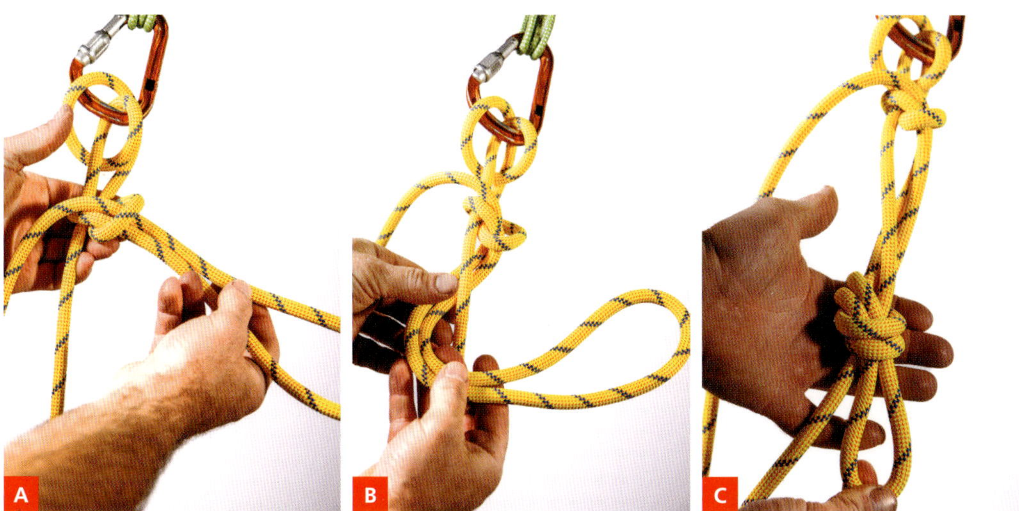

Figure 1-18. Munter-mule-overhand: **a**, *pull a foot or more of slack in the bight that finished the mule hitch;* **b**, *pass this long bight around the back of the load strand and over it;* **c**, *pass the bight up behind the load strand to create an overhand knot around the load strand and pull the overhand knot tight.* (Photos by Truc Allen)

Figure 1-19. Two munter-mule-overhands: the munter-mule-overhand combination is the foundation for most rescue systems as it provides a strong, load-releasable system that can be used to belay or lower and can be locked off at any point. Here, a klemheist friction hitch tied with the blue rope is attached to the anchor with a munter-mule-overhand (in addition to the striped yellow rope attached to the anchor with a munter-mule-overhand) to create a load-releasable system. (Photo by Jim Meyers)

hitches. Friction hitches are used in ascending and hauling systems and as rappel backups.

All friction hitches work best in situations where the difference in diameter between the cord used to tie the hitch and the rope is around 3–4 millimeters. Attempting to tie friction hitches if the difference is only 1–2 millimeters can be difficult, depending on the material, and will certainly require additional wraps. If the difference in diameter is greater than 4 millimeters, the friction hitch will bite almost too well and can be difficult to release.

There are countless friction hitches, but this section covers the five most heavily used, their best applications, and their pros and cons. A small loop of cord is used to tie friction hitches. Rock climbers commonly call this a *third hand*, but another term for it among mountaineers and alpine climbers is simply a *prusik*—which should not be confused with the prusik hitch you can also tie with this small loop of cord. To avoid confusion,this book calls the loop of cord a third hand throughout.

Prusik Hitch

The most widely known and widely used friction hitch is the prusik (fig. 1-20a). It is so widely known that to some extent a "prusik hitch" is a generic term for any friction hitch. Generally speaking, the prusik hitch itself is tied with three complete wraps—occasionally four if the difference between the diameters of the two materials is only 1–2 millimeters or the materials are unusually slick. The prusik grabs most consistently starting with the wraps in the middle and then working outward, which also makes it easy to "break" the prusik open by pushing back on the outermost wrap in a configuration commonly called the "smile" or "smiley face" (fig. 1-20b).

The prusik does have a lot of advantages: it grabs predictably, it can be loaded in either direction (toward or away from the load strand), and it is easy to loosen by pulling back on its "smiley face." Its main disadvantage

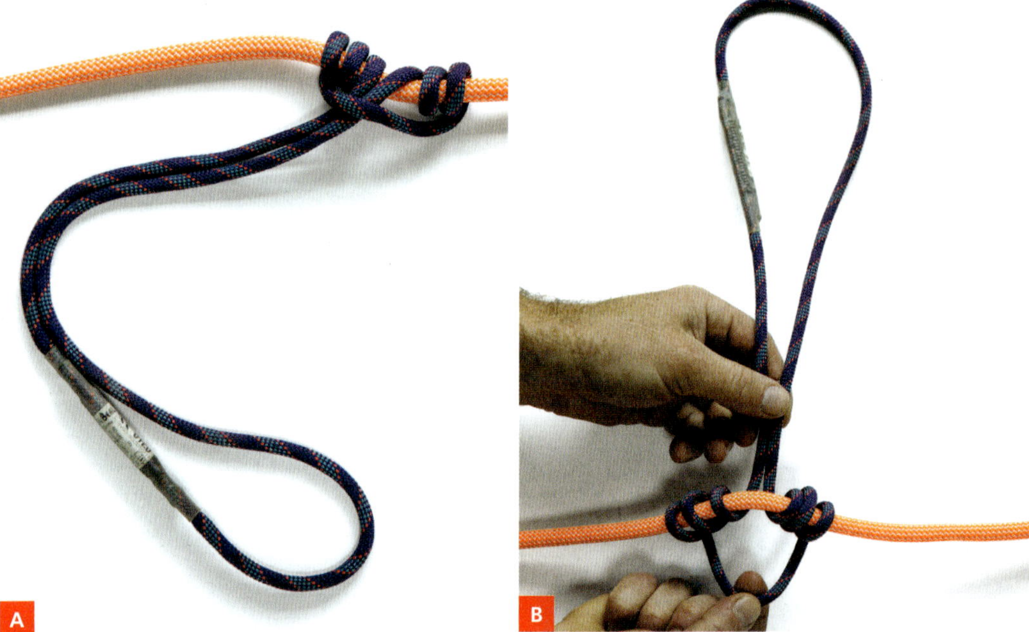

Figure 1-20. Prusik hitch: **a**, *a well-tied prusik;* **b**, *to dress the prusik hitch before tightening it, undo any twists or unnecessary overlaps so that you have a "smiley face" side and six neatly stacked strands on the other side.*

Figure 1-21. Klemheist hitch

is that it is slower to tie than other friction hitches, particularly if you are using longer pieces of material.

Klemheist Hitch

A friction hitch that is easier and more efficient to tie than a prusik if you are using longer pieces of material is the klemheist hitch (fig. 1-21). This is because the klemheist does not need to be passed through itself on every wrap. Wrapping the klemheist away from the direction of the load, wrap as many times as necessary to facilitate a good grab, then pass the long end through the short, exposed loop—the "eye"—and flip the long end back over the small loop so that you are pulling in the opposite direction of the load.

The klemheist is a good choice for ropes of similar diameters (down to 1–2 millimeters of difference), as it is easier and quicker to put more wraps on with a klemheist. A downside of the klemheist is that it generally takes a higher minimum number of wraps for it to grab the rope, and it certainly works far better in one direction (toward the "eye").

Figure 1-22. Autoblock hitch: once the appropriate number of wraps have been made, clip both ends of the material.

Tip: To get the klemheist to grab most effectively, make the "eye" as small as possible.

Autoblock Hitch

The quickest friction hitch to tie of those discussed here is the autoblock hitch (fig. 1-22); however, it offers the least grabbing power with a similar number of wraps. The autoblock also generally requires a greater difference in the diameter of ropes compared to the aforementioned friction hitches when using a similar number of wraps. If the autoblock offers enough friction for a given application, it is very easy to tighten and release. It is most commonly used as a friction-hitch backup—a "third hand"—for rappelling but it is also occasionally used as a "tractor" in hauling systems (see chapter 9).

Garda Hitch

Another rope-grabbing hitch is the garda hitch. To tie a garda, hold two similarly sized nonlocking carabiners in the same orientation and clip the rope through both carabiners (fig. 1-23a). Wrap the brake strand up and around to create a loop (fig. 1-23b), then clip the loop into only the "first" (front-load-side) carabiner (fig. 1-23c). The load will come onto the first carabiner that is clipped in the hitch and exit on the other side.

> **Tip:** Girth-hitch both carabiners together with a sling or other piece of material when attaching the hitch to keep the carabiners properly oriented.

The garda hitch has many of the same applications as other friction hitches. It works particularly well in hauling systems because, unlike most other friction hitches, it makes for a good ratchet on an anchor in a system where the rope that comes from the load and enters the ratchet changes direction 180 degrees and exits. It is also very easy to move the garda hitch in a single direction, as it can both take in slack and lock into place, making it very useful for ascending steeper terrain. However, because the garda hitch is effective in only a single direction, and is very difficult to back up, it is not the best hitch to use if it might be necessary to unweight the system or change directions.

VT Prusik

Widely used in the arborist and rope-access realms, the *Valdotain Tresse* ("Valdotain braid," from a dialect in Italy's Aosta Valley) or VT prusik has only recently become popular among climbers. The VT prusik, a hitch that allows you to ascend a weighted rope, is quickly becoming the hitch of choice for the ratchet during crevasse rescues. While less

Figure 1-23. Garda hitch: **a**, *clip the rope through two nonlocking carabiners positioned in the same orientation;* **b**, *wrap the brake strand up and around, creating a loop;* **c**, *clip the loop into just the front-load-side carabiner.*

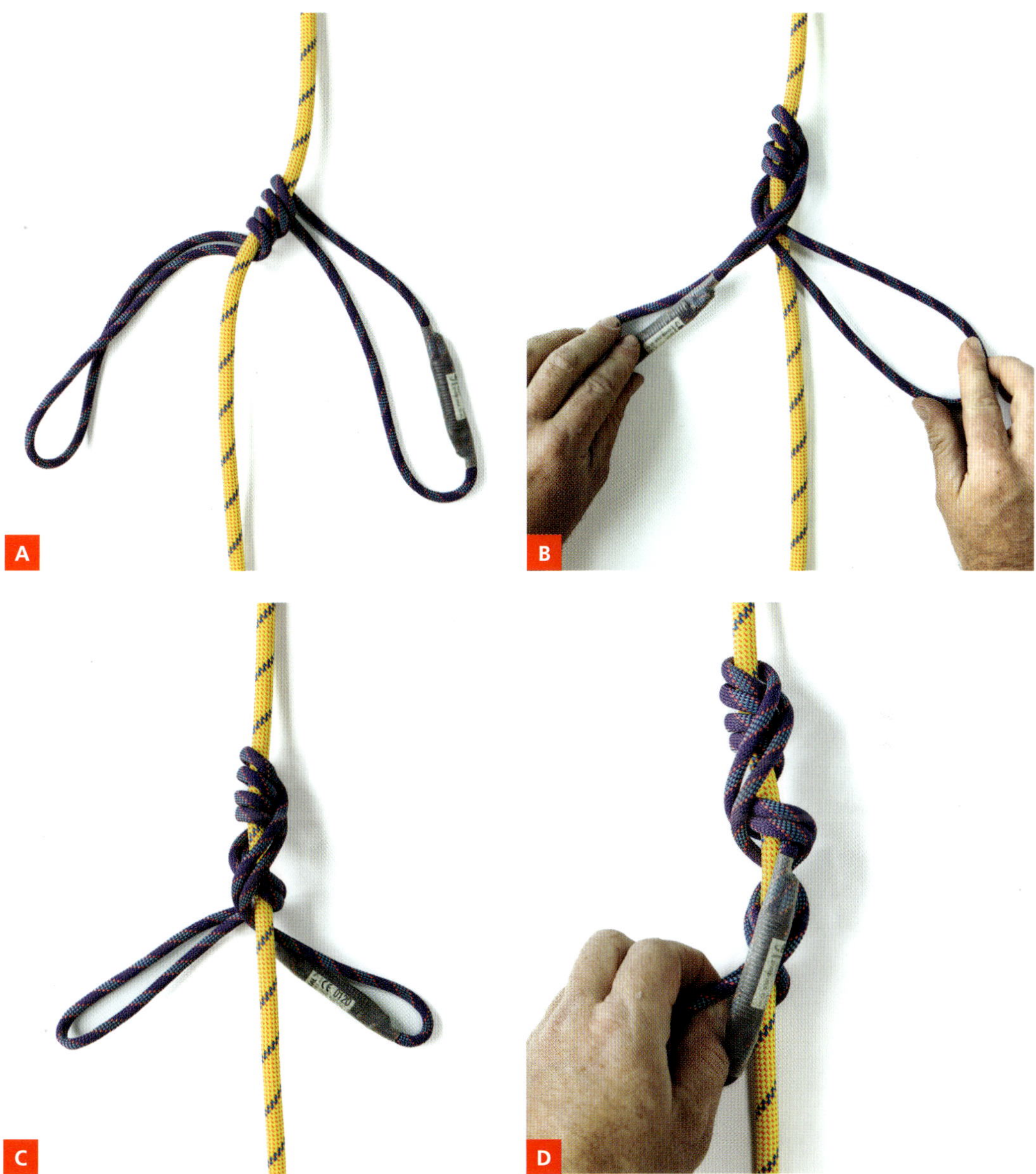

Figure 1-24. VT prusik for ascending or descending a rope: **a**, *starting from the middle of the prusik material, make two complete wraps around the rope;* **b**, *cross the two ends of the prusik material over each other, making an X on one side of the rope;* **c**, *repeat, creating an X on the other side of the rope;* **d**, *keep making Xs on alternate sides of the rope until you use up all the prusik material.* (Photos by Truc Allen)

versatile than other friction hitches, the VT prusik really excels in two applications: the first is for ascending and descending loaded ropes, and the other is as a ratchet (progress-capture technique) in hauling systems.

To tie a VT prusik, starting from the middle of the prusik material, make two complete wraps around the rope (fig. 1-24a). Cross the two ends of the VT prusik over each other, making an X on one side of the rope (fig. 1-24b), then repeat this cross on the other side of the rope (fig. 1-24c) and continue making Xs on alternating sides of the rope until you use up all of the prusik material (fig. 1-24d).

The VT prusik is one of the better options for ascending or descending a loaded line. And because it is self-minding, it makes for an excellent option as a ratchet to capture progress in complex hauling systems or crevasse rescue. If using the VT prusik as a ratchet, clip both ends of the prusik and the rope where the rope changes direction (fig. 1-25). If the VT prusik is being used as a ratchet, it is key to wrap the Xs tightly so the prusik will self-mind and not flip through the carabiner.

Figure 1-25. VT prusik for a ratchet: clip both ends of the prusik and the rope where the rope changes direction.

Opposite: *Andy Dahlen on the second pitch of* Davis-Holland, *Town Walls, Index, Washington*

CHAPTER 2

Belay Methods and Anchors

Having options for belay devices, methods, and techniques, as well as different anchor configurations using gear and, often, natural features, can easily help climbers avoid having to compromise safety if they encounter something unexpected.

Providing a good belay is one of the easiest ways to increase security for the climb's leader. The belayer should have stable footing if on the ground or on a large ledge or should hang tight against the anchor at a hanging stance. The belayer should always pay attention and work toward providing the right amount of slack to not inhibit the leader's movement without providing too much slack in the event of a fall.

BELAY DEVICES AND METHODS

This section covers a variety of effective options for belaying, each with specific advantages and disadvantages. Options include assisted-braking belay devices (fig. 2-1a), autoblocking belay devices (fig. 2-1b), and methods such as the munter hitch (fig. 2-1c). All belay devices also serve as rappel and lowering devices (described in chapters 4 and 5).

Evan Miller provides an excellent belay on the North Ridge of Eldorado Peak, North Cascades, Washington.

Figure 2-1. Belay options: **a**, *the Petzl GriGri, an assisted-braking belay device (ABD);* **b**, *the Petzl Reverso, an autoblocking belay device;* **c**, *a munter hitch.* (Photo by Truc Allen)

TRADITIONAL TUBE-STYLE DEVICE

Traditional tube-style belay devices are completely functional for rappelling, but they take more care for lead belaying and belaying a follower compared to autoblocking belay devices or assisted-braking belay devices (ABDs). You can certainly belay a follower from the top of a pitch with a traditional tube-style device, but you must use a redirect or careful body positioning to avoid being pulled in a direction that potentially compromises your belayer. Tube-style devices certainly let you belay a leader and are functional rappel tools, but they aren't nearly as versatile as other options nor do they provide even close to the level of security while belaying leaders or seconding climbers.

AUTOBLOCKING DEVICE

The autoblocking, plate, or plaquette style of belay device (fig. 2-2) is a type of tubular device that functions like a normal tube-style device while belaying the leader but has the distinct advantage of forcing the rope to bite on itself when it is used to belay from above, as well as the additional advantage of being

Connor Chilcott belays Kique Romero from above on the Cinderella to Little Sister Traverse, *Twin Sisters Range, Washington.*

able to be clipped directly to the anchor for belaying with one or two ropes.

The term *guide mode* describes using an autoblocking belay device to belay followers directly off the anchor, in a configuration that allows the device to autoblock or pinch the load strand onto the brake strand, helping to hold the load. While these devices are extremely effective at this task when set up appropriately (fig. 2-3), a few scenarios can cause them to not grab—on a high traverse, with certain rope diameters, with a slick rope, et cetera—and thus they are not considered hands-free.

The other *huge* advantage of an autoblocking belay device is that it makes it reasonable to belay two climbers seconding a pitch at the same time. The device has the

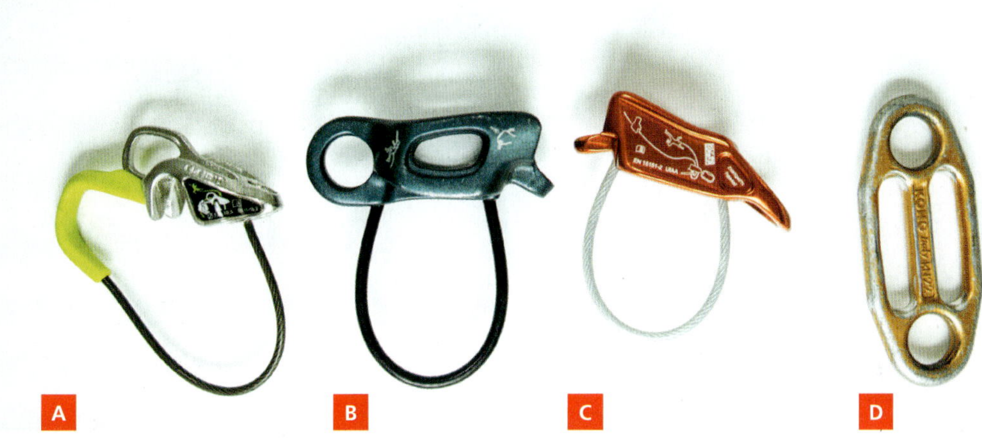

Figure 2-2. A variety of autoblocking belay devices: **a**, *Edelrid Mega Jul;* **b**, *Black Diamond ATC Guide;* **c**, *Petzl Reverso;* **d**, *Kong GiGi.* (Photo by Truc Allen)

Nate Wilhite and Keith Corbalis both following at the same time up the Purblind Pillar, *Red Rock Canyon, Nevada*

Figure 2-3. Ian Nicholson belays with an autoblocking belay device (Petzl Reverso) atop the first pitch of Blind Faith, *Eldorado Canyon, Colorado.* (Photo by Sarah Janin)

Figure 2-4. Correct setup of a Kong GiGi: **a**, *clip the device to the anchor (1) and pass a bight of rope through the device (2), then clip the "blocking" carabiner to this same bight of rope (3) ;* **b**, *clip the same carabiner to the load strand's front side;* **c**, *pull the slack out and start belaying.*

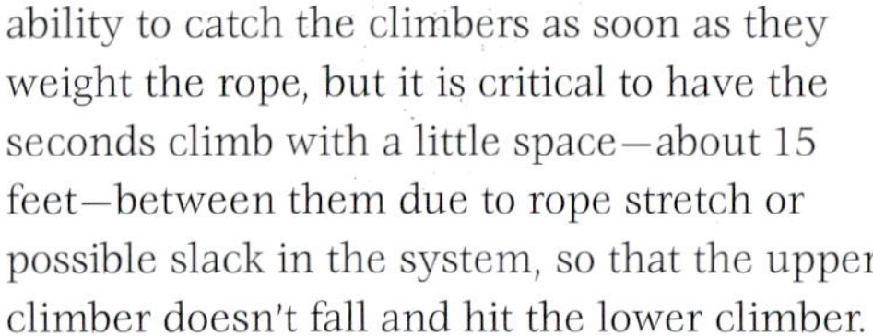

ability to catch the climbers as soon as they weight the rope, but it is critical to have the seconds climb with a little space—about 15 feet—between them due to rope stretch or possible slack in the system, so that the upper climber doesn't fall and hit the lower climber.

Kong GiGi and CAMP Ovo

The Kong GiGi and the CAMP Ovo are among the oldest autoblocking plaquette belay devices on the market. These lower-friction autoblocking belay devices are notably easier to pull rope through while belaying than models that look more like a traditional tube-style belay device, a clear advantage on longer routes or while belaying two people.

Start by clipping the device to the anchor; pass a bight of rope through the device, then clip the "blocking" carabiner to that same bight after it emerges from the belay device (fig. 2-4a). Also clip the same carabiner to the load strand (fig. 2-4b), then pull the slack out and start belaying (fig. 2-4c).

The disadvantage with the Kong GiGi, CAMP Ovo, and similar devices is that you cannot rig them in the same way you would a traditional autoblocking device, because of the real potential for the "blocking" carabiner to spin and completely nullify the device's ability to create friction (fig. 2-5). Instead, you

Figure 2-5. This Kong GiGi is incorrectly rigged—it is not clipped to the front (load) strand, nor is the "blocking" carabiner set up properly. (Photo by Jim Meyers)

Figure 2-6. This Kong GiGi belay device is set up properly for belaying a single rope, with the "blocking" carabiner clipped back around the front (load) strand. (Photo by Dale Remsberg)

must clip these devices such that the rope cannot twist the "blocking" carabiner and subsequently reduce the device's ability to create friction (fig. 2-6).

Contrary to popular belief, you can rappel with a GiGi or CAMP Ovo, though they are not intended to be used to belay leaders and they do still offer a little less friction than traditional devices. You *cannot* rappel with these devices in the same manner you would with a more traditional device, with the carabiner that the rope bends around clipped to your harness. Instead, after threading the ropes through the device's two larger (main) holes and clipping them as you normally would, clip a second locking carabiner to the smaller eyehole at the top of the belay device and clip this carabiner to your belay extension or harness belay loop before rappelling (fig. 2-7).

Figure 2-7. A Kong GiGi set up for rappelling: Thread the ropes through the device's two larger (main) holes (1) and clip them as you normally would. Then with a second carabiner (2) clip the smaller hole at the top (sometimes called the eye or, on other autoblocking belay devices, the ear) on the belay device to your belay extension or belay loop before rappelling.

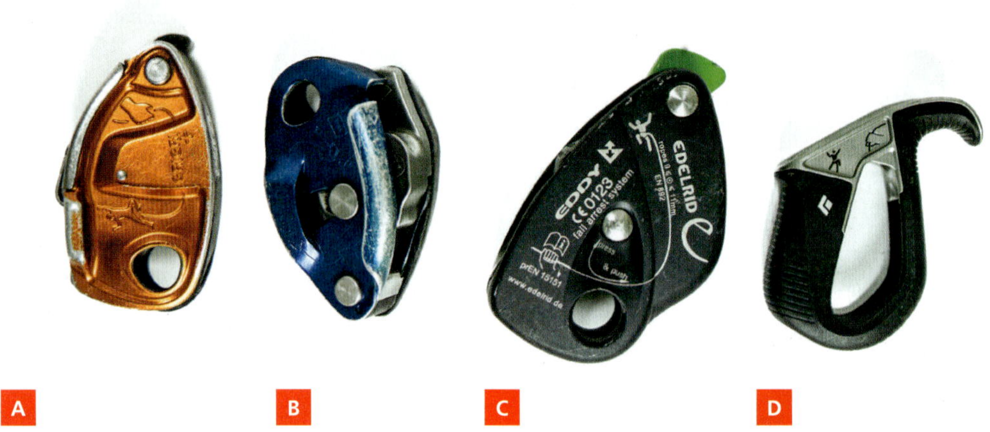

Figure 2-8. Assisted-braking belay devices: **a**, *Petzl GriGri+;* **b**, *Petzl GriGri;* **c**, *Edelrid Eddy;* **d**, *Black Diamond ATC Pilot.* (Photo by Truc Allen)

ASSISTED-BRAKING BELAY DEVICE

Belay devices that mechanically assist in stopping the rope are called assisted-braking belay devices (ABDs). There are a number of different ABDs on the market (fig. 2-8). Depending on the design, they either have some sort of cam or the entire device rotates into a position that locks the rope. These devices are both passive (the rope pulls the entire device into a position that increases friction) and active (the rope's speed activates some sort of cam inside the device to increase friction).

Similar to autoblocking belay devices, ABDs can fail to arrest the rope in some situations and thus are not considered hands-free. An ABD unquestionably increases the security and integrity of the belay; under most circumstances, the device will "bite" down on the rope once the rope reaches a certain speed, "assisting" the belayer should the leader take a longer-than-typical fall, should the belayer be pulled off their feet, or should

Cory Beal belays a follower directly off the anchor with a Petzl GriGri, an assisted-braking belay device, at Icicle Creek Canyon, Washington.

THE CASE FOR ASSISTED-BRAKING BELAY DEVICES

BY RON FUNDERBURKE

In my years as a climbing educator, I have consistently met students who have yet to fully comprehend the intersection of dynamic climbing environments and the limited capabilities all humans share. I was not any different when I first started climbing. When I began learning the sport, my brain could handle only so much. So I underestimated the scope of the subject matter; I underestimated how dynamic and variable climbing environments can be. Then I overestimated my ability to consistently maintain attention on a single task or react to violent and unexpected events like leader falls; I overestimated my ability to manage the risks in climbing using just my intellect, my muscles, and my instincts.

In time, both shortcomings were overruled by some irreversible truths. A climber who wishes to be adequately prepared for emergencies should strive to accelerate their acceptance of these truths:

- The climbing environment is dynamic and unpredictable. Spontaneous rockfall events happen; holds that have sustained hundreds of climbers suddenly break; anomalous weather bursts from above and below as if controlled by malicious gods—the list of known objective hazards continues to grow with time and experience.
- Humans are fallible and generally unaware of our fallibility. Even worse, unless we intentionally address this tendency, the more unaware we are and the more likely we are to mask our ignorance with unmerited confidence.
- Even though these truths are substantiated by significant bodies of scientific, anecdotal, and cultural evidence, the leap from awareness to action can be difficult, because it often asks a climber to unlearn something cherished or delay their climbing goals temporarily in order to learn a new skill.

That's a lot of prelude for talking about assisted-braking belay devices (ABDs), but I must say it: I have been advocating for the use of these tools for more than a decade. Yet I see climbers reflexively reach for manual-braking belay devices in contexts where they should be more suspicious of their environment and their limitations. I see accidents reported every year that correlate to the use of manual-braking devices, and I see those accidents at higher rates than those associated with ABDs.

With my failures fully disclosed, let me once again lay out the case for ABDs. I hope this challenge is one that I can meet through persistence, because the reasoning has not changed in all my years. Hopefully this time we'll convert a few more people to the cause.

1. **The human problem.** Our attention spans are limited, and even the most diligent belayers are susceptible to small lapses of attention. If those lapses coincide with falls, the resultant delay in reaction time can increase fall consequences. Additionally, some leader falls can be surprisingly violent. They can wrench the

This belayer is using an assisted-braking belay device (here, clipped to the anchor with a silver locking carabiner) to belay a follower from above. (Photo by Ron Funderburke)

belayer in different directions, high into the air, or directly into the wall, rock, ice, roof, et cetera. Having experienced this violence and successfully reacted to it many times, belayers become more skilled. In the meantime, however, lead climbers are vulnerable to a learning curve that is terribly unforgiving. ABDs provide a margin of error to belayers, a technological stopgap to a human condition that is psychologically and physiologically universal.

2. **The environmental problem.** Injuries and incidents can compromise belayers. Rockfall, icefall, falling equipment, avalanche, encounters with flora or fauna, medical conditions, the lead climber's own body; all of these can create circumstances in which a belayer, through no fault of their own, cannot maintain vigilant control of a manual-braking device. An ABD dramatically increases the likelihood of a catch in circumstances in which the belayer has been compromised.

3. **The availability problem.** There are enough different kinds of ABDs out there that conscientious consumers are not forced to conform to a tool that does not suit their handedness, number of limbs, number or size of ropes, proclivities of brand, price, fashion, or function, or whatever other quirks or preferences characterize belayers. When I first started my ABD crusade, I was trying to convince climbers to use the Petzl GriGri, because it was the only ABD readily available on the market. Nowadays, the designs and varieties are so numerous that belayers can explore myriad options.
4. **The cultural problem.** It is difficult to change behavior when faced with cultural obstacles. I believe this issue is not about reasoning or logic. In the United States in particular, our climbing culture has long been characterized by pluck, self-determination, and resilience. Those values have produced some amazing climbs and some truly heroic climbers. Those values have also taught us that greatness comes from confronting the unknown. But when belayers artificially manufacture the unknown, pretending that everything we know about climbing environments, human capability, and belay technology is somehow eclipsed by our desire to pioneer, then we're living in a dreamworld, not "living the dream." Respectfully, at some point every climber must reclaim responsibility for their knowledge and expertise. We might owe our admiration, our awe, and our culture to our mentors, our predecessors, our pioneers, but we do not owe our practice or our perception to them. At some point, we have to own those for ourselves and our posterity.
5. **The self-rescue argument.** Assisted-braking belay devices can create enormous efficiencies for self-rescue. Though it has not historically been the first thing I point out, I'd be remiss in the context of this book to ignore the utility of ABDs in small-team rescue. All of the ABDs can be used to rappel single strands of fixed or counterweighted rope, and the assisted-braking function provides an intrinsic backup that replaces the need for extensions or friction hitches. Many of these devices also make excellent progress captures in hauling systems or ascension systems. Their releasability under tension also makes them great load-transfer tools.

If it were in my power, every climber would learn to belay and rappel with simple manual-braking devices or methods. Rock climbers would start with a tube-style ATC Guide; mountaineers would start with hip belays and graduate to munter hitches. In doing so, they'd learn about sound mechanics, double-checks and communication, vigilance, and the seriousness of the belay task. But then they would graduate to an assisted-braking belay device of their choice, one uniquely suited to the climbing environment in which they find themselves most frequently.

I don't like being prescriptive, but this one adjustment to the way we think about our belay tools would help us to confront our limitations, be prepared for our environment, and have a powerful self-rescue tool at our disposal if the need ever arose.

Ron Funderburke is director of education at the Colorado Mountain School, and he has taught climbers at all levels, all over the world, as well as the teachers who teach those climbers. He has written and amended national training criteria for the American Mountain Guides Association, the American Alpine Club, and the UIAA (International Climbing and Mountaineering Federation) and has written eight books and contributed to twice that many. He has also produced public service projects and partnered with manufacturers on various promotional campaigns.

Johnny Youngs belays with a Petzl GriGri directly off a ring girth-hitch anchor on Lost in Space *at Smith Rock State Park, Oregon.*

the belayer be compromised in any way. ABDs are wonderful for belaying a leader, as they increase the belayer's ability to securely catch a fall, particularly in scenarios in which something unexpected happens, such as the leader falling suddenly, catching an unprepared belayer off guard.

While traditionally thought of as a tool for single-pitch climbing, especially sport climbing due to the generally increased odds and frequency of falling, ABDs are useful enough that they should be considered for any outing, be it sport or traditional climbing, whether single-pitch or multipitch. This is because ABDs increase the belayer's ability to catch a fall not only from a belay stance on the ground but also from a belay 1,000 feet up a route.

Rebecca Schroeder rappels with an ABD on a single strand of rope after fixing lines on the Aquarian Wall *of El Capitan, Yosemite National Park, California.*

It is also perfectly acceptable to use an ABD to belay a seconding climber from above, directly off the anchor, in a multipitch environment. In this configuration, the ABD is lower friction and easier to pull rope through than any autoblocking belay device, including options like the Kong GiGi or CAMP Ovo; this is especially true of the Petzl GriGri.. While ABDs have the disadvantage of being able to belay only one climber at a time, the notably reduced friction while belaying from above, along with their assisted-braking characteristics, make them a good choice in these settings. However, when belaying a leader or a follower, it is imperative that the person belaying remain attentive.

ABDs are the best tool for rappelling on a single strand of rope: they provide a very high level of security and do not require a backup or third hand, as it is very difficult to create a situation in which these devices are not able to engage. While it is possible to rappel in a more traditional two-rope system using an ABD, with a blocker knot or a knot that is temporarily fixed to the anchor, then untied by a second rappeller, this setup isn't ideal. Even if you have to bring a second, more traditional device for rappelling, an ABD is easily worth its weight for multipitch climbing.

BASIC ANCHORS

The goal of this book isn't to provide in-depth instruction on climbing anchors. However, it is essential to know the principles behind building solid anchors, as well as a few of the most common ways to build them, depending on the situation and the gear you have available—not only for responding to a technical rescue but also for avoiding a rescue in the first place.

SERENE, EARNEST, AND IDEAL

A lot of people learn the SERENE, EARNEST, and IDEAL acronyms to help them recall the key attributes of anchor construction but then learn or choose to construct anchors in only one or two ways. The truth is, those acronyms are just a framework in which to create anchors: the construction of anchors can even be artistic (to an extent) as long as you follow the "rules" outlined by the acronyms.

These common acronyms articulate the same basic information and principles of anchor construction: SERENE stands for Solid/Strong, Equalized, Redundant, Efficient, No Extension. EARNEST stands for Equalized, Angles/Appropriate Angles, Redundant, No

Extension, Strong, Timely. IDEAL stands for Integrity (as in the rock, the placements, and the anchor as a whole), Doubled (for redundancy), Equalized, Angles/Appropriate Angles, Loading (as in the direction of pull). All these acronyms represent the factors you should consider when building an anchor.

While all of the principles that the letters in each of these acronyms represent are important, the most crucial aspects of an anchor are that it's *strong* and *redundant*, as these are the two aspects that are most likely to kill you or your partner if you mess up, at least statistically speaking (folks die from weak anchors or when a critical component of their anchors breaks). While any of these acroynms are appropriate, for simplicity this book uses SERENE when discussing possible anchor options:

Solid/Strong: The sum of the components must make the anchor unquestionably strong and solid.

Equalized: Rig the anchor so that the load is distributed as equally as possible among the individual anchor points. Since larger angles put more force on each anchor point, try to keep the angles to 60 degrees or less.

Redundant: Build the anchor so that any one piece or part of the anchor could fail without causing complete or catastrophic failure. For example, if one piece of protection that the anchor relies on fails or part of the cordelette or sling the anchor is tied with is cut, the integral anchor should not fail catastrophically.

Efficient: Strive to be efficient in the time required to construct the anchor and with the gear used. Don't create something that is unnecessarily slow or complicated.

No **E**xtension: Construct the anchor such that if one anchor point fails, it won't cause the anchor to suddenly extend to the point where it could create shock loading (rapid loading or high impact force) to the remainder of the anchor, which could cause the entire anchor to fail catastrophically.

PRE-EQUALIZED ANCHOR

Pre-equalized anchors are among the most commonly used anchors, and with good reason: they provide a high level of security, offer both a shelf (strands above the knot area) and a master point (the knot itself) from which to operate, and are simple to construct. Pre-equalized anchors are also sometimes called traditional anchors because of their widespread and accepted use.

A pre-equalized anchor is tied to create a power point or master point with each of its legs "preset," meaning they cannot adjust if the direction of load changes. This inability to adjust is generally not a problem, as most of the time the climber will attach to or unclip from the anchor the same way—and in the event that there is a change in the direction of load, all the anchor's pieces will still be incorporated, though with reduced or no "equalization" or distribution of force.

Still, pre-equalized anchors are great at creating redundancy and incorporating as many pieces as necessary and as material will allow for, which is far more important than the ability to adjust the distribution of force to facilitate the load drastically changing directions.

Traditional Pre-Equalized Two-Piece Anchor

A pre-equalized two-piece anchor is most commonly used on bolts or ice screws or as part of a more complex alpine anchor. To tie a pre-equalized two-piece anchor, simply clip both pieces of protection (a 48-inch sling is

Figure 2-9. The most classic of pre-equalized anchors: a single sling is clipped with nonlocking carabiners to two bolts (each equipped with two steel rings) and an overhand knot is then tied to create the anchor's master point. (Photo by Dale Remsberg)

Figure 2-10. Two-piece pre-equalized anchor made with a cordelette: While it is most common to use slings or webbing, there is absolutely no reason a pre-equalized anchor cannot be constructed with a cordelette. Here, three ropes are clipped separately to the anchor's master point. (Photo by Dale Remsberg)

most common), pull in the direction of anticipated load, and tie an overhand knot (figs. 2-9 and 2-10). This knot creates the anchor's master point and isolates each strand (leg) of the sling going to the bolts, so that any one part of the system could fail (a bolt fails, one leg of the sling is cut, a carabiner comes unclipped) but the rest of the anchor would remain attached to the wall—the epitome of "redundant."

Traditional Pre-Equalized Three-Piece Anchor

When trad climbing and building anchors using traditional protection like cams and nuts, most climbers use three pieces in the majority of their anchors. There are exceptions in which four pieces are required to provide enough security, and in rare cases you might get away with two, but three-piece anchors are the most common.

There are whole books dedicated to all the different ways you can build anchors, but without question, a cordelette is most commonly used, and with good reason. It can accommodate a wide configuration of protection and provides a nice master point to work with. Setting up and taking down an anchor with a cordelette is a little slower, and the overhand knot can be difficult to untie,

Figure 2-11. The most commonly constructed three-piece anchor: **a**, *use a cordelette to clip to three pieces of protection, isolating each leg (strand) of the cordelette by tying an overhand knot;* **b**, *the same technique using a long sling.* (Photos by Dale Remsberg)

but these issues frequently don't outweigh the benefits.

To tie a traditional pre-equalized three-piece anchor, clip all three pieces of protection with nonlocking carabiners to a single strand of a 15- to 20-foot piece of 6- to 7-millimeter cordelette (already tied in a loop), then pull all the strands connecting the pieces of protection in the direction of the intended load, forming a W in the cordelette, and then tie an overhand knot with the strands to form the master point (fig. 2-11a). Similar to a two-piece anchor, the knot makes the anchor redundant: any one part of the anchor could fail without the entire anchor failing. Whatever material you choose, strength depends on the type of material and its thickness (fig. 2-11b).

Traditional Pre-Equalized Four-Piece Anchor

If one or two of the pieces in an anchor are questionable, throw in another piece and keep putting in pieces until you are positive that the anchor is adequate for the anticipated loads. A four-piece anchor (fig. 2-12) can be constructed and utilized in the exact same way as a more traditional three-piece anchor.

Girth-Hitched Pre-Equalized Two-Piece Anchor

A two-piece girth-hitched anchor is very similar in its setup to a traditional two-piece anchor, except that instead of having an overhand knot in the bottom of the anchor, it uses a girth hitch around a locking carabiner or a full-strength ring that acts as the master point. The girth-hitch anchor has been used for

Figure 2-12. A traditional pre-equalized four-piece anchor (Photo by Dale Remsberg)

Figure 2-13. A four-piece anchor with the shelf used as another full-strength clip-in point: the shelf is secure and redundant as long as there is something clipped to the master point and all the individual loops of the shelf are clipped simultaneously. (Photo by Dale Remsberg)

Tip: With pre-equalized anchors, you can use the "shelf"—as mentioned earlier, the collection of loops created between the overhand knot and the pieces of protection—as an additional secure and redundant place to clip in, as long as something is clipped to the master point (fig. 2-13). You can clip your belay device or the clove hitch that secures the belayer to the shelf, depending on the situation. It is imperative that the carabiner being used to clip to the shelf captures the loop (a.k.a. one strand) in each leg of the anchor. Again, something must be clipped to the anchor's master point; otherwise, an overly weighted shelf could invert the overhand knot, capsizing and opening it.

decades in areas of Europe but has recently been gaining popularity in North America.

To set up this anchor, clip both ends of the sling to the pieces of protection that make up the anchor and pull down on both strands to form a V, then pass a bight of both strands through a locking carabiner or fixed ring (fig. 2-14a). Pass the bight around the bottom end of the ring or locking carabiner, then bring it behind and then back to the top of the ring or locking carabiner (fig. 2-14b). Tighten the girth hitch to dress it and complete the anchor (fig. 2-14c).

The advantages of this type of anchor are mostly that the girth hitch is ultrafast to tie and easy to undo even after it has been used at a hanging belay. It also can often be tied with a shorter sling (even a 24-inch sling) since it takes up a lot less material (fig. 2-15). While this anchor might appear less secure or even dangerous, rigorous and extensive testing has shown that even if one strand (leg)

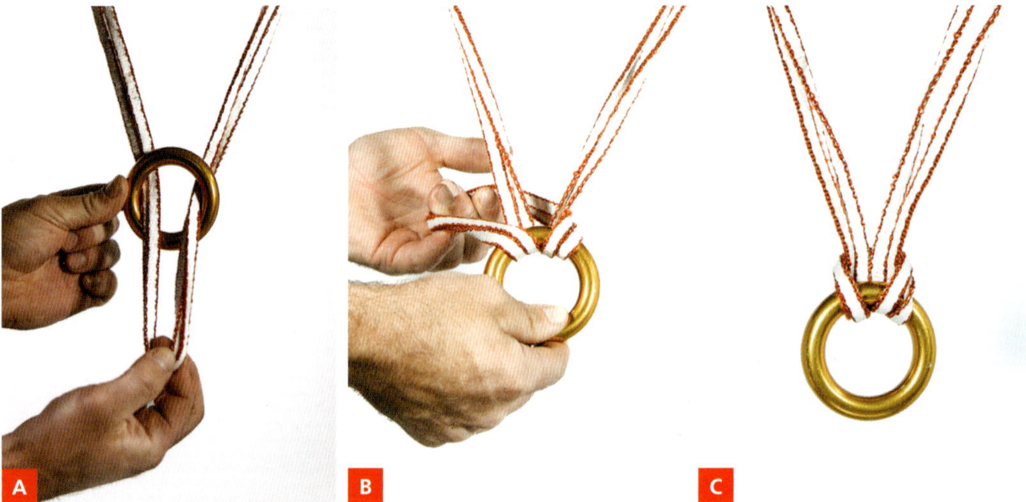

Figure 2-14. Girth-hitching an anchor's fixed ring: **a**, *after clipping both ends of the sling to the protection that makes up the anchor, pass a bight of both strands of the sling through the anchor's fixed ring;* **b**, *pass the bight around the bottom of the ring, then bring it behind and back up to the top of the ring;* **c**, *tighten the girth hitch to dress it and complete the anchor.* (Photos by Truc Allen)

of the anchor is cut or fails, the whole anchor does not fail and the girth hitch does not "slip" under climbing loads.

The downsides of the girth-hitched anchor are primarily that there is less room to work within the master point, depending on the size of the carabiner. And this anchor also requires a locking carabiner, something you may (or may not) be running short of.

Girth-Hitched Pre-Equalized Three-Piece Anchor

You can also girth-hitch the cordelette at the bottom of a pre-equalized three-piece anchor, instead of tying a knot in the cordelette. However, with three legs, this approach tends to be a little messier, particularly with 6- to 7-millimeter cord, and isn't quite as easy to untie, which reduces its advantages. Using a double-length (48-inch sling) is a less-bulky option (fig. 2-16).

QUAD ANCHORS

A "quad anchor" is another type that has been gaining popularity in recent years. For longer routes with bolted anchors, the quad can be left tied until the end of the route, eliminating the need to tie, untie, and retie your cordelette or sling, as is the case with a traditional pre-equalized anchor. The anchor is built with a doubled sling—either a "quad-length" (96-inch) one or, more frequently, a 71-inch one—with load-limiter knots tied on either side.

Two-Piece Quad Anchor

Start by folding the sling over to its midpoint on one of the two pieces of protection that make up the anchor (fig. 2-17a). A short way down from this piece of protection, tie an overhand knot, then a short distance from the other end of the sling, tie another overhand

Figure 2-15. Girth-hitched pre-equalized two-piece anchor built with a locking carabiner (Photo by Dale Remsberg)

knot (fig. 2-17b). Clip the free end of the sling to the second piece of protection in the anchor, and use either one or both of the two master points in the anchor (fig. 2-17c).

The quad anchor is best used for routes that have bolted anchors for their entirety, because once the load-limiter knots are tied, they don't have to be untied and retied, which saves time and energy for the leader and the follower. This anchor is more advantageous than the girth-hitched anchor in that it has two full-strength master points with which to work (fig. 2-18). Also, unlike the majority of anchors, it does offer some "auto-equalization" qualities, at least up to the load-limiter knots.

Three- or Four-Piece Quad Anchor

You can tie a quad anchor for a three-piece or four-piece pre-equalized anchor, but you must clearly identify the strongest piece because one

Figure 2-16. Girth-hitched pre-equalized three-piece anchor: While most people use a girth hitch for two-piece anchors, it is acceptable to also use it for three-piece anchors, as seen here. (Photo by Dale Remsberg)

of the three pieces will take half the load while the other two share the other half. In general, this anchor does not offer many benefits in time or efficiency compared to a traditional three-piece anchor built with a cordelette. With a four-piece quad, clip each piece and repeat the steps given for a two-piece.

CHAIN ANCHORS (ALPINE ANCHORS)

The chain anchor, also known as the alpine anchor, follows the same rules as a traditional anchor but is constructed with the pieces of

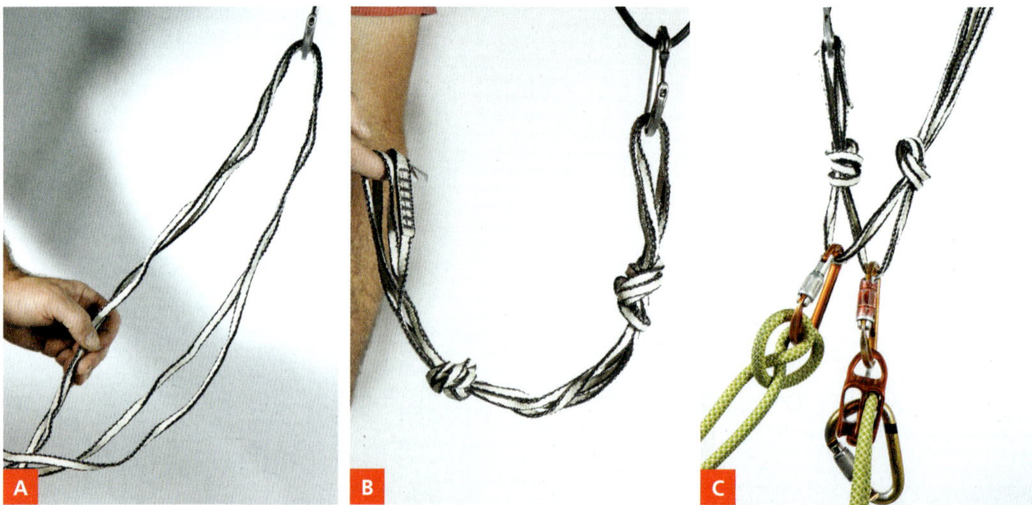

Figure 2-17. Two-piece quad anchor: **a**, *fold sling over to its midpoint on one piece of protection that makes up the anchor;* **b**, *a short way down from this piece, tie an overhand knot, then a short distance from the other end of the sling, tie another overhand knot;* **c**, *clip second end of the sling to the second piece of protection in the anchor and use either one or both of the quad's two master points.* (Photos by Truc Allen)

Figure 2-18. A two-piece quad anchor: tied with overhand load-limiting knots in a quad-length sling, this anchor has two master points. (Photo by Dale Remsberg)

Figure 2-19. A four-piece quad anchor: constructed with cordelette and an overhand knot for each "pair" of protection pieces; this anchor has two master points. (Photo by Dale Remsberg)

Figure 2-20. Chain or alpine three-piece anchors: **a**, *the left and middle two pieces of protection are clipped together, then they're clipped to the right-hand piece and to the master-point carabiner, creating a strong, redundant anchor that has little or no extension and some level of equalization;* **b**, *the left piece of protection's sling and the middle piece's built-in loop are clipped together, then they and the right-hand piece's built-in loop are clipped to the master-point carabiner.* (Photos by Dale Remsberg)

protection clipped together, rather than tied together with a sling or cordelette, in a way that creates redundancy, minimal extension, equalization, et cetera. When the rock is sound and the protection placements are sound, a "chain" or "alpine" anchor can be constructed using carabiners and the built-in loops and slings within the pieces of protection themselves (fig. 2-20a), though sometimes a small sling is used (fig. 2-20b).

The advantage of the chain anchor is that it is quicker to set up and break down, but the disadvantage is that you need the right placements in unquestionably solid rock, as the pieces of protection are generally placed close together in order to build the chain. Occasionally, the protection placements must be fine-tuned in order to be very strong and secure but also allow the anchor to be clipped in a way that creates redundancy, minimal extension, equalization, et cetera.

The possibilities are nearly endless when it comes to building anchors. Remember, though, that each piece of protection must be sound and ultimately produce an anchor that is unquestionably strong. Take care to never compromise the integrity of the placements to produce better equalization; if a chain or alpine anchor won't work in a given location, consider using other anchor techniques instead.

ROPE ANCHOR

It's bound to happen at some point in your climbing career: you're on lead, and you arrive

Figure 2-21. Two-piece equalized rope anchor: clove-hitch the rope to each piece of protection; here the length of rope between the pieces is girth-hitched to a locking carabiner to create the master point. (Photo by Dale Remsberg)

at a belay stance on a multipitch route having forgotten to bring the materials necessary to build an anchor. How will you tie together the anchor's components to create redundancy, equalization, minimal extension, et cetera? Luckily, with just a little bit of rope left in the system, you have everything you need. In this situation, using the rope itself can be an excellent option.

To use the rope to build an anchor with two pieces, clip both pieces of protection just as you would with a cordelette or sling, and once the length of rope is estimated, clove-hitch it to each piece. Then pull the rope tight between the two pieces and tie an overhand knot to create the master point, or girth-hitch the rope to a locking carabiner (fig. 2-21). In anchors with three or more pieces, clove-hitch the outermost placements and only clip the rope to the innermost placement(s).

Figure 2-22. Two-piece rope anchor: equalizing two bolts is one creative way to build an anchor with just the rope, a couple of carabiners and one overhand knot. (Photo by Silas Rossi)

There are some disadvantages to using the rope to build an anchor, mainly having to do with efficiency, and it is cumbersome if the group is leading in blocks. However, these disadvantages generally do not have to do with safety, which is obviously paramount.

OTHER ANCHORS

The purpose of the anchors in this section is to give an idea of how creative you can be when constructing anchors, as long as they meet the SERENE, EARNEST, OR IDEAL criteria discussed earlier. As an example, Figure 2-22 shows an anchor built with just the rope and carabiners; this anchor is strong, is fast to

Figure 2-23. Two-piece anchor built with only carabiners: the higher bolt is clipped with two opposite and opposed nonlocking carabiners, which are then clipped with a third nonlocker to a locking carabiner that is the master point; the locking carabiner is clipped directly to the lower ring. (Photo by Dale Remsberg)

Figure 2-24. Two-piece anchor with a fixed rappel ring: this welded chain anchor by Fixehardware, which consists of two bolts connected with a welded chain and fixed rappel ring, is rated at 25–30 kilonewtons; the master point is the locking carabiner clipped to the ring. (Photo by Dale Remsberg)

build, offers redundancy in the bolts, has minimal extension, and is equalized. Figure 2-23 shows an anchor built with just carabiners; while constructed with only metal, it still easily meets all the rules described in each of the acronyms: SERENE, EARNEST, and IDEAL.

A lot of routes are equipped with two chains leading down to a single steel ring that can rotate, which means wear will be spread out over the entire ring, increasing its longevity. These steel rings are significantly stronger than any carabiner climbers regularly carry; it is okay to clip directly to this ring and use it as a master point or to clip a "master carabiner" to it and operate off of that (fig. 2-24).

While the guideline of using two bolts or three pieces of rock protection is great, another option is to use an unquestionably sound monolithic natural feature to build a single-point anchor. These anchors can be quite secure and often are the best option at the top of a route, on a large ledge, or where good cracks might not exist. Remember,

Figure 2-25. A single-point anchor on a rock horn: the sling is doubled up, and both the "shelf" and the master point are clipped with locking carabiners for redundancy. (Photo by Dale Remsberg)

Figure 2-26. Two-piece anchor with load-limiter knots: clip one end of a shorter sling to one of the pieces of protection, tie two overhand knots in the sling, and clip the other end of the sling to the other piece of protection. Then create the sliding X by putting a half twist in one of the two strands between the load-limiter knots to make a loop—clip both this and the other strand to create the single master point and shelf. (Photo by Dale Remsberg)

though, that since there is only one "piece" of protection, these natural features must be unquestionably sound, and your soft goods (the slings or cord you use to construct the anchor) must be doubled up so that if they were to get cut in one spot, the whole anchor wouldn't fail (fig. 2-25).

Load-limiter knots can be a great way to create a secure and redundant anchor using only a shorter sling. First, clip the sling to one of your pieces of protection, then tie an overhand knot at each end—similar to a quad anchor, but the sling is not doubled over (fig. 2-26). The key to this anchor is to create a "magic" or sliding X in the middle of the sling, between the two knots. Put a half twist in one of the two strands to form a loop, and clip both this and the other strand to create the master point and shelf. (Unlike the quad anchor, which offers two master points, this setup offers just one.)

Tip: The sliding X—without load-limiter knots—should be avoided for equalizing two bolts (fig. 2-27). In an anchor built with bolts, the strength of each bolt is 23–31 kilonewtons (5,000–8,500 pounds), depending on the bolts' age, and most slings are rated to 20–23 kilonewtons (22 kilonewtons is just 4,945 pounds). This means that if you are equalizing modern bolts, the sling is the weak point, not the bolts: each bolt by itself is at least as strong as the sling. Therefore it makes more sense to beef up or make redundant the weakest part of the anchor—the sling. The advantage of the sliding X is that it comes as close as possible to splitting the load between each leg of the anchor, but the disadvantage is that it is not redundant. However, the sliding X can be a useful technique to increase the strength of a single leg of a more complex anchor.

A sliding or "magic" X is rarely the right technique for equalizing two bolts because it offers no redundancy to the weakest part of the system—the sling itself.

Opposite: *Ian Nicholson leads on a long traverse on* The Ascensionist, *Deception Crags, Washington.* (Photo by Tino Villanueva)

CHAPTER 3

Belay Escapes

Transferring the weight of a hanging climber or other loads from a belay device to the point where the load goes directly onto an anchor in a load-releasable system is called *escaping the belay*. While escaping the belay is obviously one of the most important skill sets in climbing, the concept of transferring a load from one system to another in a safe and backed-up manner has countless applications, and it is a foundation skill of technical and improvised rescue.

TYING OFF THE BELAY DEVICE

Tying off a belay device is the very first step in countless rescue techniques, but this skill can also have other applications, such as assisting in the transition from rappelling to ascending the rope to retrieve a stuck piece or simply safely going hands-free while belaying a lead climber who is resting on the rope or fiddling with a piece of protection.

TYING OFF THE BELAY DEVICE CARABINER

The current and most ideal way to tie off a belay device is by tying the rope off to the spine of the locking carabiner that attaches the belay device to the belayer's harness (the spine is the side opposite the carabiner's gate). Be sure to maintain control of the brake strand throughout this process:

1. With one hand, pin the brake strand against the underside of the belay device (fig. 3-1a).
2. Next, begin to build a mule hitch on the spine of the carabiner clipped to the belay device, making an X on the inside of the carabiner's spine by pulling a bight of rope through the carabiner and putting a half twist in it to create a small loop (fig. 3-1b).
3. With the long end of the loop, make another bight of rope and feed it around the carabiner spine and through the small loop, creating a mule hitch with around 6–8 inches of slack (fig. 3-1c).
4. Finally, tie an overhand backup knot around the load strand with the slack from the bight that finished the mule (fig. 3-1d).

TYING OFF A TRADITIONAL BELAY DEVICE

It is also possible to tie off the belay device itself. However, depending on the belay device and locking carabiner used, it can be slightly harder to keep tension during the initial pass-through of the rope. It can also be slightly more cumbersome to get enough slack to build the munter-mule-overhand compared to building it on the spine of the

Figure 3-1. Tying off the spine of the carabiner: **a**, *grip the brake strand securely against the underside of the belay device;* **b**, *pass a bight of rope through the carabiner in the belay device, putting a single twist in it that turns the bight into a loop;* **c**, *with rope from the original side of the carabiner, create another bight and pass it through the small loop, completing a "circle" around the carabiner;* **d**, *because the mule hitch is essentially a slip knot, it is imperative to back it up by tying an overhand knot around the load strand with the remaining slack.*

carabiner. Here's how to tie off the device itself:

1. Pass the brake strand of the rope through the locking carabiner that's clipped to the belay device, creating a bight (fig. 3-2a).
2. Bring the bight up so it is parallel to the load strand and fold it over, creating a loop adjacent to the load strand (fig. 3-2b).
3. With the long end of the loop, make another bight and pass it through the loop you just made, ensuring that the second bight encircles the load strand of the rope (fig. 3-2c).
4. Pull the bight tight to dress the mule hitch (fig. 3-2d).
5. Using slack from the bight, tie a backup overhand knot around the load strand of the rope (fig. 3-2e).

Figure 3-2. Tying off the device: **a**, *pass the brake strand through the locking carabiner clipped to the belay device, creating a bight;* **b**, *bring the bight up so it is parallel to the load strand and fold it over, creating a loop adjacent to the load strand;* **c**, *with the long end of the loop, make another bight and pass it through the loop that you just made, ensuring that it encircles the load strand of the rope;* **d**, *pull the bight tight;* **e**, *use slack from the bight to tie an overhand backup knot around the load strand of the rope.*

TYING OFF AN ASSISTED-BRAKING BELAY DEVICE

Tying off an assisted-braking belay device (ABD) such as a GriGri is similar to tying off a more traditional belay device around the spine of the carabiner—it is just easier to do so because the ABD is load releasable, making it hands-free; the device does the majority of the "holding" while you tie it off with an overhand stopper knot (fig. 3-3). If the device were to fail or be released in some way, the knot would jam against the device, stopping the rope from slipping any farther.

Tip: If you just want to go hands-free and are using some sort of ABD, it is okay to simply tie an overhand on a bight with a few feet of slack on the brake strand. This knot acts as a backup or "catastrophe" knot in the event that the device somehow releases.

Figure 3-3. To tie off an assisted-braking belay device (ABD), simply tie an overhand knot on the brake strand as a stopper or "catastrophe" knot.

BASELINE

Baseline is a point during technical rescues at which the load is attached directly to the anchor in a load-releasable manner. This load-releasable system is most frequently a munter-mule-overhand but could also be a belay device like a GriGri with a backup mule hitch and a backup tied on the brake strand. The concept of baseline is that it gives the rescuer a place, or baseline, from which to work or return to as needed (fig. 3-4).

Figure 3-4. Baseline: Tino Villanueva has escaped the belay—transferred the load to the anchor—and with a third hand in his left hand is ready to fire from baseline. (Photo by Jim Meyers)

Baseline is a critical place to be familiar with because working into and out of baseline is often less complicated than trying to shortcut directly between systems. In other words, it's often easier to transition to baseline, then to another technique, rather than jumping directly to the second technique unless you are sure of your ability to complete the task. Sure, there are ways to "jump" from step to step, but the vast majority of rescue techniques are most easily implemented out of baseline.

Providing an attentive belay is always an integral part of the safety system, as Dodge Garfield does here for Matt Rogers on a crux wide pitch on the East Ridge of Ingalls Peak, Stuart Range, Washington.

TRANSFERRING THE LOAD WHEN BELAYING A LEADER FROM THE HARNESS

Escaping the belay should always be thought of as a two-part system: the first part is tying off the belay, and the second part is transferring the load to an anchor. Once the belay device is tied off and the rescuer is able to go hands-free, the next step is to transition the weight or "load" from the tied-off belay device to the anchor.

On a multipitch route, whether you're leading or following, the anchor will already be built and the person belaying will be clipped in to it. In a majority of single-pitch routes, the climber will not be clipped to an anchor but will most likely be able to be lowered back to the ground. In the event that the belayer is on the ground but the climber has led too far out and can no longer be lowered to the ground, the belayer will need to build an anchor (see chapter 2) and/or ascend the rope to the climber in a counterbalanced fashion (see chapter 8).

CORDELETTE LOAD TRANSFER

The most straightforward way to transfer the load from your tied-off belay device to the anchor is to use a cordelette (usually 15–21 feet long). This method is the most straightforward visually and involves slightly fewer steps than other methods. The disadvantage is that you may not have a cordelette to work with, because it might already have been used in building your anchor. It is, however, a good technique to be familiar with, as all other systems are essentially variations of this technique.

1. Start by tying off the belay device on your harness with a mule hitch and overhand (fig. 3-5a).
2. Now find the middle of a cordelette (here, the blue cord), fold it over so you are working with two strands at a time, and with one end of the doubled-up cordelette tie a klemheist hitch around the load strand; move the klemheist to within an inch or two of the tied-off belay device. Place a carabiner on the anchor and tie the long ends of the cordelette to this carabiner with a mule hitch—this does not have to be a locking carabiner, because it should always be backed up, and while it might hold the load, it should never be used without the climbing rope itself backing up the system. Tighten the munter, taking up any slack in the cordelette (fig. 3-5b), and then add a mule hitch to it in the cordelette, and finish with an overhand backup knot (fig. 3-5c).
3. Clip a locking carabiner to the anchor and clip the brake strand coming out of the tied-off belay device to this locking carabiner (fig. 3-5d). Tie a munter hitch with this brake strand (fig. 3-5e) and tie off the munter with a mule hitch and an overhand backup knot (fig. 3-5f)—or wrap the brake strand around your hand to ensure that you do not lose control of it.
4. Slowly untie the munter-mule-overhand that is tied to the belay device itself (fig. 3-5g). Note that as you untie it, the cordelette will slowly take the weight of the load strand. Ensure that the klemheist friction hitch does not slip as it becomes weighted.
5. Remove the unweighted rope from the belay device clipped to your harness by unclipping the rope from the locking carabiner, sliding the rope out of the belay device, and removing the belay device and locking carabiner from the

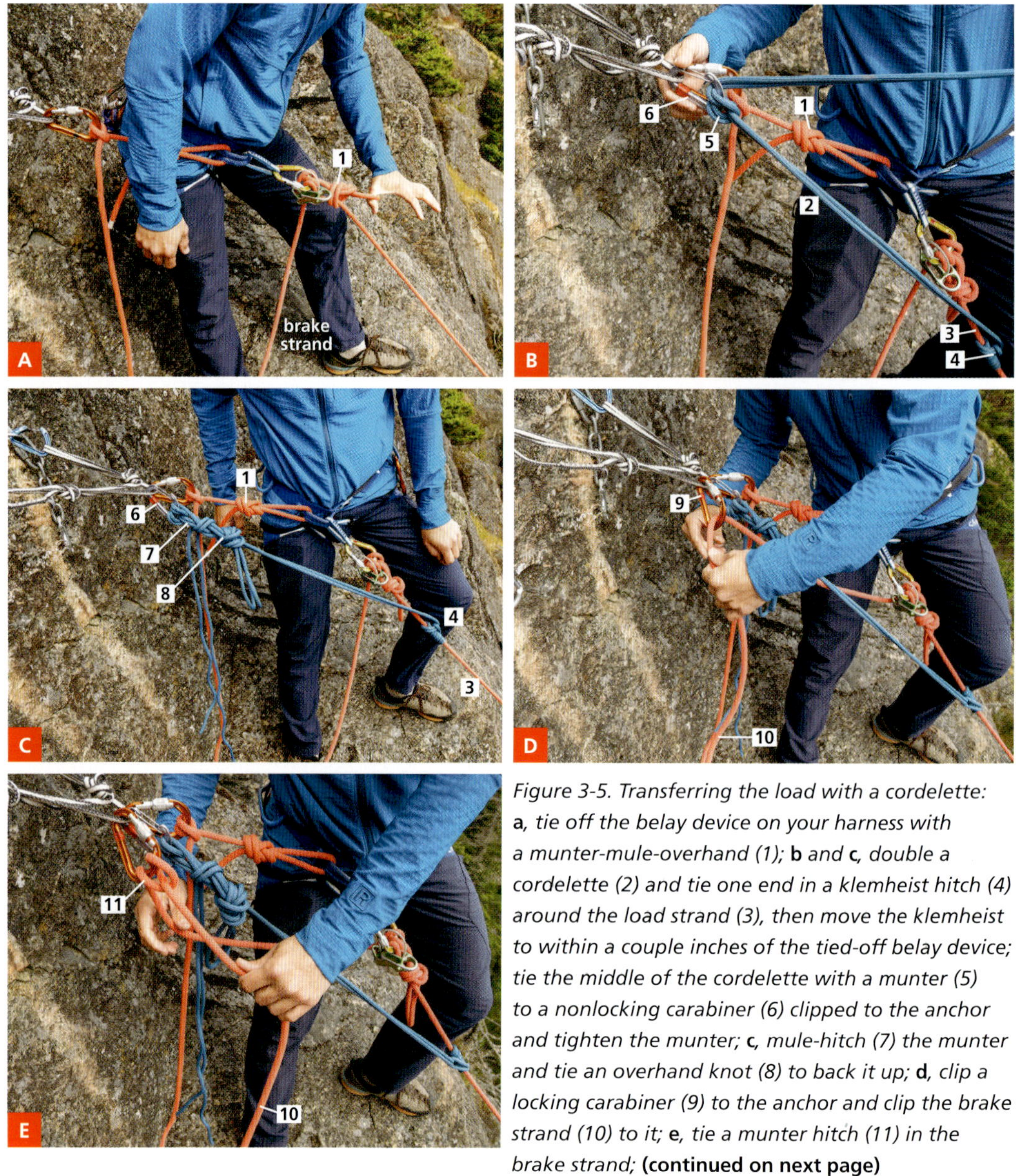

Figure 3-5. Transferring the load with a cordelette: **a**, *tie off the belay device on your harness with a munter-mule-overhand (1);* **b** *and* **c**, *double a cordelette (2) and tie one end in a klemheist hitch (4) around the load strand (3), then move the klemheist to within a couple inches of the tied-off belay device; tie the middle of the cordelette with a munter (5) to a nonlocking carabiner (6) clipped to the anchor and tighten the munter;* **c**, *mule-hitch (7) the munter and tie an overhand knot (8) to back it up;* **d**, *clip a locking carabiner (9) to the anchor and clip the brake strand (10) to it;* **e**, *tie a munter hitch (11) in the brake strand;* **(continued on next page)**

f, *mule-hitch (12) this munter and back it up with an overhand knot (13);* **g**, *untie the munter-mule-overhand (14) on your belay device (15);* **h**, *unclip your belay device from the load strand and remove the carabiner and belay device from the system;* **i**, *untie the cordelette's munter-mule-overhand clipped to the anchor;* **j**, *lower the cordelette out until the load strand (rope) holds the weight;* **k**, *once the rope has taken the weight, untie and retrieve the cordelette.*

system (fig. 3-5h)—again ensuring that you maintain control of the brake strand coming from the munter-mule-overhand tied with the brake strand to the locking carabiner clipped to the anchor. If there is too much slack, release, tighten, and retie the munter-mule-overhand in the rope clipped to the anchor with a locking carabiner.

6. It is now okay to untie the overhand backup knot and the mule hitch in the cordelette tied to the nonlocking carabiner clipped to the anchor (fig. 3-5i). Release tension on the cordelette's munter hitch (fig. 3-5j), allowing the load to transfer from the klemheist to the rope. If you do not have enough slack to lower the cordelette out, retie it and tighten the munter-mule-overhand in the rope clipped to the anchor with a locking carabiner. Once the rope has taken 100 percent of the weight, untie and retrieve the cordelette (fig. 3-5k). Welcome to baseline.

Tip: Challenge yourself to be able to tie the munter in both the lowering and belaying positions (see Figures 1-15 and 1-16 in chapter 1). Although small, this easy-to-learn technique is invaluable in complex technical rescues.

BACK-SIDE-ROPE LOAD TRANSFER

Using the climbing rope on the back side of the rescuer's clove hitch to the anchor (not the strand they're hanging from) and using a third hand or sling for the "grab" is called a *back-side load transfer*. While this technique is slightly more complicated than using the cordelette load transfer discussed above, it has the unique advantage of essentially always being viable as long as you have 2–3 feet of rope left and nearly any sort of soft good—a sling of any length, a third hand, et cetera. Start by tying off your belay device with a munter-mule-overhand (see Figure 3-2e), then follow these steps:

1. Tie a friction hitch around the load strand with any piece of soft material—a shoulder-length (24-inch) sling or a third hand works best—and clip a carabiner to the friction hitch (fig. 3-6a).
2. Clip the long end of the rope (which comes off the back side of the rescuer's clove hitch to the anchor) to the carabiner attached to the friction hitch (fig. 3-6b). This does not need to be a locking carabiner, as the load should never hang solely on the friction hitch and should be backed up with the climbing rope.
3. Pull the "back-side" rope tight and tie it to the carabiner clipped to the friction hitch with a munter-mule-overhand (fig. 3-6c).
4. Grasp the brake strand coming out of the tied-off belay device (fig. 3-6d).
5. Clip a locking carabiner to the anchor and tie this strand of rope to the carabiner with a munter hitch backed up with a mule hitch (fig. 3-6e) and back the munter-mule up with an overhand knot (fig. 3-6f).
6. Slowly untie the munter-mule-overhand on the belay device itself (fig. 3-6g). As you release the belay device, the friction hitch on the load strand will slowly take the weight. Ensure that this friction hitch does not slip as it becomes weighted.
7. Unclip the rope from the belay device on your harness (fig. 3-6h), again ensuring that you maintain control of the brake strand coming from the anchor if the

munter is not tied off with a mule hitch and overhand backup knot.

8. Untie the overhand backup and mule hitch from the back-side rope, leaving the munter clipped to the carabiner on the friction hitch (fig. 3-6i).
9. Release tension on the back-side strand's munter hitch to lower the load onto the strand tied to the anchor with a munter-mule-overhand (fig. 3-6j), allowing the friction hitch to slacken so that the climbing rope takes 100 percent of the weight. Welcome to baseline (fig. 3-6k).

ESCAPING THE BELAY WHEN BELAYING OFF AN ANCHOR FROM ABOVE

Being able to escape the belay (along with various other rescue techniques) is equally important when belaying a follower as it is when belaying a leader. It is advantageous in nearly every conceivable situation to belay directly off the anchor, ideally using an autoblocking belay device (like a Petzl Reverso or Black Diamond ATC Guide), an assisted-braking belay device (such as a GriGri), or a munter hitch. Generally speaking, belaying a second climber directly off your harness while clipped in to the anchor and belaying through a redirect on the anchor are the poorest options, for a number of reasons: they are the least efficient setups for pulling slack in as the climber ascends, the belayer is the most trapped, and they are the most difficult setups for escaping the system. While it likely isn't an issue in the case of belaying off your harness through a redirect, you are also literally doubling the forces on your anchor.

RELEASING THE BELAY DEVICE UNDER LOAD WHILE BELAYING FROM ABOVE

Suppose you are belaying from above with an autoblocking belay device, such as the Petzl Reverso or the Black Diamond ATC Guide, and are using it in autoblocking mode (a.k.a. "guide mode"). In this situation, several options exist for releasing the plate and potentially lowering the follower. The technique you choose will depend on the terrain, the condition of the person you are lowering, your skills, and the length of the lower. The following techniques can be part of releasing tension from an autoblocking belay device either to escape the belay while going to baseline or used for shorter lowers that let you escape the belay without the necessity of going to baseline.

Rocking the Carabiner

When you need to release the tension for only a little bit of slack, "rocking" the belay carabiner back and forth is a great option. This maneuver is good for when a climber has climbed too close to a piece of protection or is hanging just above a ledge, or during a belay escape when a friction hitch has been placed in front of the belay device on the load strand and the device needs to release just a small amount of tension to create the necessary slack for the friction hitch to grab the rope (and not the belay device).

Simply "rock" the belay carabiner (the one inside the device that the ropes are pinching on, not the one clipped to the anchor) back and forth (fig. 3-7). The more shape the carabiner has, the faster it will loosen, but even with the smoothest, roundest carabiner, pushing the rope in the direction you want it to go in conjunction with long "rocks" back and forth should prove effective. The

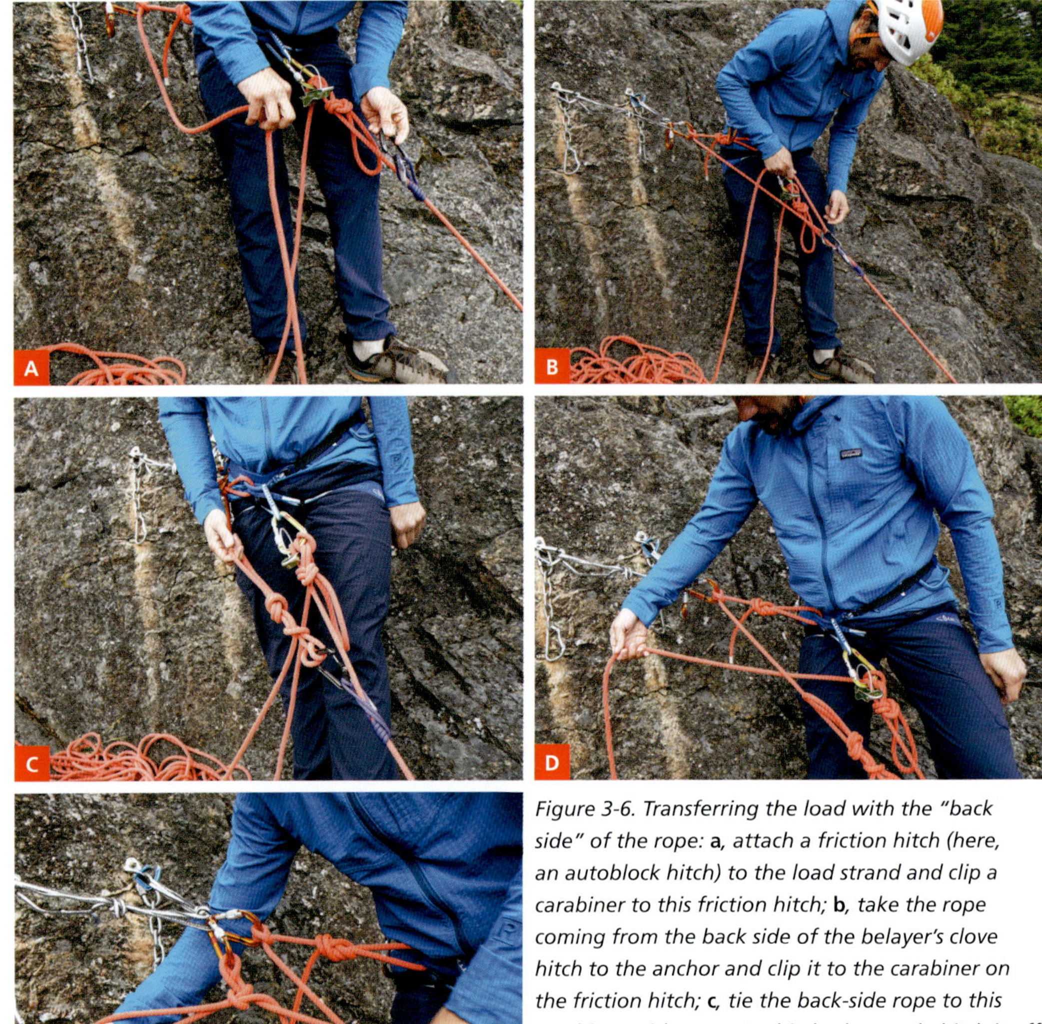

Figure 3-6. Transferring the load with the "back side" of the rope: **a**, *attach a friction hitch (here, an autoblock hitch) to the load strand and clip a carabiner to this friction hitch;* **b**, *take the rope coming from the back side of the belayer's clove hitch to the anchor and clip it to the carabiner on the friction hitch;* **c**, *tie the back-side rope to this carabiner with a munter hitch, then mule-hitch it off and tie an overhand backup knot;* **d**, *grab the brake strand coming out of the belay device;* **e**, *attach the brake strand to the anchor with a locking carabiner and tie a munter-mule;* **f**, *back up the munter-mule with an overhand knot;* **g**, *release your belay device by untying the mule and overhand on the belay device and lowering the load onto the friction hitch;* **(continued on next page)**

h, *once the friction hitch takes the load, unclip the rope from your belay device and tighten the rope going to the anchor, if necessary;* **i**, *untie the overhand backup knot and mule hitch from the back-side rope clipped to the friction hitch;* **j**, *release tension on the munter hitch to lower out the friction hitch until the rope going straight from the load to the anchor tightens and the back-side strand going to the friction hitch slackens;* **k**, *welcome to baseline.*

Fig. 3-7. "Rocking" the belay carabiner to create slack. Note that the climber can "push" slack from the brake strand into the device while still maintaining control.

downside of this trick is that you might get less than an inch of slack for every "rock," but sometimes that's all you need.

Redirected LSD (a.k.a. Redirected Load Strand Direct)

A variation on the new-wave LSD lower in which a carabiner is used to "defeat" the belay device, the redirected LSD uses a sling connected to the belayer's body that allows them to control how much the belay device is opened up in autoblocking mode and how much friction it produces. This shouldn't be your first choice for a lower, but it is the best improvised lower that does not involve completely escaping the belay device when you need to smoothly lower an injured climber a significant distance. Here's how to do it:

1. Put a third hand around the brake strand of the rope and clip it to your belay loop

Figure 3-8. Using a redirected LSD to "defeat" the autoblocking belay device: **a**, *clip the load strand in front of the belay device, then attach a double-length sling and redirect it through the anchor;* **b**, *clip it to your harness and put a third hand on the brake strand;* **c**, *lean into your harness to "defeat" the device and lower rope accordingly.*

with a locking carabiner (fig. 3-8a). This third hand is helpful, since the amount of friction can be difficult to manage and will vary according to the hanging climber's weight, the shape of the terrain, and the number of pieces the rope is running through.

2. Also clip a nonlocking carabiner to your harness belay loop and clip this carabiner to a double-length sling (fig. 3-8b). Redirect the sling through the anchor above the belay device with another nonlocking carabiner, then clip it into the load strand in front of the device.
3. To release tension, use your body weight to lean against the friction of the device, which provides a good "feel" and lets the belayer keep both hands available to manage the rope (3-8c).

The "Classic" Plate Release (a.k.a. Redirected Sling Method)

Most autoblocking belay devices feature a small fourth hole opposite the "ear"—the larger hole that clips to the anchor. This fourth hole is specifically designed for "defeating" the belay device, and it's very effective, but most devices offer only all-or-nothing results: you get a lot of friction or essentially none—nothing in between.

1. This lower can be uneven so start by putting a third hand on the brake strand of the rope.
2. Girth-hitch a sling through the fourth hole of your device (fig. 3-9a).
3. Re-direct the sling through the anchor with a nonlocking carabiner and clip it to your belay device with another nonlocking carabiner (fig. 3-9b).

Figure 3-9. "Classic" redirected-plate release: **a**, *girth-hitch a sling through the fourth (and smallest) hole on the device;* **b**, *redirect the sling through the anchor and clip it to your harness;* **c**, *attach a third hand and "lean in" to your harness.*

4. Lean away from the anchor; this will cause the belay device to rotate and release the load (fig. 3-9c). It should be noted that most devices have a very small "sweet spot" and go from holding the load to providing very little friction with just a few degrees in angle change.

Carabiner Lever

The carabiner lever method is a quick way to release the belay device without having to go to baseline and could even be used to lower your partner a short distance if they aren't seriously hurt. It is a poor option for a more severely injured (or scared) person or for any sort of long or otherwise tricky lower.

1. Put a third hand on the brake strand of the rope (fig. 3-10a). Don't skip this step: this is the most all-or-nothing feeling of all the device defeats described here, and you'll want the backup of the third hand.
2. For a smoother lower, clip the brake strand through a high redirect on the anchor (fig. 3-10b).
3. Clip a carabiner into the small hole on the bottom of the device (fig. 3-10c). (Do *not* clip the ear that is attached to the anchor nor the rope hole tubes.)
4. Ideally, the carabiner—often just the nose—clips in snugly without sliding. You do not want a loose-fitting carabiner that slides around.
5. Now pull down on the carabiner so that it acts as a lever, pivoting the device and releasing the load (fig. 3-10d).

Tip: A sling is the standard material used in the fourth hole of the belay device and redirected to "defeat" the plate and release the load. While a sling works well, you could instead use a single strand of cordelette with a blocker knot (as shown in the photo) or even pass the wire of a small nut through and clip it. Whatever you use, it needs to attach to the lower hole in the device in such a way that you can lever off of it to rotate the device and cause it to release.

Using a 5.5mm cordelette for a classic plate release

ESCAPING THE BELAY FROM ABOVE AND GOING TO BASELINE WITH A CORDELETTE

An autoblocking belay device or an assisted-braking belay device (ABD), compared with a more traditional tube-style belay device, not only provides a better belay but also another gigantic advantage when performing any sort of technical assistance or rescue. An autoblocking belay device has a third hole that is attached directly to the anchor. When set up correctly, it pinches the load strand on top of the brake strand, helping to provide security while belaying a following climber. With very few exceptions, it is generally not used in autoblocking mode to belay a leader.

Whether you're belaying with an autoblocking belay device or an ABD, neither is

Figure 3-10. Carabiner lever release: **a**, *put a third hand friction hitch on the belay device;* **b**, *redirect the brake strand coming out of the device off the anchor;* **c**, *clip a carabiner that does not easily rotate through the fourth hole;* **d**, *use the carabiner as a lever to rotate the device and "defeat" it.*

considered truly hands-free, so it is imperative to tie a stopper knot (a.k.a. "catastrophe" knot)—an overhand on a bight works great—2–3 feet behind the belay device (fig. 3-11) or tie a clove hitch and clip it to the anchor as a "fail-safe" backup, depending on whether your next step will include removing the belay device from the anchor. In the event the device were to be "defeated," the stopper knot would jam against the device and limit how far the following climber would fall.

What is nice about escaping an autoblocking belay device is that the device catches and holds a fall for you. However, there are circumstances in which these devices can fail or "creep" (slip), so it is imperative that you maintain control of the brake strand—but generally they catch and hold all or the majority of a fall.

To escape an autoblocking belay device when belaying from above:

1. Tie a stopper knot, such as an overhand knot, in the rope about 3 feet behind the belay device (fig. 3-12a). You'll find it easier to have a little slack to work with, so giving yourself 2–3 feet of space between the "catastrophe" knot and the belay device is helpful
2. Use a cordelette to tie a klemheist around the load strand (fig. 3-12b). Clip the cordelette to a new carabiner on the anchor (fig. 3-12c). This carabiner does not need to be a locking carabiner, as the load should never be exclusively on the cordelette. (It is also possible for the rescuer to use the back side of their clove-hitch attachment to the anchor—the strand they're not hanging from—as another piece of material; see Back-Side-Rope Load Transfer, above.) Tie the cordelette to this carabiner with a munter-mule overhand (fig. 3-12d).

Figure 3-11. An overhand stopper knot (a.k.a. "catastrophe" knot) is tied 2–3 feet behind the belay device, so in the event the device were to be defeated, the knot would jam against the device, limiting how far the following climber would fall.

3. Tie a munter hitch in the brake strand coming out of the belay device and clip it to a locking carabiner on the anchor (fig. 3-12e). You can either finish this with a mule hitch and an overhand backup knot (fig. 3-12f) or wrap the brake strand around your hand, but it is imperative that you maintain control of this strand over the next few steps.
4. Rock the "floating carabiner" in the autoblocking belay device (not the one clipped to the anchor) to create slack and move the weight from the belay device to the cordelette. Once the weight has been transferred to the cordelette, remove the belay device, again maintaining control of the munter hitch tied on the brake strand if it hasn't had a mule hitch and overhand backup knot added to it.
5. Untie the cordelette's overhand backup knot and mule hitch (fig. 3-12g). Lower the load using the cordelette's munter hitch until the weight is hanging on the rope and the cordelette slackens; ensure that you have enough length in the cordelette to hold the load until it is fully on the rope (fig. 3-12h). If you don't have enough material, retie the cordelette's mule hitch and overhand backup and tighten the brake strand's munter-mule-overhand. Once the rope is holding the load, untie and remove the cordelette (fig. 3-12i).
6. Welcome to baseline (fig. 3-8j).

ESCAPING THE BELAY WITH AN AUTOBLOCKING BELAY DEVICE AND A BACK-SIDE LOAD TRANSFER

Much like the back-side load transfer for escaping a lead belay, this technique can also be used to escape the belay while belaying a follower from above. Similar to a back-side load transfer for a leader, you can use the climbing rope on the back side of the rescuer's clove hitch (not the load strand) and use a third hand or sling for the friction hitch. While this technique is slightly more complicated than using the cordelette discussed above, it has the unique advantage of essentially always being viable as long as you have 2–3 feet of rope left and nearly any sort of soft goods (sling of any length, third hand, etc.).

1. Tie a stopper knot in the brake strand about 3 feet behind the belay device (fig. 3-13a).
2. Tie a friction hitch around the load strand with any piece of soft material; a prusik hitch in a third hand or a shoulder-length (24-inch) sling works best. Then attach a carabiner to the friction hitch (fig. 3-13b)—this does not need to be a locking carabiner, as the weight should never be hanging solely on the friction hitch and should be backed up with the climbing rope—and clip the long end of the rope coming off the back side of the rescuer's clove hitch to the anchor to the friction-hitch carabiner. Pull the back-side rope tight and tie it to the friction-hitch carabiner with a munter-mule-overhand (fig. 3-13c).
3. Clip a locking carabiner to the anchor and attach the brake strand coming out of the belay device to this carabiner with a munter hitch (fig. 3-13d). Either tie off the munter hitch with a mule hitch and overhand backup knot (fig. 3-13e), or wrap the brake strand around your hand to ensure that you do not lose control of it.
4. Slowly rock the locking carabiner inside the belay device (fig. 3-13f). As you do this, the friction hitch will slowly take the weight; ensure that this friction hitch does not slip as it becomes weighted. Unclip the belay device and remove the rope from it (fig. 3-13g), again ensuring that you maintain control of the brake strand coming from the anchor (if the munter hitch is not tied off with a mule hitch and overhand backup knot).
5. Untie the overhand knot and mule hitch, and pull the slack out of the munter hitch on the anchor (fig. 3-13h) so that the load tightens onto the friction hitch. Once this is tight, retie the mule hitch and overhand backup knot (fig. 3-13i).
6. Release tension on the back-side strand's munter-mule-overhand knot, allowing the friction hitch to slacken so the climbing rope is taking 100 percent of the weight (fig. 3-13j). Remove the friction hitch. Welcome to baseline.

ESCAPING THE BELAY WITH AN ASSISTED-BRAKING BELAY DEVICE

If belaying with an assisted-braking belay device (ABD), the steps are similar to those above:

1. Tie a stopper knot in the rope about 3 feet behind the ABD.
2. Tie a cordelette in a klemheist around the load strand and tie the cordelette to a new carabiner on the anchor with a munter-mule-overhand. This does not need to be a locking carabiner, as the weight should never be exclusively on the cordelette. (It is also possible to use the back side of the rescuer's clove-hitch tie-in to the anchor as another piece of material.)
3. Tie a munter hitch on the anchor with the brake strand coming out of the ABD. You

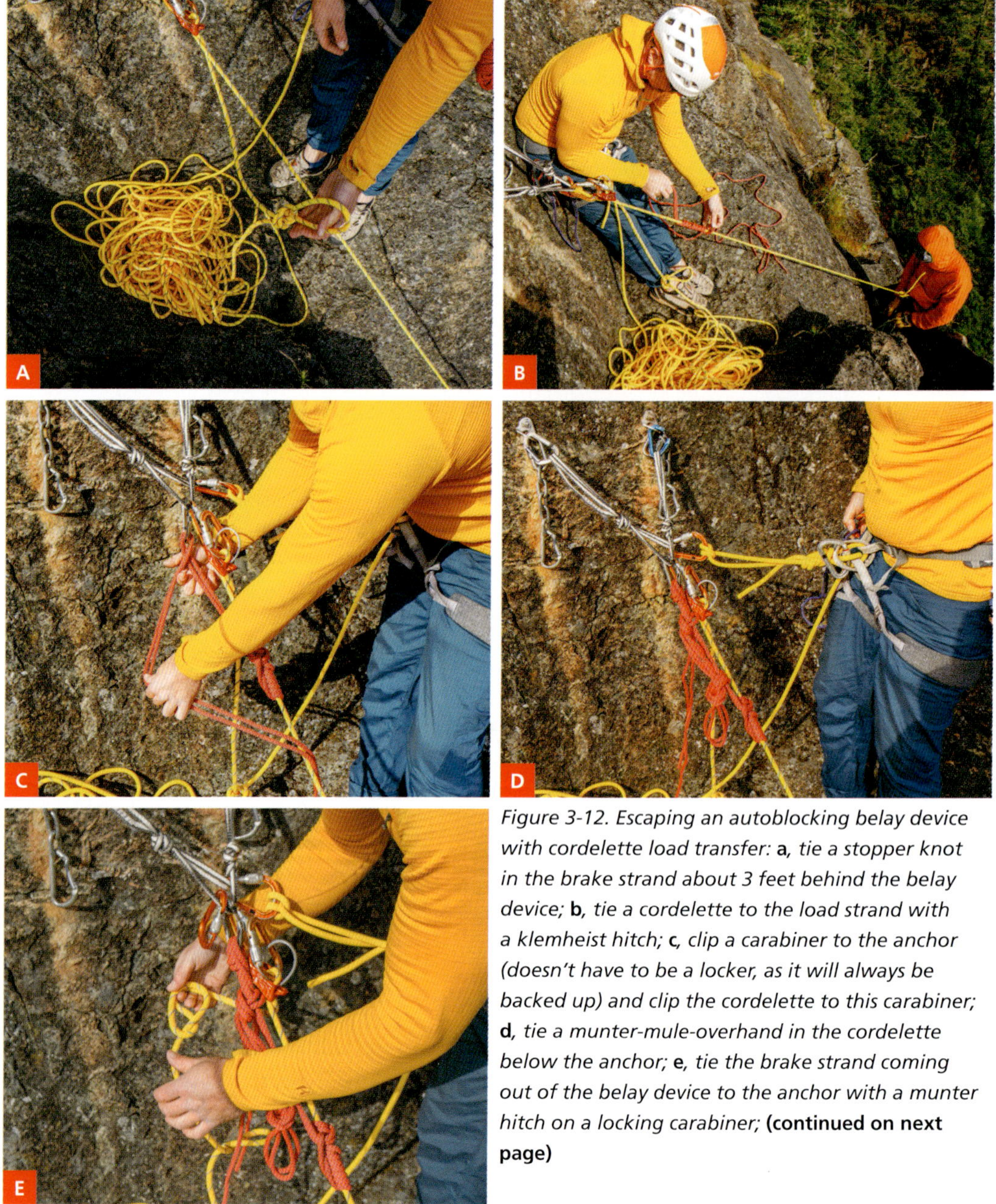

Figure 3-12. Escaping an autoblocking belay device with cordelette load transfer: **a**, *tie a stopper knot in the brake strand about 3 feet behind the belay device;* **b**, *tie a cordelette to the load strand with a klemheist hitch;* **c**, *clip a carabiner to the anchor (doesn't have to be a locker, as it will always be backed up) and clip the cordelette to this carabiner;* **d**, *tie a munter-mule-overhand in the cordelette below the anchor;* **e**, *tie the brake strand coming out of the belay device to the anchor with a munter hitch on a locking carabiner;* **(continued on next page)**

***f**, add a mule hitch and overhand knot, then rock the locking carabiner inside the belay device back and forth to slowly release tension before removing the belay device; **g**, untie the cordelette's overhand knot and mule hitch on the anchor; **h**, lower the load until the weight hangs on the rope and the cordelette slackens; **i**, untie the klemheist hitch and remove the cordelette from the rope; **j**, welcome to baseline.*

Figure 3-13. Escaping an autoblocking belay device with back-side load transfer: **a**, *tie a backup knot in the brake strand behind the belay device;* **b**, *attach a friction hitch to the load strand and clip a carabiner to it;* **c**, *take the back-side strand of the belayer's clove hitch to the anchor and clip it to the carabiner on the friction hitch with a munter-mule-overhand;* **d**, *clip a locking carabiner on the anchor and tie the brake strand from the belay device to it with a munter hitch;* **e**, *tie a mule hitch and overhand backup knot on the munter you just tied;* **(continued on next page)**

f, *rock the carabiner in the belay device (here, in the rescuer's left hand) back and forth to release tension from the belay device;* **g**, *once tension has been released from the belay device and transferred to the friction hitch, unclip the belay device and remove it;* **h**, *untie the overhand knot and mule hitch on the munter hitch on the anchor, pull the slack out of this munter, and tighten the load strand to avoid lowering the following climber unnecessarily;* **i**, *once this strand is tight, retie the mule hitch and overhand backup knot;* **j**, *release the munter-mule-overhand on the friction hitch and lower the hitch until the main load strand going directly to the anchor takes the weight, then remove the friction hitch.*

can either secure this munter with a mule hitch and overhand backup knot or wrap it around your hand, but it is imperative that you maintain control of this strand over the next few steps.

4. Pull the release lever on the ABD. This will create slack and move the weight from the belay device to the cordelette's friction hitch. Once the weight has been transferred to the cordelette, remove the belay device (again, maintaining control of the munter hitch tied on the brake strand if it hasn't been secured with a mule hitch and overhand backup knot).
5. Untie the overhand backup knot and mule hitch, then pull the slack out of the munter hitch and tie it off (again, if need be) with a mule hitch and overhand backup knot.
6. Release the cordelette so the weight is entirely on the load strand. Remove the cordelette. Welcome to baseline.

ESCAPING THE BELAY WITH TWO ROPES IN THE BELAY DEVICE

Climbing as a group of three is a lot of fun and possibly more efficient for challenging routes, as there are more climbers to share leads, carry equipment, and socialize with at the belay. It does take a little more technical prowess to keep the belay stations tidy and the ropes untangled.

If you have two ropes in the belay device while belaying two followers (or one follower because the other is injured) or while using double-rope technique, the steps required are more or less the same as for a single climber, except that you need to work on both ropes independently but at the same time—which is certainly trickier than belaying a single climber on a single rope.

Tip: Avoid putting a friction hitch around both strands of loaded rope at the same time in order to escape the belay. While it may seem like a good idea, a number of factors—including differences in rope diameter, general rope wear, sheath slickness, and how the hitch is tied—can cause one rope to slip once the belay device is removed, and there is very little you can do about this slipping once it starts. It is often better to just deal with each rope independently.

Don't capture both ropes simultaneously with a friction hitch. One rope can start to slip, and it can be difficult to stop.

GETTING TO DOUBLE BASELINE

If you already know how to escape the belay with a single rope, it isn't that different to do with two ropes, though it seems challenging.

A lot of the problems escaping the belay with two ropes come from how gear intensive it can be. It's likely that you will have only one cordelette (or only one belayer using the back side of their rope clove-hitched to the anchor, plus a piece of material like a sling or third hand), which is where it gets complicated. The key is to make sure *both* ropes are completely backed up with their own munter-mule-overhand knots on the anchor behind the belay device.

Belaying two climbers with two ropes in a device is largely the same process as belaying one climber with one rope. Here, Sara Vavra and Nate Wilhite follow the second pitch of the Tooth Fairy, *Snoqualmie Pass, Washington.*

1. Start by tying overhand stopper knots (a.k.a. "catastrophe" knots) on both brake strands 2–3 feet behind the belay device (fig. 3-14a)
2. Put a friction hitch on only one of the load strands (fig. 3-14b).
3. Clip the cordelette to the anchor and tie it off with a munter-mule-overhand knot (fig. 3-14c).
4. Clip a locking carabiner to the anchor and tie the brake strand of the same rope to the carabiner with a munter hitch (fig. 3-14d); secure this munter with a mule hitch and overhand backup knot.
5. Tie the other rope's brake strand to a new locking carabiner on the anchor with a munter-mule-overhand (fig. 3-14e).
6. Push slack into the belay device from the brake strand of the rope that is held by the friction hitch (fig. 3-14f).
7. Get that strand out of the belay device by first passing it up and around the belay device's keeper loop fig. 3-14g and h). Visualize where the belay device's keeper loop is in relation to the rope—you can remove either the inside rope or the outside rope, but make sure to pass it around the correct side of the keeper loop. Pull the strand out of the device (fig. 3-14i).
8. Tighten that strand's munter-mule-overhand knot (fig. 3-14i)
9. Release the friction hitch from the first rope.

Now repeat the process of tying a friction hitch on the second rope, which is still in the belay device, then attach a carabiner to

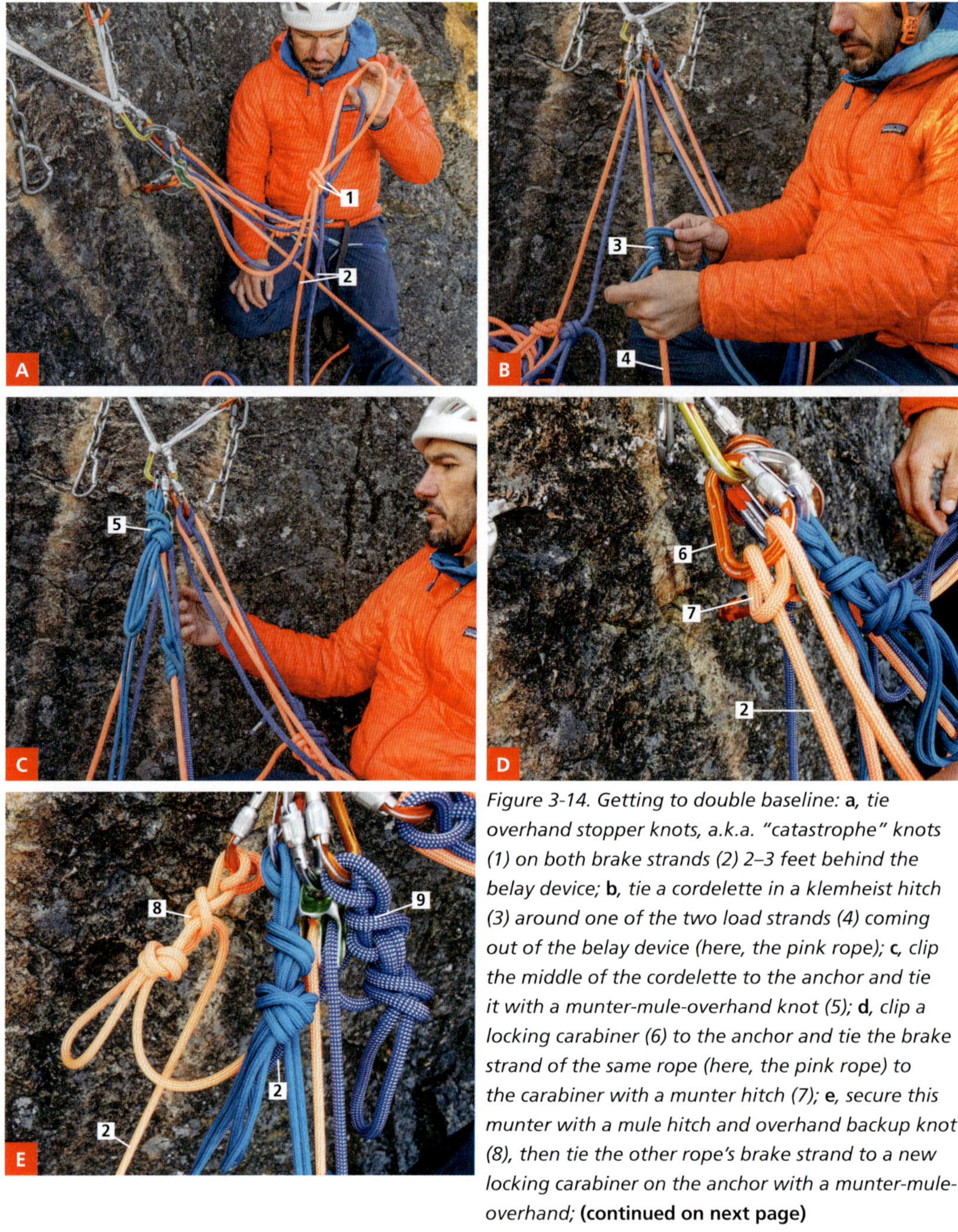

Figure 3-14. Getting to double baseline: **a**, *tie overhand stopper knots, a.k.a. "catastrophe" knots (1) on both brake strands (2) 2–3 feet behind the belay device;* **b**, *tie a cordelette in a klemheist hitch (3) around one of the two load strands (4) coming out of the belay device (here, the pink rope);* **c**, *clip the middle of the cordelette to the anchor and tie it with a munter-mule-overhand knot (5);* **d**, *clip a locking carabiner (6) to the anchor and tie the brake strand of the same rope (here, the pink rope) to the carabiner with a munter hitch (7);* **e**, *secure this munter with a mule hitch and overhand backup knot (8), then tie the other rope's brake strand to a new locking carabiner on the anchor with a munter-mule-overhand;* **(continued on next page)**

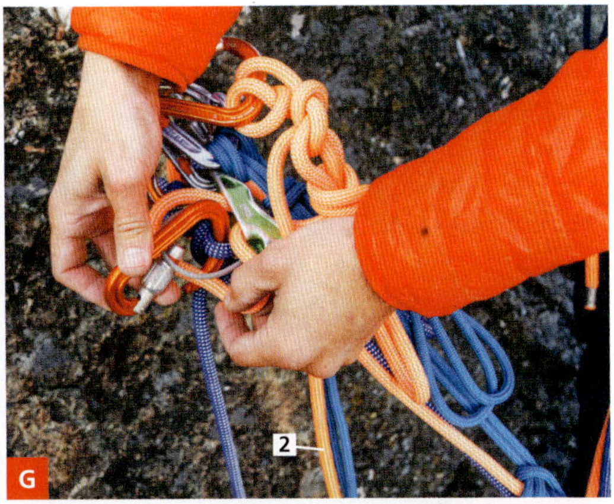

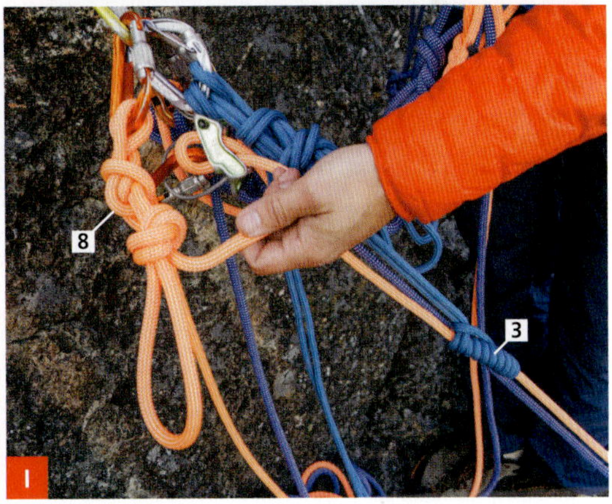

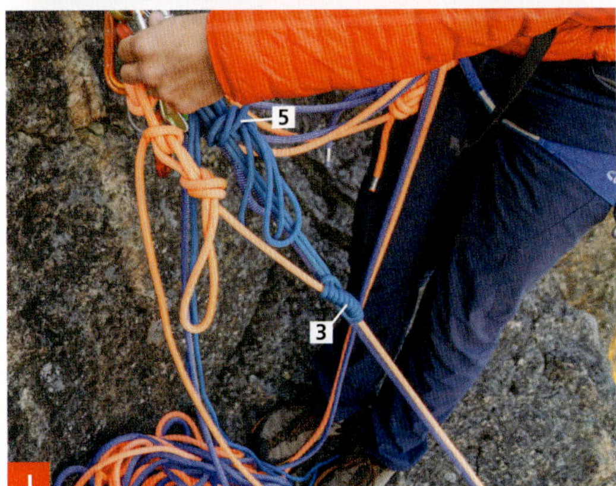

f, *push slack into the belay device from the brake strand of the rope that is held by the friction hitch (here, the pink rope);* **g**, *remove that rope from the belay device, making sure to pass it around the correct side of the device's keeper loop;* **h**, *unloop the strand being held by the friction hitch and pass it out of the belay device's carabiner;* **i**, *pull that strand out of the belay device, ensuring that it is backed up by a munter-mule-overhand (8) on the anchor and that the friction hitch (3) is holding the weight;* **j**, *release the cordelette's munter-mule-overhand (5) so that when it's untied the rope takes the weight, then remove the cordelette from the anchor and untie the klemheist (3) from the rope.*

the anchor and tie the cordelette to this new anchor with a munter-mule-overhand. To get the belay device out of the system, rock the carabiner in the belay device back and forth to release tension on the belay device until the weight has been transferred to the friction hitch on the cordelette. Pull the second rope out of the belay device and remove the belay device from the system. Untie the cordelette's munter-mule-overhand and lower the cordelette until it slackens and the rope takes the weight. Remove the cordelette from the rope; welcome to double baseline.

ESCAPING THE BELAY DEVICE WITH TWO ROPES AND ONLY ONE CLIMBER ABLE TO UNWEIGHT

While you can always opt for the procedure for getting to double baseline shown in Figure 3-14, the method described here that uses an extended master point or belay escape is simpler and quicker. If you are belaying two followers and one of them is hurt, the other one's ability to "stand up" and unweight the rope is extremely helpful. In this example, if you need to escape the belay, you need to escape the belay completely to baseline with one rope before you do so with the other rope. The follower who can unweight their rope can even climb enough to allow you to build an extended master point in front of the autoblocking belay device.

1. Tie backup knots on both brake strands 2–3 feet behind the belay device and clip them to the anchor—depending on the next step, these can be munter-mule-overhand knots or, as shown here, simple overhand knots (fig. 3-15a).
2. Attach a long sling to the anchor to create an extended master point with a locking carabiner out in front of the belay device, then have the uninjured follower ascend (generally, they will need to climb up 1.5–2 feet) so you can munter-hitch the unweighted load strand to this carabiner fig. 3-15b). Pull the slack out (fig. 3-15c). Mind your fingers: don't put them inside any loops, which would be dangerous should the hitch fail.
3. Once you have enough slack, mule-hitch this munter hitch and tie it off with an overhand backup knot (fig. 3-15d).
4. Rock the carabiner in the belay device to create slack in whichever rope is tied to the extended master point—here, the blue rope (fig. 3-15e). Once slack is created, visualize how to pass the strand out of the locking carabiner. Ensure that you did indeed clip both ropes to the anchor as a backup.
5. Push this same strand into the belay device and flip it over the belay device's keeper loop (if needed) to remove this strand from the belay device (fig. 3-15f).
6. Relock the belay device's carabiner to secure the single remaining rope (fig. 3-15g).

Figure 3-15. Escaping the belay device with only one of the two ropes: **a**, *tie overhand "catastrophe" knots (1) in the brake strand (2) of both ropes and clip them to a locking carabiner (3) on the anchor;* **b**, *attach a long sling (4) to the anchor so it hangs below the belay device and clip a locking carabiner (5) to this sling to create an extended master point, then have the uninjured follower ascend so you can tie the unweighted load strand to the extended master point's locking carabiner with a munter hitch (6);* **c**, *pull the slack out;* **d**, *then tie a mule hitch and an overhand backup knot (7) to the munter hitch;* **(continued on next page)**

e, *push slack into the belay device from the rope you just tied off on the extended master point (here, the blue rope);* **f**, *open the belay device's locking carabiner and pass the strand tied in a munter-mule-overhand to the extended master point (here, the blue rope) out of the belay device;* **g**, *relock the belay device's carabiner to secure the single remaining rope (here, the pink rope).*

Opposite: *A climber rappelling into a storm in Patagonia uses saddlebags to manage the ropes.* (Photo by Mikey Schaefer)

CHAPTER 4

Rappelling and Descending

John Willard rappels with an extension down the South Face of Ingalls Peak, Stuart Range, Washington.

If you climb, you will inevitably have to get down. It is often said that rappelling is one of the most dangerous parts of climbing, because you are completely reliant on a technical system—unlike climbing upward, in which the technical system and belayer serve only as a backup in the event of a fall. Having a thorough knowledge of rappelling systems and methods will provide you with options in the event you encounter something unexpected.

Rappelling is one of the basic but essential technical aspects of climbing, and it's well known that it's where the greatest number of accidents happen—rappelling systems get tested each and every time they are used. That these systems need to be sound goes without saying, but the stakes are raised in a rescue scenario, in which the loads are often larger (two people), more complex, and less familiar, all while being operated in what is likely a stressful situation.

RAPPEL EXTENSIONS

When making multiple consecutive rappels—or even a single rappel—a rappel extension provides a lot of advantages and a lot more options over simply clipping your belay device to your harness's belay loop. Prefabricated products designed specifically for this

Figure 4-1. The Petzl Dual Connect is one of many prefabricated rappel extensions. It offers an adjustable-length clip-in point—the end in the climber's right hand (the belay device is clipped to the other end)—and is dynamic, very durable, and heat resistant. While prefabricated options like the Dual Connect are dedicated tools, meaning you are "carrying something extra," they serve their purpose extremely well.

Figure 4-2. A rappel extension can be created by girth-hitching a double-length sling to your harness, then tying an overhand knot in the middle of the sling and clipping your belay device's locking carabiner to the loop between the knot and your harness. This is a great option for consecutive-step rappels, because it gives you a lot of length to be clipped in to a potentially high anchor while you prepare the next rappel.

Figure 4-3. To fix the belay device carabiner in place, tie an overhand on a bight in the middle of the double-length sling; this setup provides slightly more redundancy but does not allow as much length for clipping anchors.

Figure 4-4. For another rappel extension option using a double-length sling, pass the sling through your harness belay loop with the ends offset, then gather both ends and tie an overhand on a bight in front of the belay loop; clip the belay device to the shorter end of the sling.

purpose include the Metolius PAS and the Petzl Dual Connect (fig. 4-1), but you can also simply tie a knot in the middle of a 48-inch sling and girth-hitch it to your harness (fig. 4-2). Another popular option is to tie a small overhand on a bight in the sling to create even more redundancy and a specific spot to clip your belay device (figs. 4-3 and 4-4).

You will see many different styles of rappel extensions, and while rappelling with any extension offers a *huge* advantage over simply rappelling off your belay loop, different types of extensions have different pros and cons. All of the options shown here are accepted practices. Regardless of which model or technique you select, the goal is to give you two clip-in points: one for securing yourself to an anchor and another for extending your belay device above your harness.

Tip: Nylon is a more durable, heat-resistant, and elastic material than Dyneema and thus is more desirable for an extension and tether. It isn't necessarily dangerous to use Dyneema or a similar material for your extension, but take greater care to keep the rope from running over these materials and to prevent them from coming into contact with extremely hot belay devices after long, steep rappels.

IMPROVISED RAPPELS

If you or your partner drops or completely forgets their belay device, you have a few options in order to get down. The first is to consider simply lowering the climber with no belay device down to the ground or the next anchor. This is certainly more straightforward but isn't always an option, particularly if you have several rappels remaining or you don't have a good idea of where you are going. For more on lowering, see chapter 5.

DOUBLE-LOCKER RAPPEL

The simplest option is to rappel with a double-locker rappel. Many people are familiar with a double-carabiner-brake rappel; the double-locker rappel is a simplified version that is far quicker and more straightforward to set up and break down, while providing nearly as much friction. It can be used for the majority of rappels on single ropes (which are generally greater than 8.5 millimeters in diameter), and it is also perfectly acceptable for dead-vertical rappels, even single-stranded.

This setup is called a double-locker rappel due to the minimum number of locking carabiners needed, but these two locking carabiners should not be clipped directly to your harness belay loop or rappel extension; instead, there are two options for attaching the double-locker-rappel setup to your harness belay loop or rappel extension. In addition to the two similar-sized locking carabiners, you will

Figure 4-5. Opposite (black), opposed (orange), and opposite and opposed (blue) pairs of carabiners. For opposite and opposed the gates are on opposite sides and their hinges are on the same end so they're opposed when both are open.

Figure 4-6. Double-locker-rappel setup: **a**, *pass a bight in both ropes through a closed locking carabiner;* **b**, *clip a second locking carabiner in to both bights and the load strands of the ropes you will rappel on;* **c**, *clip two nonlocking carabiners that are opposite and opposed to the first locker and to your rappel extension or harness belay loop;* **d**, *alternatively, clip a third locker to the first locker and to your rappel extension or harness belay loop.* (Photos by Jim Meyers)

need either two nonlockers used opposite and opposed (fig. 4-5) or a third locking carabiner.

Here's how to set up the double-locker rappel:

1. First, pass a bight from the ropes (or rope, if performing a single-strand rappel) through the first (closed) locking carabiner (fig. 4-6a).
2. With the second locking carabiner, clip the "bottom" four strands coming *into* and exiting the first locker (fig. 4-6b), without actually clipping the two carabiners together. It is helpful to think of making an S shape with the rope that you are attaching to the two carabiners.
3. Now either set up two nonlocking carabiners to be opposite and opposed (fig. 4-6c), or use a third locking carabiner (fig. 4-6d); with either option, clip the carabiner(s) to the first locking carabiner and to either your rappel extension or harness belay loop.

DOUBLE-CARABINER-BRAKE RAPPEL

The double-carabiner-brake rappel is essentially a subtle variation of the double-locker rappel, and contrary to popular belief, it does not need to be set up with oval carabiners—even most wire-gate carabiners work fine. This technique is best done with at least midsized

Figure 4.7. Double-carabiner-brake rappel: **a**, *push a bight from both strands of rope through two nonlocking carabiners that are opposite and opposed;* **b**, *clip a second set of nonlocking carabiners—opposed but not opposite, so their spines are on the same side—in to the bight as well as around both strands of rope exiting the first set of carabiners;* **c**, *now the trickier part—invert and pivot the second set of carabiners;* **d**, *push them horizontally into the first set, confirming that the ropes do not run over any carabiner gates;* **e**, *clip an additional locker (or two more nonlockers opposite and opposed) to the first set of carabiners as well as to your rappel extension or harness belay loop.*

Rappelling with a munter hitch will likely result in vicious twists in the rope.

or larger-than-average nonlocking carabiners though you can use smaller carabiners. All the carabiners do not need to be exactly the same model, but they do need to at least be similar in size.

1. Start by passing a bight from the rope(s) through two nonlocking carabiners that are opposite and opposed (fig. 4-7a).
2. Then position two more nonlockers to be opposed but *not* opposite (you do not want the rope pressing onto the gates) and oriented so the rope will run over the carabiners' spines. Clip these two carabiners in to the bight made by all the strands coming through the first set of carabiners *and* the strands that are above them (without actually clipping any of the carabiners together). It is helpful to think of making an S shape that you'll be clipping in to (fig. 4-7b).
3. Now invert the two (opposite but not opposed carabiners (fig. 4-7c) and pass them down onto the two lower opposite and opposed carabiners (fig. 4-7d). Double-check that the rope is running against two spines and not a combination of gates and spines.
4. It is imperative that you do not attach these four carabiners directly to your harness belay loop or rappel extension. Instead, clip two more opposite and opposed nonlockers or another locking carabiner (fig. 4-7e) to the first pair of opposite and opposed nonlockers, then clip this new attachment to your belay loop or rappel extension. Do *not* clip the original four carabiners directly to your belay loop.

AVOID RAPPELLING WITH A MUNTER HITCH

In general, rappelling with a munter hitch is not advised and is even discouraged. It isn't that it won't provide enough friction, but it is impossible to avoid getting twists in the rope—and with a long, near-vertical rappel, the twisting is likely to be dramatic and require repeated flaking of the rope to remove. If it is a single rappel, you can get away with rappelling with a munter, because you can flake the rope once you are back on the ground, but if you have three or more rappels ahead of you, a double-locker rappel—or simply lowering—is strongly preferred.

RAPPEL BACKUPS

Several practices provide a backup for rappelling: friction hitches, knots in the ends of the rope(s), and a firefighter's belay.

Figure 4-8. Rachel Spitzer gets rigged for a rappel near Leavenworth, Washington. To significantly improve her safety, she has tied an autoblock hitch below her belay device and clipped it to her harness belay loop. (Photo by Jim Meyers)

Figure 4-9. Don't use Dyneema or similar materials as your third hand for a friction-hitch backup—they work in a pinch but have a much lower melting point; the odds of compromising the strength of a Dyneema sling after just a few rappels are pretty high. (Photo by Jim Meyers)

FRICTION-HITCH BACKUP

Placing a friction-hitch backup on the brake side of the belay device allows the rappeller to go hands-free. This makes it easier and safer for the rappeller to build and/or clip in to the next anchor, deal with a tangled or stuck rope, manage rope saddlebags, retrieve a stuck piece of protection, and/or swing around to look for the next rappel station. It also provides essential security in the event that the rappeller is struck by a falling rock—or is otherwise compromised—and lets go of the rope.

The key to making a friction-hitch backup work is that under no circumstances can it come into contact with the belay device itself. If this happens, more often than not the device will *tend* or *mind* the friction hitch, which causes it to release and keeps it from grabbing, rendering it useless. A number of climbers have died as a result of having their friction-hitch backup accidentally get minded by their belay device due to inadequate extension: the belay device was too close to their friction hitch.

Tip: Before committing to a rappel, do a quick "lean" while still tethered to the anchor to make sure all your systems are set up correctly: check whether the carabiner in your belay device is clipped through both strands of rope, the friction hitch grabs appropriately, and it cannot be minded by the belay device.

The most common backup is an autoblock hitch (fig. 4-8), as it is the quickest to wrap around the rope. A prusik hitch is perfectly acceptable but is slower to tie and untie. As with all friction hitches, the rappeller should test the friction hitch prior to unclipping from the top anchor and starting their rappel.

Figure 4-10. Tie a barrel knot in the end of each rope before rappelling. (Photo by Jim Meyers)

KNOTS IN THE ENDS OF THE RAPPEL ROPE

It is a good idea to get in the habit of always tying knots in the ends of your ropes before rappelling (fig. 4-10). This once hotly debated topic in climbing has swung decisively toward defaulting to tying knots. The argument in favor is clear: the knots will protect the rappeller from unintentionally rappelling off one (or both) strands of rope—an accident that happens far too frequently and can easily be prevented. The argument against is that the knots could get stuck or you could forget to untie them. A stuck rope is an inconvenience and unquestionably a pain to fix; however, at the time of this writing, no one has actually died as a direct result of their ropes getting stuck, whereas climbers die each year from rappelling off the ends of their ropes. So tie knots in *every* case—even if you are rappelling a single-pitch route and can see both ends on the ground. This simple step could save your life someday.

FIREFIGHTER'S BELAY

Once one rappeller gets down to the ground or the lower belay station, they have the ability to provide some additional security to the next rappeller by maintaining a loose grip on both strands of the rope as that person rappels: from this position they can pull down tight to lock up the rappeller's belay device, should the rappeller lose control. This technique, called a firefighter's belay, should be implemented any time there is a new rappeller, the rappel is off the fall line, a large roof needs to be negotiated, the group is fatigued, or any other factor might compromise the rappeller's ability to maintain complete and unquestionable control of their rappel.

Just as important as performing a firefighter's belay is paying close attention to the rappeller: watching them around tricky features

A firefighter's belay protects the final rappel off the Opossum *in the Marsupials, Smith Rock, Oregon.*

A student on an American Mountain Guides Association rock-guide course implements the firefighter's belay for a fellow student in an area known for its steep routes and steep rappels: the Shawangunks (a.k.a. the Gunks), New York. (Photo by Silas Rossi)

such roofs, or anticipating if they need to traverse off the fall line. Don't hold the ropes tight while they rappel, as this can make it more difficult for them to smoothly slide down the rope. Aim for readiness, without holding the rope too tight.

THE "J RIG"

Clipping the ropes directly to the next (lower) anchor is a technique called the "J rig" because of the J shape the rope makes hanging with slack from the upper station to the lower station. The J rig increases team security during rappels and is a great technique for any consecutive rappels, as it makes it impossible for the subsequent rappeller to miss the belay station or rappel off the ends of the rope. It is particularly useful for steep stances or rappel stations situated diagonally from one another, as well as when it's dark or the group is tired. Use the J rig for any consecutive rappels, but particularly if the rappels involve rope *stretching* in which you barely reach the next set of anchors, the rappels traverse significantly, or there are consecutive steep rappels from hanging stances. For rappels that traverse significantly, the J rig makes it far easier and safer for the second rappeller to get down to the lower anchor, as they can

Figure 4-11. The J-rig prevents subsequent rappellers from rappelling off the end of the rope. (Photo by Dale Remsberg)

rappel in line or even slightly below the lower anchor, lock off their brake strands, and get "towed in" to the lower belay by the climber already there.

The first rappeller sets up the J rig: with the rope still hanging from the upper anchor, use a clove hitch or overhand knot to clip both strands to the anchor you have just rappelled to, leaving some slack in the system—which creates the J shape in the rope (fig. 4-11). The J rig helps the group maintain control of the ends of the rope—especially helpful if it is windy, there are rope-eating flakes nearby, or the rappels follow a diagonal trajectory.

MANAGING ROPES WHILE DESCENDING

One of the most common and easiest-to-make mistakes that even experienced climbers are guilty of is wasting time while rappelling due to poor rope management. Not every rappel is down a clean, steep slab or off an overhang into space, so a few extra seconds to better manage the ropes before starting a rappel can easily save minutes of fighting rope snarls and twists. This becomes an even bigger deal when routes require two ropes to descend, as there is just more rope to get tangled and exponentially more twisted.

If the cliff face below is steep and smooth, then by all means just toss or pay out the rope as it falls. In lower-angle or ledgy terrain, make hand coils and simply clip them to extra quickdraws or slings on your harness rather than throwing them down the cliff, where they will inevitably get tangled. However, if the descent is covered in trees, has traverses of any significant length, or the weather is windy, strongly consider saddlebagging.

Mimi Eckhardt prepares two 60-meter ropes for saddlebagging during rappels from the top of the Red Wall, Smith Rock, Oregon.

SADDLEBAGGING

Many climbers just deal with twists and tangles while rappelling, but the truth is, saddlebagging the ropes takes only a few additional seconds compared with just tossing the ropes down the cliff. Saddlebagging ropes is not just for lower-angle or ledgy terrain; it is also an excellent technique for windy or stormy conditions in which your rope could be blown around, increasing the odds of it getting stuck in a difficult-to-reach place. Saddlebagging keeps the rope with you and lets you take it where you want to go.

Saddlebags don't need to be perfect. The goal is to have multiple points during the rappel when the rappeller can "drop" or throw the

Silas Rossi enjoys some hang time while rappelling the overhanging final pitch of Le Mulot *(WI6+ R), Quebec, Canada.* (Photo by Dustin Portzline)

Tip: It takes very little extra time to create saddlebags if done efficiently, and they will certainly more than make up for the additional few seconds on lower-angle rappels, in which the first rappeller may spend a minute or more untangling ropes that have tumbled down the cliff.

different sections of rope rather than having to take the time to pay out the strands perfectly, coil by coil.

1. As with any rappel, feed as much rope as you can (20–50 feet) down the cliff below so that it hangs straight down more or less directly on the anchor. Even on the lowest-angle rappels, this is still around 20–40 feet.
2. Start making butterfly coils the same way you would if you were going to throw them. Try to make them relatively uniform in size (fig. 4-12a).
3. Use a medium-length quickdraw or tripled-up runner to "basket" the coils together on your harness (fig. 4-12b). Create at least two sets of coils/baskets to further break up the rappel. Even with just a single 60-meter rope, create two or three groups of coils that can be dropped as you go. While two is the minimum, as many as five or six could be used.
4. Start rappelling until the rope coming out of your belay device almost reaches the next stack of coils. If the rope is coming readily off the top, or if the "bottom" of the rope is toward the bottom of the stack, the coil may pay out nicely for a while; keep rappelling. However, if the rope hangs up in the slightest, unclip a coil (fig. 4-12c).

Figure 4-12. Saddlebagging: **a**, *ideally starting from the ends of the rope, start making hand coils as you would if you were going to toss the ropes down the face;* **b**, *clip the coils to your harness gear loops using slings or quickdraws;* **c**, *rappel as the rope pays out nicely, but when it stops paying out or starts to tangle, unclip a coil;* **d**, *drop or toss the coil.*

5. Drop or throw that set of coils (fig. 4-12d). Avoid rappelling to the point where the belay device comes tight to the stack; toss the coils at the first signs of snarls or tangles. Repeat until you run out of coils or you reach the next belay.

Tip: Saddlebags work better if you have less gear or other items on your harness for the coils to get hung up on. Take any unnecessary gear off your harness, especially things like cams and nuts, and carry them in a backpack or give them to your partner.

USING THE BASEBALL OR MISSILE METHOD

Sometimes you need to toss the rappel rope some amount of horizontal distance. A good technique for this is commonly called the baseball or missile method.

To start, take the end of the rope that is going down the cliff—ideally with a knot in the end of it (fig. 4-13a)—and wrap the rope around itself, almost like a ball of yarn (fig. 4-13b). The bigger this ball, the better, but it becomes harder to throw if it gets bigger than the size of a soccer ball (fig. 4-13c). Be sure to

REEPSCHNUR RAPPEL OVERCOMES MURPHY'S LAW

BY MIKE SOUCY

The Diamond, on the East Face of Longs Peak in Rocky Mountain National Park, Colorado, is a classic (and often crowded) alpine big wall. On a beautiful but waning August afternoon, my partner and I find ourselves sitting in a major traffic jam of climbers three-quarters of the way up the wall. Due to the time of day, we are left with no choice but to bail down the series of 50-meter rappels back to the talus. Fortunately, we have two 60-meter ropes and are familiar with the bolted rappel route to our right. The only hurdle that remains is making a long *diagonal rappel* to get from our location to these bolted anchors. . . .

Murphy's Law is clipped to the rack that day, which results in our lead line getting wrapped around a flake shortly after we pull it through the first anchor. If you have been in this scenario before, you're aware that it's a tricky one for rope retrieval. You are forced to tie in to your other rope end, lead back up to free the stuck rope, and set a new anchor to rap back down to your belayer. Not ideal.

After much flipping, whipping, pulling, and cussing, we determine that the rope end is hopelessly stuck and that leading up and across the wall will be too time-consuming and dangerous. Out comes the pocketknife and we chop 40 meters off my partner's new 60-meter lead line. Bummer.

Currently in our possession we have the remaining 20 meters of lead rope plus a 60-meter twin rope that we have been using as our rap/haul line. The length of the following rappels is known to be about 50 meters each. Certainly not the best of situations, but we also have a plan.

I will lower my partner to the next rap station using the intact 60-meter rope. I'm fine lowering him on this skinny rope, because of the clean fall line with a low likelihood of a pendulum over a sharp edge. Once he hits the next anchor, I will fix his side of the rope using a Reepschnur (alpine butterfly knot clipped back to the loaded side with a locking carabiner). I will rappel down this rope, clipped to the remaining end (which I know is short of the next anchor). When I get to the short end, I will tie on to the remaining 20 meters of the lead line, plus whatever else is needed (slings, cordelette, pants, etc.) to reach the rap anchor. I can now pull down my clipped-together "vertical yard sale," along with the intact 60-meter rope. We repeat this all the way to the base of the wall.

In the end, this proves to be a very workable but less-than-perfect solution. I have to lower my partner in steep, rocky terrain on a single strand of twin rope, and the normally speedy rappels take us about twice as long.

There are other solutions available here. Making 30-meter rappels on the intact 60-meter rope and building additional anchors (leaving your own gear) could also be a safe albeit less known and certainly more expensive option. So would being patient while the teams above clear out, as well as maybe walking off in the dark, assuming Murphy didn't steal your headlamp.

The Reepschnur-tag method is worth practicing for situations when you don't have enough rope to reach rappel stations or, like us, you are forced to cut your rope.

Mike Soucy is an International Federation of Mountain Guides Associations–certified mountain guide based in Longmont, Colorado.

One of Colorado's most famous climbing features, the Diamond on the East Face of Longs Peak sports numerous steep and sustained routes requiring technical climbing above 13,000 feet. (Photo by Mike Soucy)

Figure 4-13. Baseball or missile method: **a**, *tie a knot in the end of the rope;* **b**, *start wrapping the rope around itself;* **c**, *wrap until it is not quite the size of a soccer ball;* **d**, *maximize the baseball's direction of travel when you throw it.*

create enough slack "behind the ball," on the back side of the rope, so the slack rope doesn't tighten too early and the baseball or missile doesn't get hung up, throwing off its trajectory or reducing the distance it can travel. It is amazing how far and effectively the "baseball" can travel in the direction you toss it (fig. 4-13d), depending on your throwing skills.

LOWERING

Lowering instead of rappelling is another method of getting down, underutilized even by experienced climbers. Lowering allows you to get both ends of the ropes down to where you want them, even under the windiest conditions. It also allows the climber being lowered to construct an anchor without needing to lock themself off. For details about lowering, see chapter 5.

Tip: If it's super windy or the weather is otherwise gnarly, consider lowering your partner to the next anchor with both ends of the rope attached to them as a way to get the rope down and perhaps also set up a J rig. This eliminates the need to manage the ropes on rappel.

JOINING ROPES

If a rappel requires more than one rope, a.k.a. a double-rope rappel, the flat overhand is the best knot for the job (fig. 4-14). The flat overhand presents a number of advantages while still providing more than enough strength for

Figure 4-14. The flat overhand is the best knot for joining two ropes for rappelling—it is strong and low profile, with a tendency to "stand up" under tension, further reducing its chances of getting stuck. (Photo by Dale Remsberg)

rappelling despite its relatively small size and simplicity. Its small size is actually one of its major benefits, as it is significantly less likely to get stuck than a Flemish bend or a double fisherman's bend. Additionally, because the flat overhand is offset from the axis of tension, it tends to "stand up," allowing it to more easily slide over rough surfaces.

The key to tying a strong and safe flat overhand is to leave around 1 foot of tail. Leaving more isn't necessarily safer: it increases the chance of the knot catching when the rope is pulled and risks the rappeller accidentally threading one of the short ends into their belay device. Once the knot is tied, pull each of the four strands coming out of the knot independently to snug it up (see Figure 1-6 in chapter 1); avoid pulling on two strands simultaneously, as this is significantly less effective at tightening the knot.

SPECIALIZED RAPPEL TECHNIQUES

This section covers some strategies that you might not use often, but that are, nonetheless, useful tools to be familiar with when unusual situations arise.

REEPSCHNUR RAPPEL

The Reepschnur rappel has countless applications. It is a way to use a blocking knot to rappel farther than half a rope length and still be able to retrieve your rope. When setting up a Reepschnur, you need to either know how far you have to go or lower the first person to determine the exact length of the rappel (see chapter 5 for details on lowering). Here's how to set up the Reepschnur rappel:

1. Lower the first climber or otherwise figure out the exact length of the rappel (fig. 4-15a).
2. Tie a knot (most commonly an alpine butterfly) on the shorter of the two strands of rope threaded through the anchor (not the longer side that the climber was lowered on), then clip the knot to the other (longer) strand of rope with a locking carabiner (fig. 4-15b). The lower the profile in this setup, the better.
3. Set up a single-strand rappel on the long strand of rope and begin your rappel, keeping both strands of rope close to you (fig. 4-15c). It is better to rappel on the side of rope that the alpine butterfly is clipped to rather than the strand it's tied with, so you get the benefit of the knot jamming against the rappel anchor. It is imperative that you not lose control of the short end of the rope; it is an excellent idea to clip this pull side directly to yourself since unlike in a normal rappel, in which both strands are running through your belay

Figure 4-15. Reepschnur rappel: **a**, *lower a climber to figure out the exact length of the rappel;* **b**, *tie an alpine butterfly on the short side of the rappel rope and clip this knot to the long strand of rope with a locking carabiner;* **c**, *set up a single-strand rappel and keep both strands of rope close to you;* **d**, *once you get to the end of the shorter strand of the rope, tie items to it that will allow you to "pull" it at the bottom of the rappel;* **e**, *rappel all the way to the ground (or the next anchor) on the longer strand;* **f**, *at the bottom of the rappel, pull the chained-together side of the rope to retrieve it.*

device, it is easy for the short strand to get hung up on a ledge or otherwise creep out of your control.

4. When the short strand comes tight on your harness as you rappel down the long end, remove the short strand and start tying things to it that will allow you to "pull" it from lower down (fig. 4-15d). Use longer items first, such as cordelette or long slings, but anything goes—even cams and nuts "chained" together.
5. Rappel all the way to the ground or the next anchor on the longer strand (fig. 4-15e), then retrieve the rope by pulling down on the slings, cams, cordelette, et cetera (fig. 4-15f). When you pull the "chained-together" side of the rope, you will see the importance of putting the alpine butterfly on this side of the rope, as it (as well as the items attached to the short end) would not be able to pass through the rappel rings.

Tip: The Reepschnur isn't a technique you'll use all the time, but if you climb long enough it will inevitably be an incredibly useful tool to smoothly overcome a rappel that is too long for your ropes.

BEAL ESCAPER

The Beal Escaper is a unique product that has gained a lot of popularity since it was first released. Made up of an elastic cord connected to Dyneema webbing, the latter woven in a configuration similar to a VT prusik, the Escaper facilitates relatively long single-strand rappels plus rope retrieval. The elastic cord lets the hitch creep when the rope is unweighted at the end of the rappel, enabling you to pull your rope.

David Allfrey tandem rappels with a haul bag on the descent after climbing a new big wall route on the northwest face of Kichatna Spire, Alaska Range. (Photo by Graham Zimmerman)

While this device might seem sketchy, it is actually quite robust, but its bigger problem is that it can introduce too much friction into the system if the rappel is too low-angle; in that situation, the elastic cord is not able to spring upward and allow the Dyneema sling to slowly creep off. Also be cautious of *super-long* rappels (greater than 40 meters), as the Escaper's "spring" action is lessened, making it more difficult to release the rope.

The Beal Escaper isn't a tool to use if you know you will have to make a number of double-rope rappels, but it can help you get through a few longer rappels that you might not have seen coming. It can also minimize how much equipment you have to leave

RESCUE ON NORTH EARLY WINTERS SPIRE

BY LARRY GOLDIE

One midsummer afternoon when I had just returned to our office in Mazama, Washington, from guiding on the Goat Wall, a rescue call came in over the radio. The report was of a climber who had taken an estimated 80-foot fall on North Early Winters Spire and had badly injured at least one of their lower legs, inhibiting their ability to stand or walk, much less descend a technical rock route. The incident was witnessed by a climber on the adjacent spire, who was, remarkably, able to radio someone in the parking lot who relayed the message. It was incredibly lucky that they were able to make a rescue call of any kind, as the area has little to no cell service.

Being on our local high-angle rescue team, I was asked if I could hike up there and help out with the rescue while the rest of the team mobilized from down in the Methow Valley, which would bring a paramedic as well as all of the rescue gear from our main rescue headquarters.

I met a few other members of the team at the parking lot, and we quickly hiked up to the base to establish contact with the injured party. We were able to establish some basic dialogue via shouting and learned that they were in the process of self-evacuating, but that things were going very slowly and they could certainly use some help. While the initial plan was to wait for the rest of the team to arrive with all of the heavy-duty rescue gear, I began to get impatient and knew that it was going to be a long time coming.

Finally, knowing the techniques the injured climber would likely need to get down and how simple it would be for me to get up there using the climbing gear I had with me, I took a belay from one of the other members of my team and climbed up to the injured party. They had done a good job of splinting his injured ankle and wrist, and he had a bandage on his head. They were helping him slide on his butt down some scree and talus toward a rappel anchor below. I assisted by supporting the injured person's leg as we slowly scooched down to the *Chockstone* anchor.

At this point, I rigged a tandem rappel out of a cordelette, making sure to put the injured person on the longer end of the cordelette. I then ran his strand of the rope over my shoulder in an effort to keep his back off the wall as we descended. We did two more rappels like this, which brought us to the base of the spire, where the paramedic had finally arrived. The paramedic did a full assessment and redressed the injured person's wounds. From there, the full team moved him a bit lower to a suitable location for a helicopter pickup.

Larry Goldie, an IFMGA/UIAGM mountain guide and co-owner of North Cascades Mountain Guides, is based in Winthrop, Washington.

Figure 4-16. The Beal Escaper: **a**, *thread the "rope" side of the Escaper through the anchor you will rappel from;* **b**, *feed the "rope" end into the Escaper's webbing, carefully following the device's arrows and directions;* **c**, *pass the Escaper's "rope" through all strands of the webbing;* **d**, *pull the climbing rope through the "eye" end of the Escaper, far enough that the Escaper's black marker is beyond the webbing;* **e**, *tie the climbing rope directly to the Escaper using a secure knot like a rewoven figure eight or a rewoven overhand, then rappel on a single strand of rope;* **f**, *after the rappel, pull the rope roughly 20–30 times to retrieve it.*

behind in an emergency if you need to retreat down a rarely rappelled section of terrain.

1. Start by passing the Escaper through the anchor (fig. 4-16a).
2. Follow several arrows that show where the device's tapered rope is threaded through webbing (fig. 4-16b) until the tapered rope is completely through (fig. 4-16c).

3. Pass the climbing rope through the Escaper's "eye" (fig. 4-16d).
4. Tie it directly to the Escaper with a secure knot like a rewoven figure 8 or rewoven overhand. Now you're ready to rappel (fig. 4-16e).

While this device appears like it will pull through easily after the rappel, it is surprisingly difficult to get the rope to release. For moderate-length rappels, expect more than 20 pulls to get it to release (fig. 4-16f).

TANDEM RAPPELS

A tandem rappel is when two climbers, or one person and multiple generally heavy objects, descend from a single belay device and are tethered to it in various configurations. The reasons for a tandem rappel are numerous: if one climber has sustained an injury, particularly to either their lower- or upper-body extremities, or if their level of consciousness has been recently compromised; if a climber is scared; if a climber is too light, such as a young child, to easily rappel solo; or if a climber is otherwise unable to rappel. In these situations, the tandem rappel is an excellent option for getting them down. For big wall climbers, the technique for rappelling with a haul bag is identical to rappelling with an unconscious climber.

At the belay station, generally speaking, you girth-hitch (or clip) the (injured or not) second climber's harness belay loop—or a haul bag's haul loop—to a double-length sling (fig. 4-17a) that will be clipped to the belay device. Tie an overhand knot in the middle of the sling (fig. 4-17b) and clip the locking carabiner that connects to the belay device to the loops in the sling on either side of the knot (fig. 4-17c). You, as the primary rappeller, rescuer, or hauler, clip the free end of the sling to your belay loop (fig. 4-17d). You clip in to the tether rather than tying in to the system, which keeps you from becoming trapped should the situation change.

Tip: A third-hand backup should unquestionably be used if you are doing a tandem rappel, since it is not just your life in your hands but the other person's as well. Because there is significantly more weight on the belay device in a tandem rappel than in a solo rappel, an additional wrap or two in the friction hitch is generally required.

Depending on the situation, it is rarely advised to rappel truly side by side in a tandem rappel, so considering whether to put the second climber above or below the rescuer is important. If the second climber has a lower-leg injury, is scared, or is too light to rappel (as in the case of a small child), it is generally advised that you hang them above you rather than beside or below. For a climber with lower-leg injuries, this position lets the rescuer "cradle" and protect them during the rappel. The same is true for nervous people or children: having them above you lets you steer them more easily. If the second climber has an arm injury or is a lot bigger than you (or if you are tandem rappelling with a haul bag), it can be easier to rappel with them below you; if they can manage themself, it allows you a little more freedom of movement.

COUNTERBALANCED RAPPELS

Also sometimes referred to as a pick-off rappel, a counterbalanced rappel is a technique that can be used to rescue a leader or a seconding climber while they are hanging in the middle of a pitch, whether they are

Figure 4-17. Setting up a tandem rappel: **a**, *girth-hitch a double-length sling to the harness belay loop of the second climber (here, the climber in the white helmet);* **b**, *tie an overhand knot in the middle of the sling;* **c**, *clip a locking carabiner to the sling loops on either side of the knot, then clip this carabiner to the belay device;* **d**, *clip the free end of the sling to the first climber's belay loop.*

leading or following the pitch. The name stems from the fact that the two climbers counterbalance one another on either side of the rappel rope as they descend. Unlike a tandem rappel, in which two climbers hang from one belay device, in a counterbalanced rappel each climber is on one side of the rope with the rope fixed to one climber and the other operating a belay device.

If a following climber gets hurt or incapacitated while seconding a pitch, a tandem rappel is not an option: a counterbalanced rappel must be implemented. If the second climber is injured in any way and is unable to complete the pitch, first escape the belay (see chapter 3). Once you've escaped the belay (see Figure 3-13j), follow these steps to set up the counterbalanced rappel:

Figure 4-18. Setting up a counterbalanced rappel: **a**, *after escaping the belay, clip a sacrificial locking carabiner to the brake strand (1) coming out of the munter-mule-overhand (2);* **b**, *thread the rope into the rappel anchor;* **c**, *rig an extended single-strand rappel (3) on the brake side (non–belay-device side) of the anchor;* **d**, *untie and remove the munter-mule-overhand tied in the rope;* **(continued on next page)**

e, *release the cordelette's munter-mule-overhand on the anchor until the belay device is weighted through the rappel anchor, and leave the friction hitch (4) on the rope;* **f**, *tie off the long end of the cordelette and clip it to your harness belay loop (5), then remove your attachment system from the anchor and begin descending;* **g**, *as you rappel, mind the friction hitch, and when you reach the injured climber, let the friction hitch catch (grab).*

1. Clip a sacrificial locking carabiner to the brake strand coming out of the munter-mule-overhand (fig. 4-18a), then clip the rope in to the rappel anchor (fig. 4-18b). (On an anchor with fixed rings, the rescuer must attach themself with a tether to the free end of the rope in order to thread the rings).
2. Build a rappel extension on your harness (see Figures 4-1 through 4-4), clip your belay device to the rappel extension, and set up your rappel on the brake strand where you added the sacrificial locking carabiner, making sure to add a well-tied friction-hitch backup (fig. 4-18c).
3. Release and remove the brake strand's munter-mule-overhand and associated carabiners from the anchor (fig. 4-18d).
4. Lower out and remove the cordelette's munter-mule-overhand attached to the anchor until the weight comes tight on your belay device in a "counterbalanced" fashion through the rappel anchor (fig. 4-18e). Leave the friction hitch on the rope.
5. Tie an overhand knot in the long (now open) end of the cordelette and clip it to the belay loop on your harness. (Attaching the cordelette to your harness enables you either to rappel in opposition to the other person, with them staying in one place, or to move downward simultaneously by letting the friction hitch grab.) Remove your attachment system from the anchor and begin descending (fig. 4-18f).
6. Rappel, minding the friction hitch as you go (fig. 4-18g). Managing the friction hitch lets you choose when the injured climber remains stationary and when they descend with you. When you reach the injured climber, let the friction hitch catch (grab), so it will move the injured climber down at the same rate as your rappel.

TRANSITIONING WITH AN INJURED OR UNCONSCIOUS CLIMBER AT A STEEP ANCHOR

If you are rappelling with an unconscious climber, one of the trickiest maneuvers is attaching them to and unattaching them from the anchor between rappels at a steep stance. A great way to do this is with the rope, but it can also be accomplished with a doubled-up cordelette or other long pieces of material. This maneuver can be done from a tandem rappel or a counterbalanced rappel. Even if a counterbalanced rappel was used initially, switching to tandem rappels is generally easier once both climbers have arrived at an anchor together.

Rappel until you reach the next rappel station and build a new anchor from which to operate—any anchor with a master point will do. Be careful to not rappel too low; a good guideline is to rappel until the master point of the next anchor will be at roughly waist level. Then follow these same steps:

1. Rappel down until you are level with the lower anchor (fig. 4-19a).
2. Clip a locking carabiner to the master point, then take the rope leading directly from the rescuer's tie-in, clip it through this locking carabiner, and attach it to the injured climber's harness belay loop with a munter hitch on a locking carabiner (fig. 4-19b). Back this up with a mule hitch and an overhand knot (fig. 4-19c); the rescuer is now "counterbalanced" with the injured climber, which allows the rescuer to use their body weight to move the injured climber slightly.

Evan Davis and Andrew Lamb perform a tandem rappel in Oak Creek Canyon, Red Rock, Nevada.

3. Remove the belay device (fig. 4-19d) and friction-hitch backup, then remove the cordelette and friction hitch that assisted in "pulling" the injured climber down (fig. 4-19e). Untie the rope from the injured climber's harness (fig. 4-19f).
4. Take the end of the rope that you just untied from the injured climber and thread the new anchor you will be rappelling from to the middle mark of the rope (fig. 4-19g). Do *not* use the same locking carabiner that you are already hanging counterbalanced from. It is *very* easy to trap the team this way and is complicated to get out of.
5. Thread both strands of rope into your belay device (fig. 4-19h). Rig your device such that it is captured by the rappel extension on both sides of the knot and tie a third-hand friction-hitch backup, making sure it has enough wraps—an extra one or two wraps compared to what you normally do—to account for the increased load.
6. Clip the other end of your rappel extension to the injured climber with a locking carabiner (fig. 4-19i). Your options are to (a) clip the shorter side of the tether to you to hang the other climber below you, (b) clip the shorter side of the tether to the injured person if you want them to hang above you, or (c) tie the extension's knot in the middle if the other person is scared but relatively uninjured (you will bang into them the most with this setup, but for them it is the most "comforting" spot).
7. Release the munter-mule-overhand on the injured climber's harness that is "counterbalancing" you with the other climber until they are loading the rappel extension connected to the belay device (fig. 4-19j).
8. Remove the extra locking carabiner from the anchor and start rappelling (fig. 4-19k).

Tip: Whether performing a counterbalanced rappel or a tandem rappel, remember that it is easy to descend but very difficult to go back up, so clip yourself and the other climber in close to the anchor and keep slack tolerances tight. Clipping the injured climber tightly and as close to the anchor as possible makes transitioning to a subsequent rappel much easier.

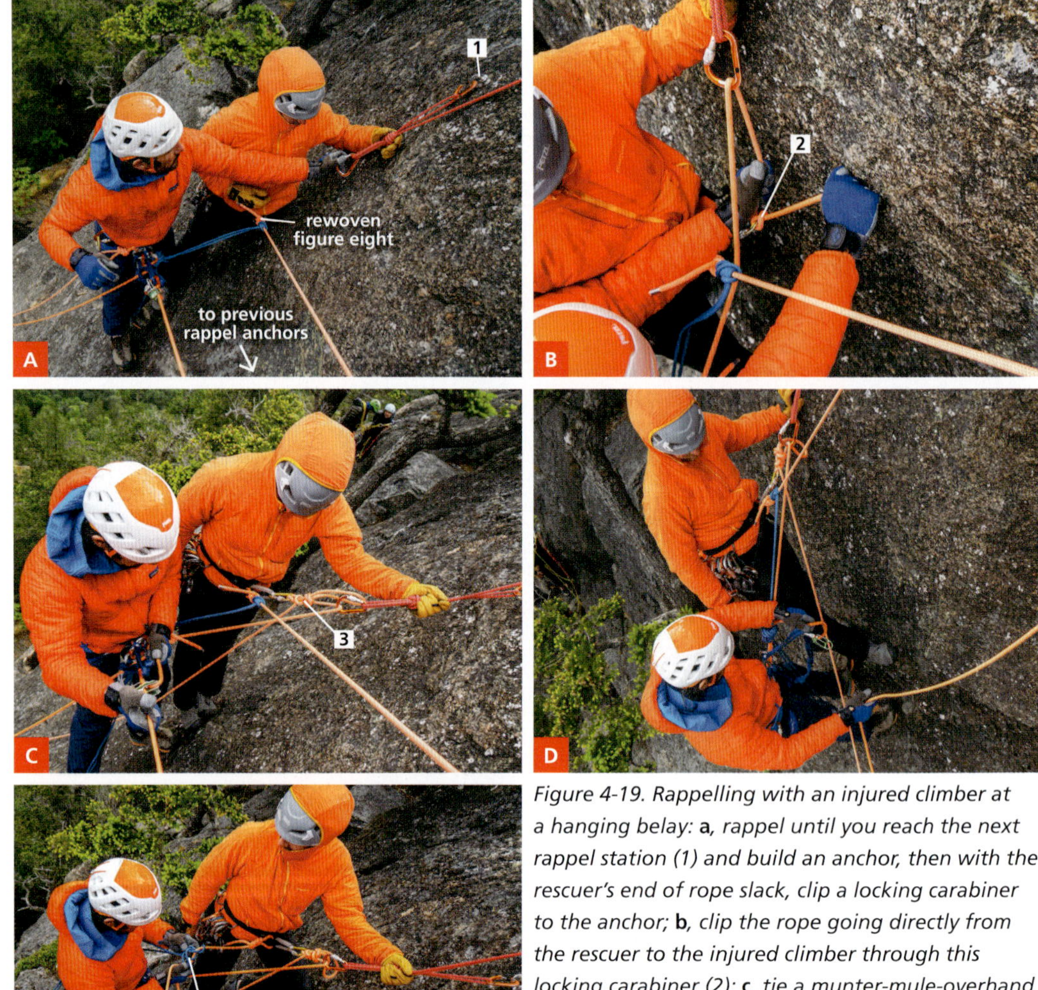

Figure 4-19. Rappelling with an injured climber at a hanging belay: **a**, *rappel until you reach the next rappel station (1) and build an anchor, then with the rescuer's end of rope slack, clip a locking carabiner to the anchor;* **b**, *clip the rope going directly from the rescuer to the injured climber through this locking carabiner (2);* **c**, *tie a munter-mule-overhand (3) on the injured climber's harness using a locking carabiner;* **d**, *let the new counterbalanced clip-in take the weight, then remove the belay device;* **e**, *remove the friction-hitch backup (4);* **f**, *remove the cordelette and friction hitch that assisted in "pulling" the injured climber down, then untie the rope from the injured climber's harness;* **g**, *thread the just-untied end of the rope through the anchor to the rope's midpoint;* **(continued on next page)**

h, *thread both strands of rope into your belay device and tie a third-hand friction-hitch backup, making sure it has enough wraps to match the additional load;* **i**, *clip the other end of your rappel extension to the injured climber with a locking carabiner (5);* **j**, *untie and release the munter-mule-overhand on the injured climber's harness and lower them until they are weighting the rappel extension connected to the belay device;* **k**, *remove the extra locking carabiner from the anchor and start rappelling.*

REQUISITE SKILLS FOR REMOTE MOUNTAINS

BY MIKEY SCHAEFER

Micah Dash and I are attempting a new route on the South Face of Mount Combatant in British Columbia's Waddington Range. Micah is slowly navigating his way up the fifth pitch, gingerly tiptoeing his way around small bits of precarious choss sitting on every ledge we pass. The south face is a massive series of buttresses and ridges that gain more than 4,500 feet of elevation. As I hang from the belay looking around, I feel small in the massive and remote landscape. I try not to feel overwhelmed with the task at hand, but my mind wanders to all of the "what ifs" and worst-case scenarios that can happen.

I think back on my first expedition to Patagonia eight years prior, when I became so overwhelmed with fear and apprehension that midway up a new route I bailed on my partner. At the time, I was a fairly inexperienced climber and realized I truly lacked the requisite skills for climbing in such remote mountains. I knew that I barely had the skills to get up and down safely, and that if there was bad weather or an accident, I wouldn't be able to rescue myself or my partner. After that trip, I promised myself I wouldn't come back to the mountains until I had gained the necessary skills.

Fast-forward from those eight years ago: small pebbles shower me at the belay as Micah cleans off hand- and footholds, when all of a sudden much larger blocks start careering toward me. As I look up, I see Micah tumbling down the wall, then flying past me. The rope comes taut as he stops 20 feet below the belay. He instantly starts moaning in pain and grasping his ankles. He has just taken close to a 50-foot fall, hitting multiple ledges on the way down. I instantly know I have to figure out how to get us down.

His injuries aren't life-threatening, but both his ankles appear to be unstable, and he can't put weight on them. He isn't going to be able to make it back to the belay unassisted, and the best plan is for me to rappel to him. Since he can't get an anchor in, I set up a counterbalanced rappel to get to his position. I then clip a double-length runner between us and position him in my lap so I can keep his ankles from hitting the wall. We rap down for about 100 feet and get an anchor in. For the next rap, I decide a tandem rap is the way to go, though in reality it is more like a triple as I also have to hang our pack, which weighs nearly 50 pounds. We make our way down with Micah straddling my lap.

After a few uneventful rappels, we find ourselves down on the Tiedemen Glacier and a long way from our base camp. With little choice, we decide to radio in a helicopter pickup for Micah. As the excitement of the accident starts to recede, I replay the last few hours in my head and feel thankful that I'm no longer paralyzed by fear and apprehension but empowered with the knowledge I've gained.

Mikey Schaefer is a world-famous photographer, filmmaker, and climber based in Reno, Nevada.

Opposite: *Rebecca Schroeder is lowered out on a traversing pitch 1,500 feet up the* Muir Wall, *El Capitan, Yosemite National Park, California.*

CHAPTER 5

Lowering

There are countless reasons to lower someone: it's an excellent way to get the rope down if it's windy or the next rappel must be constructed (for example, the team is retreating downward); it can be faster or more efficient depending on the terrain; it might be the best or only option for those less experienced with rappelling or who do not know how to do it at all.

There are, however, a few things to consider when lowering. Avoid lowering over loose terrain, because the rope can dislodge rocks that can strike the person being lowered. Also, always close the system by tying in to the system or attaching it physically to the anchor to eliminate the potential for lowering someone off the end of the rope. It is strongly recommended that you use a friction-hitch backup with any lowering method. This chapter provides a number of different lowering methods.

REDIRECTED PLATE

A redirected plate is the smoothest lower, and it puts the absolute least amount of twists into the rope. The only disadvantage to it is that it is marginally slower to set up than other methods and it requires a second locking carabiner. With a redirected-plate lower, the load travels up through a locking carabiner and down to a belay device, with a third-hand friction hitch.

1. Thread the rope into the belay device as you would if you were belaying a leader, but instead of clipping the device to your harness, clip it to the anchor with a locking carabiner (fig. 5-1a).
2. Clip a second locking carabiner to the anchor and attach the brake strand of the rope with a clove hitch. It is helpful if the second locker—which creates the redirect—is similar-sized or smaller than the one clipped in the belay device (fig. 5-1b).
3. Wrap a third-hand friction hitch around the brake strand and clip this hitch to your harness belay loop using a locking carabiner.
4. Close the system by tying a knot, such as a rewoven figure eight, on your harness.
5. Stack the rope neatly to ensure a smooth lower.

Tip: Rather than lowering from your harness through a redirect up above you, try a redirected plate. It is far easier to provide a smooth lower that offers greater security than a lower off your harness, while also allowing for options should something unexpected arise.

Figure 5-1. The redirected-plate lower: **a**, *the rope is threaded into the belay device (1) as you would for belaying a leader, but the device is clipped to the anchor with a locking carabiner (2);* **b**, *second locker (3) is clipped to the anchor and attached to the brake strand (4) with a clove hitch. A third-hand friction hitch (5; here an autoblock) is placed between the device and a locker (6) on the belay loop, then the system is closed with a knot (7; here a rewoven figure eight) on your harness.*

If there are fixed rappel anchors, you can thread the end of the rope through the chains prior to lowering, not only to use the lowest link to redirect the belay device but also to simultaneously pull the rope through the chains. To do this, simply pass the rope through the chains or rappel point and have the person being lowered tie in to that end. Next, rig your belay device in the same manner listed above for a redirected plate, but use the anchor chains instead of a second carabiner (fig. 5-2).

Tip: If you use the technique of redirecting through a fixed rappel anchor's chains, it is imperative that the belay device be lower than the chains so that you are able to achieve adequate friction.

REDIRECTED CLIP-BACK

Similar to the more traditional redirected-plate lower, the redirected clip-back lower doesn't

Figure 5-2. Redirecting through a fixed rappel anchor's chains: thread the end of the rope through the chains of a fixed rappel anchor, not only to use the lowest link to redirect the belay device but also to simultaneously pull the rope through the chains.

LOWERING IN NUCLEAR WINDS IN PATAGONIA

BY IAN NICHOLSON

My longtime climbing partner Graham Zimmerman and I flew down to Chilean Patagonia to try to climb a new route on some of the monstrous rock formations lining the French Valley in Torres del Paine. We walked in the 20-plus miles and set up camp at Campo Britanico, but after a few carries we learned that the cost of the ferry was well worth saving the 10 or so miles.

The weather was particularly stormy that year, and after a few brief attempts on some slightly larger formations on the other side of the valley, it finally looked like we had around 24 hours of decent weather between storms. We hiked over to a feature named Los Gemelos, which had seen only two other ascents total, with one of those ascents the year prior.

From the base, the bottom of a route called the *Slash* looked like fairly run-out granite overlaps on steep slabs. With a little bit of aid here and there, we got to more continuous cracks and pushed upward.

Around 1,000 feet up, darkness began to fall; a few pitches higher and, just past midnight, we found ourselves on the summit in complete darkness with snow lightly falling. The storm had already started to show up earlier than expected, and just a few raps into the descent the winds began raging. We had some information about the previous party (Mark Matthews and Dave Turner) and how they had gotten down but couldn't find any of their anchors.

Just two rappels into the descent, the wind turned nuclear and traditional rappels were no longer an option. Graham and I could *barely* hear each other even while standing side by side. If we let go of the rope (let alone tried to throw it), the wind could support more than 50 feet of the rope completely horizontally, and it was strong enough to forcefully slam us into the wall even while we hung off the anchor. The idea of "throwing the ropes" was laughable, plus we had no idea how to get down nor would we be able to communicate.

So we decided Graham would lower me (using a redirected plate with a third hand) to basically within 30 feet or so of the end of the rope. I would then build an anchor, and if I had to ascend to do so, that would just have to be the case. Then Graham would start rappelling (because the rope was unweighted) once he could, and we wouldn't have to verbally communicate.

The descent was *steep* and mostly dead-vertical, with lots of small overhangs. On each lower, Graham would lower me past what seemed like massive stretches of blank granite, but at each stop I lucked out by being near a crack that accepted a few pitons or nuts.

All in all, it was about as smooth a descent on a previously undescended mini–big wall in the dark in a full-blown Patagonian storm as it could get. Save for one slightly spicy snow-bollard rappel a couple of raps from the glacier, the descent was fast and efficient. Once down and walking back to camp, we both discussed how slow and difficult it would have been trying to throw ropes or even saddlebag them in such strong winds. Lowering got both ropes where we wanted them, I didn't have to lock off any rappel, and it gave us both more options should the situation have required it.

Graham Zimmerman is at a belay about halfway up Los Gemelos *in the French Valley, Torres del Paine National Park, Chile.*

require any additional carabiners (fig. 5-3). It is quite smooth and, with care in its construction and rope management, will minimize twisting as the rope flows through the system. Overall this method causes far fewer twists in the rope compared to lowering with a munter hitch, but on longer lowers this method will introduce a few more twists than the more traditional redirected plate. Here's how to set it up:

1. Clip a locking carabiner to the anchor and attach the belay device, inserting the device in an upside-down V shape. Do *not* lower in this orientation.
2. Thread a bight of rope into the belay device and clip it directly to the anchor so that both the load and brake strands are pointed down (fig. 5-4a). Don't clip the device's attachment point used for belaying climbers from above (the third hole); the only part of the plaquette attached to the anchor should be its "keeper loop," if it has one.

Figure 5-3. A redirected clip-back lower is simpler and quicker to set up than a redirected plate and provides plenty of strength, but it requires a little more care to prevent twisting in the rope. (Photo by Dale Remsberg)

3. Wrap the brake strand around back toward the device (rather than away) in a circular motion (fig. 5-4b) and reclip the original locking carabiner through which the bight of rope is running (fig. 5-4c).
4. Lock the carabiner (fig. 5-4d), tie on a third-hand friction-hitch backup (fig. 5-4e), and ensure that the system is closed.

Tip: When performing a redirected clip-back lower, keep the rope running in line with the belay device rather than creating a right angle from the brake hand to the locking carabiner, which creates twists in the rope.

THE MUNTER LOWER

Knowing how to lower with a munter hitch is a great skill for any climber. All it takes is a single locking carabiner, and, contrary to popular belief, a munter can provide a tremendous amount of friction and can smoothly lower large loads. The disadvantage is that on longer lowers it is very hard to avoid putting twists in the rope. This means the munter hitch is best for short lowers or even a single longer lower, but attempting to perform several consecutive long lowers with a munter will result in an extremely twisty rope that has the potential to be, at the very least, severely problematic to deal with or get so snarled that it could become a hazard.

To minimize twists, keep the load strand and brake strand as close as possible (fig. 5-5a). It is important to remember that when lowering with a munter hitch, "braking" involves bringing the load strand and brake strand closer to parallel rather than creating more angle, as you typically would while belaying off your harness (fig. 5-5b).

Figure 5-4. The redirected clip-back lower: **a**, *clip a locking carabiner (1) to the anchor and attach the belay device (2), inserting the belay device in an upside-down V shape;* **b**, *wrap the brake strand (3) coming out of the "teethed" side of the device in a circular motion;* **c**, *clip this bight in to the locking carabiner (1) holding the belay device;* **d**, *lock the carabiner;* **e**, *tie on a third-hand friction-hitch backup (4) and ensure that the system is closed.*

Figure 5-5. Lowering with a munter hitch: **a**, *good technique keeps the brake strand and load strand close to parallel to reduce the number of twists in the rope during the lower;* **b**, *poor technique creates a large angle between the load strand and the brake strand, which introduces many more twists in the rope.*

Figure 5-6. An HMS-style (pear-shaped) carabiner is wide enough to allow the munter hitch to easily flip back and forth during a lower, which will not only be easier to work with but also put far fewer twists in the rope. (Photo by Truc Allen)

Additionally, keep an eye on the rope—you'll be able to seee it twisting as the rope passes through the munter hitch. A way to reduce twists is to force your own twists into the rope going in the opposite direction as the rope enters the munter hitch, which will then spin the other way, reducing the amount of twisting your rope suffers over the duration of the lower.

Tip: When lowering with a munter hitch, using an HMS-style (pear shaped) locking carabiner provides enough "room" for the munter to flip freely and will reduce twists compared to a smaller or more heavily tapered locking carabiner, which can cause one or both strands to ride (and subsequently twist) on the spine and/or gate of the carabiner. HMS stands for the German *halbmastwurf sicherung*, which means "half clove-hitch belay"—or munter hitch.

Figure 5-7. Lowering with an ABD—here, a GriGri: clip the locking carabiner directly to the anchor and thread the rope through the GriGri the way you would if you were lead belaying, then fold the brake strand over the device's round edge and redirect it through a second locking carabiner clipped to the anchor. Keep one hand on the brake strand while the other hand manages the release lever, and if the GriGri is not hanging in space, take care that the lever does not jam against the wall, potentially releasing the lower climber.

ASSISTED-BRAKING BELAY DEVICE

The more lowering techniques you become familiar with, the more places you'll see to implement them. When lowering off an assisted-braking belay device (ABD) like the Petzl GriGri, a friction-hitch backup is not recommended. In the event you let go of the release lever, the device locks up automatically, and managing a friction-hitch backup while attempting to manage the release lever during a lower with an ABD is problematic and makes it difficult to achieve a smooth lower.

To set up this lower, clip a locking carabiner directly to the anchor and thread the rope through the ABD in the same manner you would if you were lead belaying. Now fold the brake strand over the device's round edge and redirect it through a second locking carabiner clipped to the anchor. When lowering, keep one hand on the brake strand while the other hand manages the release lever (fig. 5-7). If

Figure 5-8. Using an autoblocking belay device for a very short lower: **a**, *if the device is weighted but the lower climber needs just a little bit of slack, "rock" the locking carabiner that the rope runs around back and forth;* **b**, *moving the carabiner in its full range of motion is more effective than shorter "rocks."*

the ABD is not hanging in space, take care that the lever does not jam against the wall, potentially releasing the lower climber.

AUTOBLOCKING BELAY DEVICE IN GUIDE MODE

If you are belaying from above with an autoblocking belay device such as the Petzl Reverso or the Black Diamond ATC Guide and using it in guide mode, there are several considerations for lowering, depending on the terrain, your skills, and the length of the lower.

SUPER-SHORT LOWERS

Say your second climber ascends close to a bolt or piece of protection and can't get enough slack to clean it. You can simply "rock" the carabiner in the belay device back and forth to create a few inches of slack, even if the second climber is fully weighting the rope (fig. 5-8a). Generally, longer "rocks" that move the carabiner in its full range of motion are more effective than shorter "rocks" (fig. 5-8b).

SHORT TO MEDIUM-LENGTH LOWERS

If the person being lowered needs more than a foot but less than 30 feet, the next option is to briefly "defeat" the device. This method allows you to control the speed of the lower with your body weight by leaning back in to your harness while still controlling the brake strand with two hands. A friction-hitch backup is strongly encouraged due to the all-or-nothing nature of this lower and how easy it is to lose control.

1. Girth-hitch a sling to the fourth, small (bottom) hole featured on the majority of autoblocking belay devices on the market (fig. 5-9a).
2. Redirect the sling through a carabiner clipped to the anchor (fig. 5-9b).
3. Clip the sling to your harness's belay loop (fig. 5-9c) and tie a friction-hitch backup on the brake strand coming out of the belay device.
4. Lean back onto the sling (fig. 5-9d), which changes the orientation of the belay device and "defeats" autoblocking mode, allowing the rope to run through the device.

Figure 5-9. Using an autoblocking belay device for a short to medium-length lower: **a**, *girth-hitch a sling to the bottom hole in the autoblocking belay device;* **b**, *redirect this sling through a carabiner clipped to the anchor;* **c**, *clip the redirected sling to your harness belay loop and add a third-hand friction-hitch backup to the brake strand from the belay device;* **d**, *lean back on the sling using your body weight to rotate and "defeat" the braking power of the device as you manage the friction hitch during the lower.*

This technique is great for relatively short lowers; however, if you have a full-length lower, one of the other methods is worth the extra time to set up, as it will prove faster and smoother by the time you've lowered someone more than 100 feet.

LOAD STRAND DIRECT LOWERS

The load strand direct (LSD) is the simplest option for longer lowers while belaying off an anchor with an autoblocking belay device. However, it shouldn't be a go-to technique if you and the other climber are at the belay station together. The LSD offers a reasonably smooth lower that is very easy to set up if the seconding climber can stand up and unweight the device, creating just a small amount of slack in the system. Here's how to do it

1. Starting from a position where you are belaying directly off the anchor, put a

Figure 5-10. A load strand direct lower with an autoblocking belay device: **a**, *put a third-hand friction hitch on the brake strand and clip a nonlocking carabiner to the anchor next to the locking carabiner the belay device is clipped to (on the side of the device where the brake and load strands exit, opposite the keeper loop);* **b**, *have the climber being lowered stand up to create a little bit of slack in the load strand, then clip the load strand to the nonlocking carabiner;* **c**, *with the nonlocking carabiner "defeating" the device, lower the climber while managing the friction-hitch backup.*

friction-hitch backup on the brake strand and clip a nonlocking carabiner to the anchor next to the locking carabiner the autoblocking belay device is clipped to (fig. 5-10a). The nonlocking carabiner should be on the side of the device where the brake and load strands exit.

2. If the climber being lowered can stand up and unweight the device, pull up a bit of slack in the load strand and clip it to the nonlocking carabiner (fig. 5-10b).
3. With this additional carabiner "defeating" the device (fig. 5-10c), lower the climber while managing the friction-hitch backup.

Opposite: *Ian Nicholson above the Crooked River on the third pitch of* Sky Ridge, *Smith Rock, Oregon* (Photo by Ryan Minton)

CHAPTER 6

Knot Passes

This chapter offers strategies for dealing with two issues affecting the climbing rope that you'll most likely encounter at some point: knots in the rope that must pass through the safety system and the rope getting stuck.

PASSING KNOTS DURING A LOWER

An invaluable skill for climbers is the ability to pass a knot, whether it is the random figure-eight skeleton that has somehow worked its way into the middle of the rope or an intentionally tied overhand or alpine butterfly to "isolate" a damaged section of the rope. There are several ways to pass a knot, depending on the circumstances; however, they all work by one of three principles: using a load transfer to pass the knot, using an extension to pass the knot, or physically passing the knot through a lowering system.

OVERHAND KNOT PULL-THROUGH (A.K.A. THE "MUNTER POP")

If you are passing a flat overhand knot joining two ropes tied together or an overhand isolating a section of rope that has been damaged, lowering with a munter hitch and subsequently pulling the overhand knot slowly through the munter hitch itself can be easy, fast, and safe as long as the loads aren't too big.

1. With a munter hitch built on an HMS (pear-shaped) carabiner and a friction-hitch backup, let the overhand knot run completely into the munter hitch from which you are performing the lower (fig. 6-1a).
2. Pull the tails of the overhand knot through the first overlap or bight in the munter hitch (fig. 6-1b). If the overhand knot hangs up, give the tails a sharp tug to get the overhand knot to "pop" through.
3. Do this two more times, passing the tails forward through the next bight (fig. 6-1c) toward where you want the rest of the knot to travel.
4. On the final pop, make sure the knot doesn't get hung up on the "tongue" (the final bight) of the munter, which creates a ton of slack in the system (fig. 6-1d).
5. Pull the knot through the munter's final bight to complete the knot pass (fig. 6-1e).

Tip: Remember that the "munter pop" works only with a flat overhand. It will *not* work with a figure eight, a "skeleton" found in the rope, or an alpine butterfly.

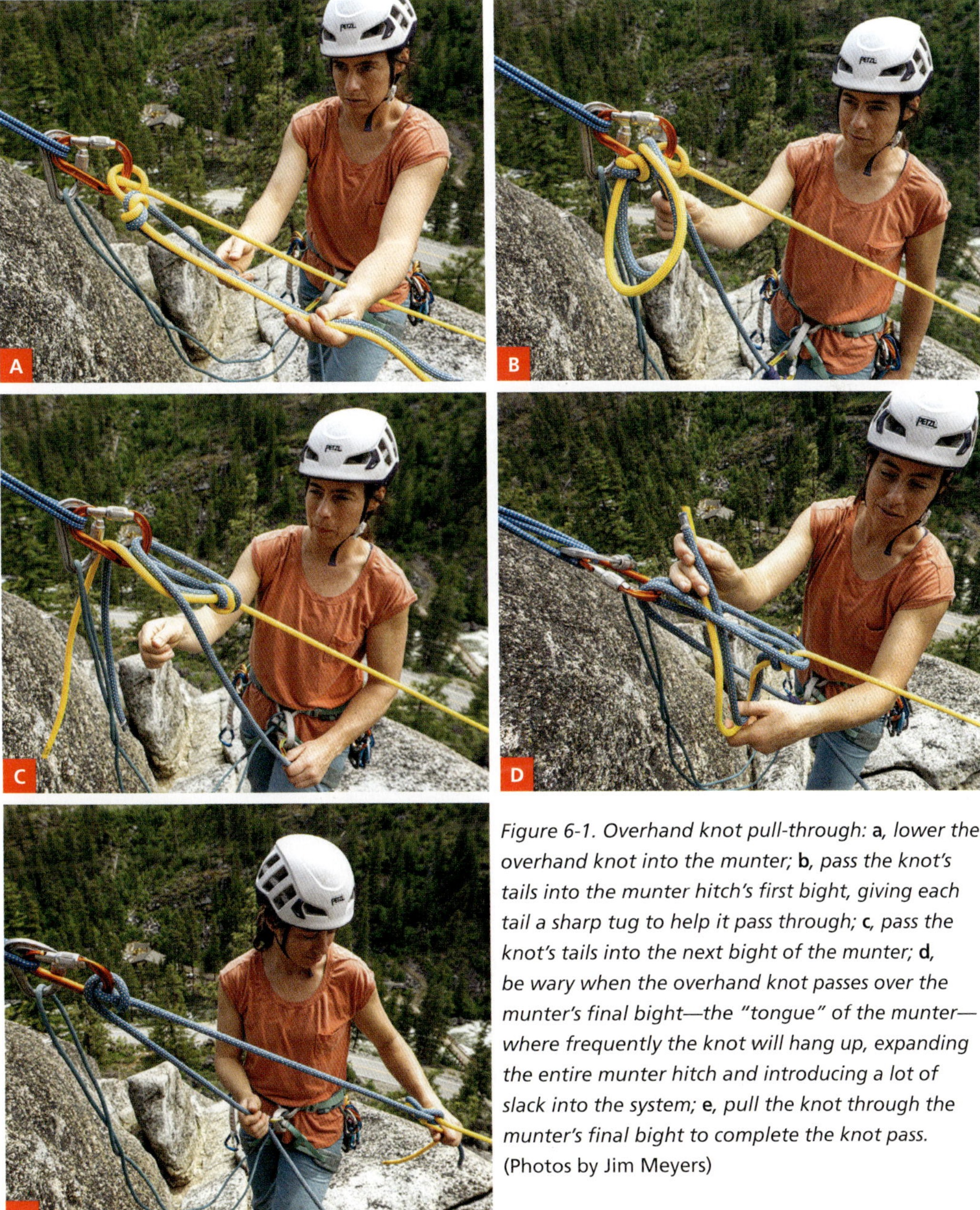

Figure 6-1. Overhand knot pull-through: **a**, *lower the overhand knot into the munter;* **b**, *pass the knot's tails into the munter hitch's first bight, giving each tail a sharp tug to help it pass through;* **c**, *pass the knot's tails into the next bight of the munter;* **d**, *be wary when the overhand knot passes over the munter's final bight—the "tongue" of the munter—where frequently the knot will hang up, expanding the entire munter hitch and introducing a lot of slack into the system;* **e**, *pull the knot through the munter's final bight to complete the knot pass.* (Photos by Jim Meyers)

NEARLY BLINDED ON MOUNT BRADLEY

BY ALAN ROUSSEAU

As usual, things were going really well . . . until they were not. Jackson Marvell and I were 10 days into our first big trip together and had established a new route on the east face of Mount Dickey (M7 AI6+; 5,000 feet) and repeated *Trailer Park* (WI6- M6; 3,000 feet) on the west face of London Tower. With a couple days left in the trip, we launched again. Our sights were set on an unclimbed system on Mount Bradley. The first 3,000 feet of the face climbed very quickly; we soon found ourselves in the steepest zone of our route and entered an overhanging, ice-choked dihedral.

Jackson climbed delicately above the belay through a very impressive lead, but near the end of his pitch, a fist-sized piece of ice fell and connected directly with my left eye and nose. I didn't see it coming and was completely blindsided—no pun intended. It hit me with such force that I collapsed onto the anchor, and I just remember blood everywhere. The next thing I realized was that I had zero vision in my left eye. My interocular pressure skyrocketed and I quickly became dizzy and nauseated, vomiting a few times. It was immediately clear that we were not climbing any higher, and with a single rack of gear, Jackson needed to get us down 3,000 feet of technical terrain.

Once Jackson rappelled down to me, he saw how serious the situation was and took over with calm confidence. We began rappelling; Jackson prerigged my rappels with an extension and a backup through the steeper portions of our descent. Once the terrain eased, he lowered me a few times onto ledges and down-climbed to where I was. As we reached the lower apron, even though the terrain eased, we still had a long way to go. Jackson opted to tie two ropes together and lower me 120 meters at a time, using a munter over-hand knot pull-through/munter pop–style knot pass since the terrain wasn't as steep and speed was essential. Jackson would then down-climb to me and repeat the process.

In just two hours we reached the Ruth Glacier. We contacted Talkeetna Air Taxi and told them while we did not require emergency medical service, we would need to be picked up in two hours from our camp. The skin back to camp was a blur of dizzy dry heaves for me. Jackson broke down our camp with impressive speed, and as we zipped the last duffel shut, the pilot pulled the wing of his plane over us and we were off.

One eye surgery and three years later, I have 20/70 vision in my left eye and 20/20 vision with both eyes open. My surgeon told me that if I had been out for two days longer, my left eye would have needed to be removed.

Since that trip, I've climbed in the Alaska Range seven more times and it remains my favorite place to climb. I'm grateful Jackson was on his A game that day. Remember, if you are going to enter big terrain, make sure you go with someone who knows how to get you out of it!

Alan Rousseau is an International Federation of Mountain Guides Associations–certified mountain guide based in Salt Lake City, Utah.

Moments before the accident, Jackson Marvell leads a steep pitch a little over 3,000 feet up a new route on Mount Bradley in the Alaska Range. (Photo by Alan Rousseau)

IN-LINE KNOT PASS

The fastest and smoothest way to pass any form of knot is the in-line knot pass, which uses an extended master point for a second lowering system and can be done with large loads. The downside of the in-line knot pass is that you have to *know* you'll be doing a knot pass, whereas with other knot passes, such as the improvised knot pass, you can execute them mid-lower regardless of which lowering technique you might be using.

The in-line knot pass is also sometimes called the "knuckle-breaker knot pass" or the "knuckle breaker," due to the tendency of the extension's carabiner to pinch or "bite" your fingers if you don't use certain techniques or don't take care. Luckily, avoiding the knuckle-breaker part of the transition is easy if you keep a few things in mind.

1. Build your second lowering system by putting an extension on the anchor pre-tied with a mule hitch in the rope, so that

Figure 6-2. In-line knot pass: **a**, *set up an extended master point with a sling and munter hitch, then tie a munter-mule-overhand on the anchor (not on the extended master point) just past (on the brake side of) the knot you intend to pass;* **b**, *start lowering with a third-hand friction-hitch backup (here, hidden by the climber's right hand);* **c**, *remove your friction-hitch backup (untied third hand hangs by the climber's left leg) just before the munter-mule-overhand of the initial lowering system becomes loaded, then finish lowering until the munter on the extended master point comes taut, with tension provided by the munter-mule-overhand on the anchor;* **d**, *move your friction-hitch backup to the brake-side strand of the munter-mule-overhand on the anchor;* **(continued on next page)**

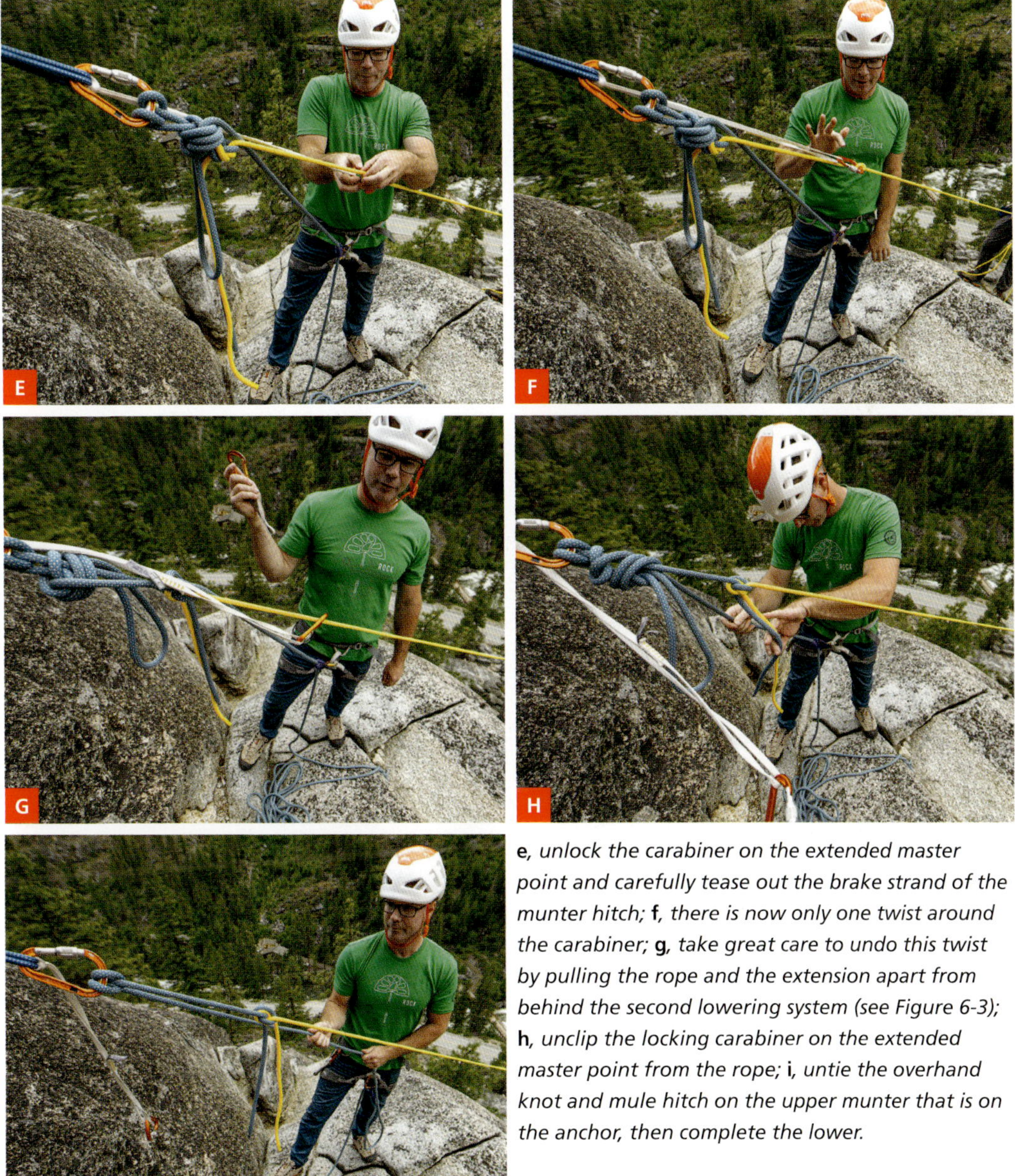

e, *unlock the carabiner on the extended master point and carefully tease out the brake strand of the munter hitch;* **f**, *there is now only one twist around the carabiner;* **g**, *take great care to undo this twist by pulling the rope and the extension apart from behind the second lowering system (see Figure 6-3);* **h**, *unclip the locking carabiner on the extended master point from the rope;* **i**, *untie the overhand knot and mule hitch on the upper munter that is on the anchor, then complete the lower.*

your initial lowering point is at least 24 inches above the second lowering system's master point; the lower on the extended master point must be performed with a munter hitch. Add a munter-mule-overhand to the initial lowering point and have the knot you need to pass as close as possible to the initial lowering system's munter-mule-overhand (or redirected belay device or whatever method you are using for lowering). Ideally, the knot that needs to be passed is within 4 inches of the initial tied-off lowering system, but basically the closer the better (fig. 6-2a).

2. Put a third-hand friction-hitch backup on the brake strand of the second lowering system's munter hitch and begin lowering (fig. 6-2b). When the rope *nearly* comes tight to your friction-hitch backup on the second lowering system, stop lowering and remove your friction-hitch backup.
3. Finish lowering, letting the rope come tight on the initial munter-mule-overhand, with the brake strand coming tight on the pretied-off second lowering system (fig. 6-2c).
4. Move your friction-hitch backup to the brake-side strand of the munter-mule-overhand on the anchor (fig. 6-2d).
5. Unlock the locking carabiner that is holding the second lowering system's munter hitch. Open the gate and carefully tease out the brake strand (fig. 6-2e); despite the load, this is very easy to do because of all the rope in play in the system. At this point, the rope will go around the second lowering system's locking carabiner one time, creating a single twist, and care must be taken to remove it (fig. 6-2f). Carelessness or improper technique during this stage will earn this knot its nickname the "knuckle breaker." To remove this twist, you can pull the rope and the extension apart from behind the second lowering system (see Figure 6-3, as well as the Tip below).
6. Once you have removed the twist, the locking carabiner will hang slack while still clipped on to the rope being lowered (fig. 6-2g); unclip this carabiner from the rope (fig. 6-2h).
7. Remove the overhand backup knot and mule hitch from the new lowering system, then continue lowering (fig. 6-2i).

Tip: The potential for the "knuckle-breaker" aspect of the in-line knot pass comes when you are taking the rope out of the lower locking carabiner on the extension that has been lowered tight to the initial lowering system. While it's easy to remove the rope by opening the carabiner's gate and pushing it out regardless of load, due to the volume of rope in the system, getting the twist off the extension's lowering carabiner is the tricky part. With light loads or body-weight loads with a lot of friction or that are being lowered down a low-angle slab, you can "grab" the carabiner rather than poking it or flicking it, which is most people's initial response and the most likely way to have your fingers "bit" by the carabiner untwisting. The easiest way to get the twist out of the carabiner is to simply pull the rope and the extension's sling apart with your hands above the knot pass (fig. 6-3a). If this doesn't work, one of the easier techniques for releasing this twist is to clip a quickdraw or sling to the brake strand and give a sharp pull perpendicular toward the loaded carabiner (fig. 6-3b).

TRIPLE IN-LINE KNOT PASSES TO ESCAPE EL CAPITAN

BY IAN NICHOLSON

On the third morning of a late-fall trip to Yosemite National Park to climb El Capitan with Graham Zimmerman and Jason Broman, we woke up to plummeting temperatures 12 pitches up the *North America Wall*. Even in the sunshine, we could barely stay warm while wearing all of our clothes, including the same jackets we use for midwinter ice climbing. The day before we'd launched, we had seen the chance of a snowstorm go from unlikely to a sure bet. We could see the clouds starting to build, and we made the tough decision to descend.

We were prepared with food and water for all three of us for six days on the wall, and our haul bags were still quite heavy. We packed up the portaledge, rigged the haul bags, and—wearing the majority of our clothing—began to descend. We lowered the bags directly off the anchor with a GriGri, while one of the three of us rappelled next to the bags, attempting to wrangle them in to the next anchor, all the while the frigid winds increased and the sky darkened.

We slowly made our way down, but it was time-consuming swinging our still very heavy bags side to side. When we were still five pitches off the ground, it started to snow, and we all knew the intensity of that snowfall was about to skyrocket. Sensing the urgency of the situation, we decided to tie all three of our ropes together and perform two knot passes in order to lower our bags nearly 600 feet straight to the ground.

Graham attached himself to the bags while I set up two in-line knot passes. As the load was so big—more than 350 pounds between our food, water, gear, and Graham—I used a GriGri as my third hand, but despite lowering such a heavy load, the system performed flawlessly and the entire process of lowering Graham and the bags took less than 10 minutes. Once that was complete, Jason and I made the remaining rappels quickly with no weight and no bags. It was a good thing, too, because just as we hit the ground, the snowfall reached its maximum intensity and we could barely see 50 feet in front of us.

The group listens to the weather report calling for the arrival of a full-on winter storm in a few hours. At this point, despite being in the sun and wearing all of our clothes, we are extremely cold. Graham Zimmerman and Jason Broman are literally "chilling" on the portaledge.

Figure 6-3. Two techniques to avoid the in-line knot pass's "knuckle-breaker" effects: **a**, *to remove the twist from the extended master point's locking carabiner during the in-line knot pass, bend the rope from the "uphill" side of the munter-mule-overhand on the anchor, which keeps your hands safe when the locking carabiner on the extended master point spins and travels up the rope—this technique creates a "bumper" so that the carabiner can't hit you;* **b**, *alternatively, use a sling or a quickdraw to pull the strand.*

IMPROVISED KNOT PASS

Though the improvised (often called "traditional") knot pass is not the easiest or the fastest knot pass to perform, it has the distinct advantage of working in essentially any situation. Unlike the in-line knot pass, the improvised knot pass does not need to be "prerigged," so if an unexpected figure-eight skeleton or a damaged section of rope comes up, you can perform this knot pass on the fly. And unlike the overhand knot pull-through (a.k.a. the "munter pop"), the improvised knot pass works with any type of knot that you might need to pass.

1. Start by lowering with whatever lowering system you desire, with a friction-hitch backup (fig. 6-4a).
2. Lower until the knot that needs to be passed creeps as close to the lowering system as is reasonable, given the stance and anchor position and knowing the closer you get it, the easier your job will be (fig. 6-4b).
3. When the knot that needs to be passed runs into the friction-hitch backup, use a long piece of material like a cordelette or a long runner to tie a klemheist around the load strand of the rope, and tie the other end of the cordelette to the anchor with a munter-mule-overhand (fig. 6-4c).
4. Build a new lowering system with a munter on the back side of the knot you want to pass and behind the initial lowering system (fig. 6-4d). Back up this munter with a mule hitch and an overhand backup knot (fig. 6-4e).
5. Transfer your friction-hitch backup to the new brake strand of the secondary lowering system (fig. 6-4f).
6. Release the cordelette's munter-mule-overhand on the anchor (fig. 6-4g) and lower the cordelette until it slackens

and the weight comes tight on the munter-mule-overhand in the rope behind the knot you wish to pass (fig. 6-4h).

7. Remove the cordelette's klemheist from the rope (fig. 6-4i).
8. To continue lowering, untie the overhand knot and mule hitch backing up the new munter on the anchor.

Tip: If you don't have a long piece of material like a cordelette, a great option is to use the back-side strand of the rescuer's clove hitch (their primary attachment to the anchor) plus some other type of small friction hitch. The friction hitch is used to "hold" the load while the knot is passed and the weight is transitioned from one lowering system to the other.

RAPPELLING PAST A KNOT

It is best to rappel past a knot while rappelling from an extension in a manner similar to an improvised knot pass. While this can be done without an extension, you just need to make sure that whatever friction hitch you use to briefly hold the weight is long enough to overcome any slack you create while transferring the initial rappel system to a secondary rappel system.

1. Start rappelling with an extension and a backup. It is important that you have an extension but can still reach the rope beyond (or above) your belay device. Rappel until the knot that needs to be passed comes tight to your friction-hitch backup (fig. 6-5a).
2. Put a knot (a clove hitch or a figure eight on a bight) in the rope and clip it to your harness belay loop with a few feet of slack in it (see Figure 6-5a). This is to protect you in the event you mess something up, so that you do not accidentally fall to your death.
3. Tie a friction hitch above (beyond) your belay device (fig. 6-5b) and attach it to your belay loop with a munter hitch (fig. 6-5c), then finish it with a mule hitch and overhand backup knot (fig. 6-5d).
4. Rappel slightly so that the friction hitch takes the weight (fig. 6-5e). Remove your belay device from the rope (fig. 6-5f).
5. Rebuild your original rappel system right off your belay loop—it is easiest if this is not on an extension. Rerig your belay device and friction-hitch backup below the knot you wish to pass (fig. 6-5g). It's a good idea to move your backup clove hitch or figure eight on a bight farther down the rope so you don't come tight on it while passing the knot..
6. Remove the first rappel system (fig. 6-5i).
7. Release the munter-mule-overhand that attaches the cordelette to your harness, and lower yourself down onto your "new" rappel device (fig. 6-5j). Now untie the cordelette's friction hitch on the rope, lowering the cordelette out until it slackens. Don't forget to remove the cordelette from the rope so that it does not get caught when you pull the rope at the end of the rappel.
8. Continue rappelling (fig. 6-5k).

DEALING WITH A STUCK ROPE

It happens to most climbers at some point or another: either during a rappel or on the ground at the end of the rappel, the rope won't come free. Here are some steps for retrieving a stuck rope:

1. First give the rope a few good flicks to see if you can free it before pulling hard.

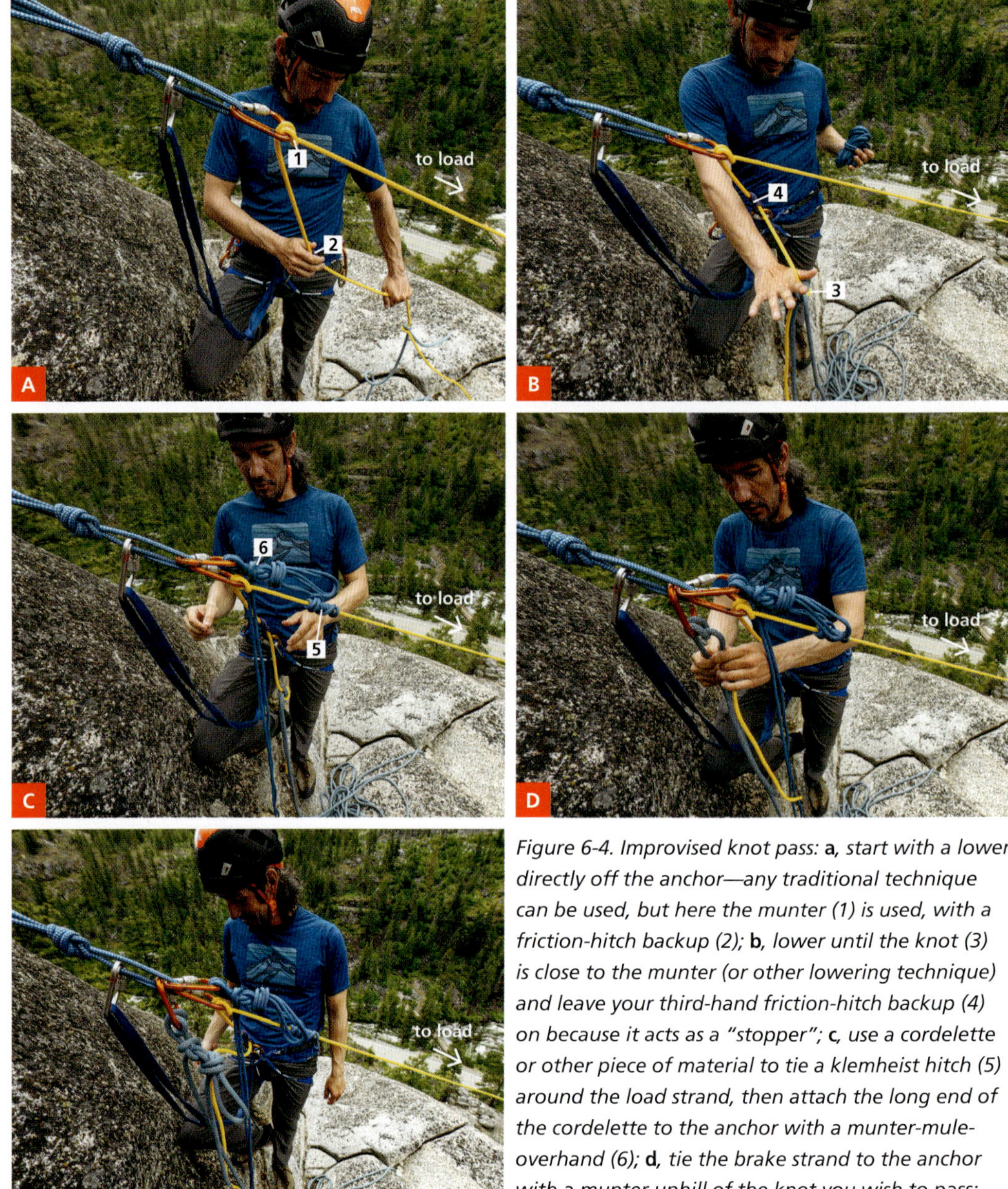

Figure 6-4. Improvised knot pass: **a**, *start with a lower directly off the anchor—any traditional technique can be used, but here the munter (1) is used, with a friction-hitch backup (2);* **b**, *lower until the knot (3) is close to the munter (or other lowering technique) and leave your third-hand friction-hitch backup (4) on because it acts as a "stopper";* **c**, *use a cordelette or other piece of material to tie a klemheist hitch (5) around the load strand, then attach the long end of the cordelette to the anchor with a munter-mule-overhand (6);* **d**, *tie the brake strand to the anchor with a munter uphill of the knot you wish to pass;* **e**, *mule this munter off and tie an overhand knot;* **(continued on next page)**

f, *move your friction-hitch backup to the brake side of the munter-mule-overhand you just tied (here, from the yellow rope to the light-blue rope) and undo the initial lowering system (here, the munter on the yellow rope);* **g**, *release the cordelette's munter-mule-overhand;* **h**, *lower the cordelette until it slackens and the munter-mule-overhand tied in the rope behind the knot you wish to pass tightens;* **i**, *remove the cordelette from the rope and continue lowering, you will need to untie the overhand knot and mule hitch backing up the new munter on the anchor.*

Figure 6-5. Rappelling past a knot: **a**, *rappel until the knot you wish to pass is very close to your friction-hitch backup, then tie a clove hitch or figure eight on a bight in the rope and clip it to your harness belay loop;* **b**, *tie a friction hitch above your belay device using a cordelette or long sling;* **c**, *use the cordelette (or long sling) to tie a munter on your belay loop;* **d**, *mule this munter off and tie an overhand backup;* **e**, *rappel until the cordelette takes the weight and your belay device slackens;* **f**, *remove your belay device from the rope;* **g**, *rerig your belay device and friction-hitch backup below the knot you wish to pass;* **h**, *untie the overhand knot and mule hitch from the cordelette on your harness;* **(continued on next page)**

i, *lower yourself until the cordelette slackens and your belay device takes the tension;* **j**, *remove the cordelette from your harness and untie it from the rope;* **k**, *finish the rappel.*

2. If you are on a large ledge or on the ground, walk away from the base of the cliff (fig. 6-6). This will reduce friction and change the direction of pull, increasing the odds of the rope being freed. Walking away from the cliff can sometimes help lift the rope over the obstructing or constricting feature, allowing the rope to run more freely.
3. Attempt the same tactic by walking to each side; this generally is less effective than walking away from the cliff, but it is worth a try before taking more drastic measures.
4. The final step is to pull *hard*. Use a friction hitch (like a VT prusik, which can be released under load) or an assisted-braking belay device (ABD) to pull the rope and hold it. Use both your and your partner's weight on the rope.

Tip: Never ascend a single strand of stuck rope after the rope has been pulled through the rappel anchor. If the rope fails to pull, it is rarely a good idea to ascend the rope, because you have *no* idea why it won't come down. Even if you and your partner have tried every trick in the book and have both pulled as hard as you can to attempt to retrieve a stuck rope, trusting your life to some unknown knot jam or constriction is just not worth it. Either use the rope you have to lead-climb back up to the stuck portion of the rope, or cut it and continue rappelling, building anchors as needed—or use the Reepschnur rappel (discussed in chapter 4), which allows you to make 30-meter rappels with less than 60 meters of rope.

LEADING WITH HALF THE ROPE

If one side of the rappel rope hangs up and you have only one strand, a common technique is for one climber to tie in to the end they have access to and for the other to put them on belay. The climber who ties in to the end then lead-climbs up, placing gear or clipping bolts as they go, as if they were leading normally. Depending on the situation, it may be easiest to relead to the previous anchor, being sure to make any adjustments necessary to prevent the rope from getting stuck again—or consider building a new rappel anchor. This strategy requires that the terrain you rappelled is climbable and protectable, but this is usually the case, since a large percentage of descent/rappel routes follow the ascent line or the easiest route on the formation. Obviously, if a given route's descent involves rappels down a steep, blank slab, this strategy will not be an option.

Never ascend a stuck single rope if you don't know how it's attached to the rock. (Photo by Silas Rossi)

Figure 6-6. If the rope won't pull easily, before really pulling hard, try walking the rope away from the cliff, which does multiple things: it reduces friction as less rope rubs on the rock, and it also changes the angle of pull on the rope. As you lift the rope from the rock's surface features, it lessens the chance of the rope getting caught. (Photo by Sheila Walsh)

THE LAST RESORT: CUTTING THE ROPE

If you have exhausted all other techniques, then the only remaining option is cutting the rope and building new rappel anchors or using a Reepschnur rappel (see chapter 4). If you are going to cut the rope, get as much rope as possible. Pull the stuck rope as tight as you can using a GriGri or autoblock device and even consider a 3:1 mechanical advantage (discussed in chapter 9), as every inch of rope you are able to maintain possession of will make the rest of your descent potentially easier, depending on the length of the rappels. Once the rope is *drum* tight, and only then, cut the rope as high as is safely possible.

Ian Nicholson and Tino Villanueva have just been forced to cut their rope—visible left of and parallel to the dark crack—with a long way to go to get down off El Capitan, Yosemite National Park, California. (Photo by Tom Evans)

Opposite: *Ian Nicholson jugs the wickedly steep* Tangerine Trip, *El Capitan, Yosemite National Park, California.* (Photo by Ryan O'Connell)

CHAPTER 7

Improvised Ascension and Aid-Climbing Techniques

This chapter focuses on improvised ascension techniques rather than full-on big-wall jugging methods for which you might have more specific equipment like ascenders, daisy chains, etriers, or stirrups. However, many of the tips and techniques in this chapter can help solve a number of common problems you might encounter in this type of environment. Similar to other rescue techniques, an improvised ascension of a rope isn't something that climbers will have to do with any sort of regularity, but for most climbers it will happen at some point for any number of reasons.

There are countless techniques for ascending a rope, but having a few in your back pocket is an unquestionably invaluable strategy. Situations such as ascending back to an anchor you mistakenly passed, assisting in retrieving a stuck rope, ascending a single fixed line as part of a greater rescue system, or escaping from a plunge into a hidden crevasse are things that nearly every climber will need to do at some point. Knowing how to use the gear you likely already have on your harness to ascend either a single strand of rope or two ropes in a more traditional rappelling setting has many applications. Fixed lines on big mountains in the Himalaya or on Alaska's Denali are best ascended with a combination of the techniques described in this chapter and a more dedicated tool like an ascender.

Tip: If you are planning to climb a big wall, a dedicated, nonimprovised setup is ideal. While the methods described in this chapter will work for climbing a big wall, they are vastly less efficient compared to ascending with dedicated tools like ascenders (jumars), aiders (etriers), adjustable foot stirrups, and/or adjustable daisies.

ROPE-ASCENSION METHODS

There are countless ascension methods, but fundamentally they all work the same. They all "grab" the rope in two places using either friction hitches or some sort of mechanical device(s). One of these friction hitches or mechanical devices attaches to your waist, and the other attaches to your foot (or a pair attaches to both feet). To ascend, you alternate between sitting in your harness and stepping up on first one foot, then the other. All rope-ascension systems work by alternately weighting one rope-grabbing system then allowing you to slide the other rope-grabbing system upward.

While these systems all function fairly similarly, some offer unique advantages and

A climber ascends Washburn's Thumb on a fixed line on Denali's upper West Buttress, Alaska.

disadvantages, such as efficiency in steep terrain or the ability to ascend two strands of rope. The keys to every ascension system are (1) making sure the rope-grabbing mechanisms slide easily while still grabbing the rope, and (2) balancing the amount of vertical gain with efficiency based on the ascension system and the angle of the terrain being ascended.

MECHANICAL PRUSIKS

Examples of mechanical prusiks include products like the Petzl Tibloc and WIld Country Ropeman. While they are a little more on the "luxury" side of equipment, for the weight of two locking carabiners they make the majority of ascension and raising systems more streamlined and faster to implement.

Figure 7-1. Backup knots for ascension systems: **a***, an overhand on a bight tied with one or two strands of rope is among the more commonly used backup knots while ascending a rope;* **b***, another commonly used "backup" hitch while ascending is the clove hitch, which can be used with two strands of rope although it is a little messy—and more care must be taken when adjusting it.*

Tip: Whether you are ascending a rope with a more traditional rope-ascension system or an improvised one, it is critical to *always* have some type of backup to the system. This can be an overhand on a bight (fig. 7-1a), a clove hitch through which slack is pushed or "milked" (fig. 7-1b), a succession of figure eights clipped collectively to (or swapped out on) a large locking carabiner on the climber's harness, or another "hard" knot that keeps you from falling the distance of the rope (or worse) should some portion of your ascension system fail.

COMMON IMPROVISED TECHNIQUES

Assisted-braking belay device (ABD) plus foot loop: Using an ABD on the harness and a double-length sling tied with a klemheist hitch as a foot loop is very fast for ascending a single strand of rope (fig. 7-2a) and can be used in steep terrain, but it's not an option for ascending two ropes.

Ratchet plus foot loop: Using a Petzl Micro Traxion on the harness (fig. 7-2b) and a double-length sling tied with a klemheist hitch as a foot loop is also very fast for ascending a single strand of rope and can be used in steep terrain, but again, it's not an option for ascending two ropes.

Autoblocking belay device plus foot loop: Using an autoblocking belay device on the harness, with it rigged in guide mode, and a double-length sling tied with a klemheist as a foot loop (fig. 7-2c) can be used on one or two strands of rope, but it is difficult to pull slack through this system in steep terrain.

Mechanical prusik plus soft goods: Using a mechanical prusik such as a Tibloc, which is much quicker to release than a friction hitch, with a combination of slings and/or a cordelette allows you to ascend either one or two ropes. While this method isn't as efficient for ascending a single strand, it is *vastly* faster and more efficient for ascending two strands than using an autoblocking belay device.

Figure 7-2. Improvised ascension methods: **a**, *an ABD (here, a GriGri) on the harness for a waist prusik and a double-length sling with a klemheist for a foot prusik;* **b**, *a Micro Traxion on the harness for a waist prusik (add a double-length sling with a klemheist for a foot prusik);* **c**, *an autoblocking belay device (rigged in guide mode) on the harness for a waist prusik and a double-length sling with a klemheist as a foot prusik;* **d**, *a sling on the harness for a waist prusik, tied with a friction hitch around the rope, and a sling with a garda hitch for a foot prusik.*

All soft goods with a garda hitch: Using two slings—one clipped to the harness and tied with a friction hitch around the rope and one with a garda hitch for a foot loop (fig. 7-2d)—takes very little gear, but it is low friction. It is okay in steep terrain but not an option for ascending two ropes.

ASCENDING ONE STRAND OF ROPE

Ascending a single strand of rope is the most straightforward ascension technique, offers the simplest solutions, and allows for the most options and tools to be used. For example, an

Tip: While the garda hitch on the harness seems like a great idea—it undoubtedly facilitates efficient movement—it has one big disadvantage to be aware of: it has the potential of unclipping itself when it is rapidly weighted and of tightening itself when followed by complete unloading and rapid tightening. During many guide-level exams, I have seen climbers reach to pull up on the garda on their waist only to unclip one carabiner, resulting in a complete failure of the hitch and an unexpected backward flip until their true backup knot catches.

assisted-braking belay device (ABD) such as a Petzl GriGri or Trango Vergo, a ratchet such as a Petzl Micro Traxion or an Edelrid Spoc, or a mechanical prusik such as a Petzl Tibloc or a Wild Country Ropeman are fantastically easy to use for ascending a single strand of rope. However, none of these present a good option (and sometimes no option at all) for ascending two ropes, depending on the tactics used.

USING ONLY SOFT GOODS

Make sure you start with a backup knot, and place a locking carabiner on your harness belay loop that will be your "backup" carabiner. A lot of people may want to tie on a clove hitch that they will slowly adjust as they ascend. Adjust your clove hitch so that you are never exposed to a fall of greater than 6 feet.

1. Tie a klemheist hitch with a double-length (48-inch) runner around the rope and clip it to your belay loop—this is your "waist prusik."
2. Build a garda hitch (see Figure 1-23) on the rope below the klemheist hitch. Girth-hitch a single-length (24-inch) runner to the garda hitch (fig. 7-3b), to help keep it from getting twisted or falling apart as you climb upward, and put your foot in the sling's loop—this is your "foot prusik" (fig. 7-3c).
3. Hang on the waist prusik and pull up on the brake strand, then stand in the foot prusik and push the klemheist hitch up the rope to make upward progress (fig. 7-3d). Continue alternating between weighting the waist prusik and standing up in the foot prusik.

USING AN ASSISTED-BRAKING BELAY DEVICE

If you have an assisted-braking belay device (ABD) such as a GriGri, clip the device to your

Figure 7-3. Ascending a single rope using only soft goods: **a**, *tie a sling with a friction hitch like a klemheist to the rope and clip it to your harness's belay loop for a waist prusik, then tie a garda hitch on the rope below the klemheist;* **b**, *girth-hitch a single-length runner (1) to both carabiners of the garda hitch;* **c**, *put one foot into this runner's loop—this is your "foot prusik";* **d**, *to ascend, weight your waist prusik and pull up on the brake strand, then stand up in the foot prusik and push the klemheist hitch up the rope.*

harness belay loop as a "waist prusik" and tie a klemheist hitch using a double-length (48-inch) runner above the ABD (fig. 7-4a). Stand in the bottom of the runner's loop for a "foot prusik" (fig. 7-4b). To ascend, hang on the waist prusik and push the klemheist hitch up the rope, then stand up in the foot prusik and take in slack with the ABD to make upward progress. Continue alternating between weighting the waist prusik and standing up in the foot prusik.

> **Tip:** While an autoblocking belay device like a Petzl Reverso or Black Diamond ATC Guide might appear to work similarly to an ABD like a GriGri, the autoblocking belay devices have far more friction—too much friction—for most people to use them in place of a waist prusik if there is any significant distance that must be ascended or if the terrain is steep.

USING AN ABD WITH 3:1 MECHANICAL ADVANTAGE ON STEEP TERRAIN

Another option to make ascending a rope easier, particularly on steeper terrain, is to create a 3:1 hauling system (see chapter 9) to "pull" yourself upward as you ascend. A 3:1 system is overkill and less efficient for

to klemheist hitch
A
B
1
C
D

IMPROVING AFTER LOSING AN AIDER ON THE NOSE

BY CHANTEL ASTORGA

"*Noooooooo,*" I thought as I watched my ascender and attached etrier (aider) unclip from my harness and fall into the abyss, bouncing off the lower-angle rock and narrowly missing the eight teams spread out on various pitches below me. I was attached to my anchor at the top of the 3,000-foot Great Roof pitch on the *Nose*, on Yosemite's El Capitan. It was hour nine of an attempt to rope-solo the route in under 24 hours. I had been using a self-belay system that allowed me to rope-solo the route. However, this technique also required me to lead, rappel, and jug every pitch, essentially going over each pitch three times. I had been making great progress despite the crowds, but now it was starting to get dark, and soon I'd be entering the steepest part of the wall—and now I had only one ascender.

Of course, it would still be possible to complete the climb safely with some creativity, but having only one ascender and one etrier would slow things down significantly. I had started the route with very little gear, trying to keep my systems simple and the load I carried as light as possible. I had prusiked ropes several times before, but it had always been a somewhat slow and tedious task; it also required more energy than I wanted to use, especially given the 1,000-plus feet of overhanging wall above me. I had not brought a Micro Traxion, which essentially works like a micro ascender, because I was climbing the route in a single day.

I had never been in this position before—by myself in the middle of a big wall with only a single ascender—so I had to consider my options. Similar to how I'd climbed the previous 20 pitches, I climbed the Pancake Flake pitch and rappelled on my GriGri back down to the previous anchor. However, this time I left the GriGri on my belay loop and kept it attached to the rope, then I connected my single ascender to the rope above, with an etrier hanging down that acted as a foot loop. I started making upward progress, sliding the ascender up, standing up in the foot loop, then pulling the slack through the GriGri, weighting it, and moving the ascender up again.

While this worked for a while, the steepness of the upper portion of the *Nose* made it feel very energy intensive. As I ascended I started thinking, "There has to be a better way." I climbed the next pitch and started to think about pulley systems, and then it occurred to me that I could "haul" myself upward, which would greatly increase my efficiency due to the steepness of the terrain.

After completing another pitch, I rappelled back to my previous anchor, leaving the GriGri on my belay loop with the rope attached just as before. I followed the same steps as the previous pitch, clipping my ascender above the GriGri, with my etrier attached as a foot loop. This time, however, I clipped an additional carabiner to my ascender and clipped the (brake-side) rope coming out of the GriGri up through that carabiner on my ascender. So now I could pull down as I stepped up and would essentially create a 3-to-1

Chantel Astorga tackles pitch 17 during a 2014 attempt to solo the Nose *on El Capitan in under 24 hours, just before dropping an ascender and etrier on the classic 31-pitch route in Yosemite National Park, California.* (Photo by Tom Evans)

Chantel in the Karakoram (Photo by Jean Thompson)

mechanical advantage to haul myself upward: voilà—fluidity. In vertical or less-than-vertical terrain, or if the distance I needed to cover hadn't been so great, simply replacing my ascender with my GriGri would have been enough—but with a thousand feet of overhanging rock still above me, using the 3:1 hauling system was the ticket for efficiency. Despite the major hiccup of losing an ascender and etrier, I was able to reach the top, thanks to my knowledge of a few different techniques and some time spent working through them . . . even if it took a bit longer than I had hoped!

Chantel Astorga is an avalanche forecaster for the Idaho Transportation Department; she has also worked as a mountain guide and for Yosemite Search and Rescue. She has ascended some of the most difficult routes on the planet in lightning-fast times.

Figure 7-4. Ascending a single rope using an assisted-braking belay device (ABD): **a**, *with the ABD rigged on your belay loop as your "waist prusik," backed up with a knot on the brake-side strand (also clipped to the belay loop, hidden here by climber's jacket), tie a long sling to the rope above the ABD with a klemheist hitch;* **b**, *step into this sling—your "foot prusik"—and start ascending, alternately weighting the ABD and the sling.*

lower-angled terrain, where slack might be problematic to pull through whatever ratchet you are using, but it is the perfect solution for ascending steeper or otherwise physically demanding terrain.

In setting up this system, it is extremely helpful to have an assisted-braking belay device (ABD) such as a Petzl GriGri or a mechanical ratchet like a Micro Traxion, due to the reduction in friction when hauling yourself upward.

Conversely, an autoblocking belay device like a Petzl Reverso or Black Diamond ATC Guide is significantly less efficient when it comes to pulling rope through (a.k.a. hauling) because of the increased friction in the device itself. Here's how to set up a 3:1 mechanical advantage for ascending the rope using an ABD:

1. Rig your ABD on the rope, and clip the device to your harness belay loop with a locking carabiner (fig. 7-5a).
2. Pull up a length of rope on the brake strand and clove-hitch it to a locking carabiner on your belay loop (fig. 7-5b). This is your backup and should be adjusted as you climb.
3. Tie a friction hitch on—or attach a mechanical ascender to—the load strand above the ABD. Clip a long sling to this friction

Figure 7-5. Using an assisted-braking belay device (ABD) with a 3:1 mechanical advantage: **a**, *rig your ABD on the rope and clip the device to your harness belay loop;* **b**, *pull up a length of rope on the brake strand and clove-hitch it to a locking carabiner on your belay loop as a backup;* **c**, *tie a friction hitch on the load strand above the ABD, clip a long sling to this hitch for a foot prusik, and clip the brake strand up through a second carabiner clipped to the friction hitch's carabiner;* **d**, *as you stand up in the foot prusik, pull down on the brake strand coming down from the friction hitch to create a 3:1 mechanical advantage.*

hitch or mechanical ascender to act as a "foot prusik." Clip the brake strand back up through a second carabiner on the friction hitch's or mechanical ascender's carabiner so that you are able to pull down on the brake strand (fig. 7-5c). This second carabiner (not the one the foot prusik is attached to) reduces friction because the rope runs over the carabiner's aluminum versus whatever the foot prusik's sling is made of, which also limits wear on that material.

The keys to making this technique so efficient are rhythm and timing. When you stand up in the foot prusik, pull down on the brake strand that comes down from the friction hitch or mechanical ascender, giving yourself a 3:1 mechanical advantage (fig. 7-5d).

ASCENDING TWO STRANDS OF ROPE

Ascending two strands of a rope is a more common scenario than ascending a single strand. This often happens after a team has rappelled and attempted to retrieve the rope but, for any number of reasons, the rope just won't budge (see chapter 6).

USING ONLY SOFT GOODS

If you have to ascend a significant distance (which will likely be the case), use two pieces of soft goods (slings, cordelette, etc.) to set up the waist and foot prusiks. As always, put a backup knot on the rope—a figure eight on a bight, a clove hitch, or something similar—and clip it to a locking carabiner on your harness belay loop.

1. Use a shorter piece of material, such as your third-hand rappel backup or a shoulder-length (24-inch) sling, to tie a prusik hitch around both strands of the rope that must be ascended. Clip this prusik to your belay loop as your "waist prusik" (fig. 7-6a).
2. Use a slightly longer piece of material, such as a double-length (48-inch) sling or two shoulder-length slings girth-hitched or clipped together, to tie a second friction hitch on both strands below the waist prusik. This is your "foot prusik." (In Figure 7-6, the lower sling that makes up the foot prusik is doubled up and tied with an overhand knot to create a hole for the climber's foot).
3. Alternate weighting the waist prusik while sliding up the rope on the unweighted foot prusik (fig. 7-6b), then standing in the foot prusik while sliding on the waist prusik up the rope.
4. Adjust or retie your backup knot(s) to minimize fall potential to no more than 6 feet.

USING AN AUTOBLOCKING BELAY DEVICE

To incorporate an autoblocking belay device (such as a Petzl Reverso) in guide mode, start by, as always, putting a figure eight on a bight (or similar) backup knot on the rope and clipping it to a locking carabiner on your belay loop. Then follow these steps:

1. Clip an autoblocking belay device to your belay loop and run both strands of rope through it—this is your "waist prusik."
2. Use a double-length (48-inch) sling or two shoulder-length slings girth-hitched together to tie a friction hitch on both strands of rope for your "foot prusik." (In Figure 7-7, this is a long cordelette.)
3. Alternate weighting the waist prusik while sliding the unweighted foot prusik up the rope, then standing in the foot prusik while sliding the rope up through the autoblocking belay device (fig. 7-7).

Figure 7-6. Using only soft goods to ascend two strands of rope: **a**, *for your "waist prusik," friction-hitch one end of a single-length sling (1) to both strands of rope and clip the other end to your harness belay loop; and for your "foot prusik," friction-hitch one end of a longer sling (here, a neon-green sling is hard to see behind the rope, clipped to a blue sling) to both strands below the first friction hitch and clip to a single-length runner (here, dark blue);* **b**, *weight the waist prusik and slide the unweighted foot prusik up the rope (then weight the foot prusik to slide the waist prusik up the rope).*

4. Adjust or retie your backup knot(s) to minimize fall potential to no more than 6 feet.

TRANSITIONING FROM RAPPELLING TO ASCENDING

In the event that you rappel past the next rappel anchor without realizing it, you will have to ascend back up to that anchor. If the terrain being rappelled is low-angle enough and/or the distance to that anchor is relatively short, you can tie a backup "blocking knot" and just pull the rope back up through your device by pushing your feet against the rock. However, in vertical terrain or if a longer distance needs to be covered, it will likely be worth it to transition from rappelling to some sort of improvised ascension system in order to regain the passed anchor.

ON A SINGLE ROPE

To transition from a rappel to some form of improvised ascension on a single rope, you can use an assisted-braking belay device (ABD) like a GriGri or a Micro Traxion (if you find yourself traveling on glaciers) on your

Figure 7-7. Using an autoblocking belay device to ascend two strands of rope: the belay device clipped to the harness belay loop is the waist prusik; a double-length sling (cordelette here)friction-hitched to both strands of rope is the foot prusik

harness for a waist prusik and a garda hitch for your foot prusik.

1. When you stop the rappel, ensure that your third-hand friction hitch catches below your belay device (fig. 7-8a), then tie a figure eight on a bight, a clove hitch, or a similar backup knot and clip it to your belay loop with a locking carabiner (fig. 7-8b). Ensure that this backup knot is not "tight" and you have a few feet of rope to work with.
2. Next, use a single (24-inch) sling, or a double (48-inch) sling with a knot tied in the middle, to tie a friction hitch around the strand of rope about 3–5 inches above the belay device (fig. 7-8c). Measure out the distance to your belay loop and tie an overhand knot in the sling (fig. 7-8d) so that it is clipped snugly to your belay loop (fig. 7-8e). A nonlocking carabiner is fine, as this will hold only your body weight but your life will never depend on it.
3. Rappel until the friction hitch takes the weight and the belay device becomes slack (fig. 7-8f).
4. Push a little slack into the belay device (fig. 7-8g), then clip the "eye" (top hole) of the device into your belay loop and remove the main locker attached to the device from your belay loop or rappel extension, leaving the rope attached to this locker (fig. 7-8h); this puts the belay device in guide mode. Rock upward on the belay device while pulling up on the brake strand, so that the device takes your weight (fig. 7-8i).
5. Unclip the sling from your belay loop (fig. 7-8j).
6. Put your foot in the unclipped end of the sling as your "foot prusik" (fig. 7-8k). A garda hitch also works well here.
7. Alternate weighting the belay device attached to your harness (your "waist prusik") while sliding the unweighted "foot prusik" up the rope, then standing in the foot prusik while taking in slack through the belay device.
8. Adjust or retie your backup knot(s) to minimize fall potential to no more than 6 feet.

Figure 7-8. Transitioning from rappelling to ascending on a single strand of rope: **a**, *stop the rappel if you've passed the next rappel anchor;* **b**, *tie a backup knot and clip it to your belay loop with a locking carabiner;* **c**, *friction-hitch a sling above the belay device;* **d**, *tie a knot in the other end of the sling so it's short enough that when you rappel onto the sling you can still reach the friction hitch;* **e**, *clip this end of the sling to your belay loop;* **(continued on next page)**

f, *rappel until the belay device becomes slack and the sling takes the weight;* **g**, *push a little slack into the belay device;* **h**, *clip the "eye" (top hole) of the belay device in to your belay loop and remove the main locker attached to the device from your belay loop or rappel extension, leaving the rope attached to this locker;* **i**, *rock upward on the belay device (now in guide mode) while pulling up on the brake strand and transferring your weight from the sling to the device;* **j**, *unclip the sling from your belay loop;* **k**, *place the unclipped end of the sling on your foot and start ascending.*

A BASIC ASCENDING SYSTEM SAVES A TRIP TO THE KICHATNAS

BY IAN NICHOLSON

Graham Zimmerman, Ryan O'Connell, and I attempted the northwest face of Kichatna Spire, a roughly 3,000-foot route in Alaska that starts with around 2,000 feet of ice and mixed climbing and is capped by a headwall of steep rock and ridge climbing. We started the route ascending 12 long pitches to the point where the route transitioned from ice to difficult aid up a fairly blank wall. With the weather moving and the difficulty of the climbing increasing (plus being a little scared), we decided to bail. We rappelled all the way to the base of the route using a mix of V-threads, nuts, and pins and pulled the ropes from the final rappel after around 24 hours on the move.

Exhausted but relieved, we started preparing to travel down the glacier back to camp. I wanted to remove my beanie from beneath my helmet, so I took off my helmet and (mistake!) set it down next to me . . . only to watch it slide roughly 50 feet downhill and fly over the lip of a huge crevasse. Ryan, Graham, and I stared wide-eyed for a moment, no one speaking. This was only the fourth day of a two-week trip, and we were trying to climb massive new routes in a remote corner of the Alaska Range: helmets were a must. Losing my helmet would either be a deal-breaker or at least make it a lot scarier to continue.

I built an anchor and had Ryan and Graham belay me to the lip of the crevasse. By some miracle, there my helmet was, sitting on a ledge 70–80 feet down in an otherwise bottomless crevasse. All of us were so tired, but with snow falling and a storm in the forecast, we knew we had to get the helmet then.

I set an anchor, made the 70-plus-foot complete free-hanging rappel into the crevasse—taking care not to knock my helmet deeper into the crevasse—and snagged the helmet. I then ascended back out using a GriGri on my waist and a small prusik attached to a double-length sling. It was a little physical, but the whole transition from rappelling to ascending was far quicker than expected, and it let us continue the trip after the months of planning, preparation, and training we had put in.

Our intended route on the imposing Kichatna Spire in the Alaska Range ascended the deep V notch just right of center; the final headwall is visible on the upper face.

Ryan O'Connell climbs the 5.10 sections but skips the thin 5.11 slab with a few moves of aid by pulling on quickdraws and standing on bolt hangers on the Direct East Buttress *of South Early Winters Spire, North Cascades, Washington.* (Photo by Andew Burr)

ON A DOUBLE ROPE

The steps required to transition from a rappel to some form of improvised ascension on two strands of rope are nearly identical to those on a single rope, except for the differences in the belay devices (steps 4 and 5 here; steps 4, 5, and 6 above).

1. Make sure that your third-hand friction hitch catches below your belay device, then tie a figure eight on a bight (or similar) backup knot and clip it to your harness belay loop with a locking carabiner (fig. 7-9a). Ensure that this backup knot is not "tight" and you have a few feet of rope to work with.
2. Use a single (24-inch) sling, or a double (48-inch) sling with a knot in it, to tie a friction hitch around both strands of rope about 3–5 inches above the device (fig. 7-9b). Measure out the distance to your belay loop and tie an overhand knot in the sling so that it clips snugly to your belay loop (fig. 7-9c). A nonlocking carabiner is fine, as it will hold only your body weight but never your life.
3. Rappel until the friction hitch takes the weight and the belay device becomes slack (fig. 7-9d).
4. Remove the belay device from the rope and your belay loop or rappel extension (fig. 7-9e).
5. Remove the third-hand friction-hitch backup that was below your rappel device, then take a longer piece of material—like a double-length (48-inch) sling or two shoulder-length slings girth-hitched together—and friction-hitch it below the sling that is clipped to your harness (fig. 7-9f). This will be your "foot prusik."
6. Alternate weighting the "waist prusik" attached to your harness while sliding the unweighted foot prusik up the rope (fig. 7-9g), then standing in the foot prusik and sliding the waist prusik up the rope.
7. Adjust or retie your backup knot(s) to minimize fall potential to no more than 6 feet.

Tip: If you know you might need to transition from a rappel to an improvised ascent, make sure your rappel extension is on the shorter side. This will keep it within reach when you tie the friction hitch that will help you unweight the belay device.

TIPS FOR BASIC AID-CLIMBING TECHNIQUES

We all like free climbing, and certainly it's nice to climb a challenging pitch without taking or weighting the rope. However, there comes a time, particularly on longer routes where you just have to get up the route, when being able to efficiently aid something with just the gear on your harness can save hours. Most climbers recognize that they can pull on a piece of gear to make upward progress, but some basic knowledge of aid climbing can help you reach so much farther and travel faster in terrain that is just a little too difficult to free-climb.

STAND IN SLINGS

Simply pulling on gear can assist you, but to extend your reach much farther, put your foot in a single-length (24-inch) sling and step up (fig. 7-10).

USE A FIFI

While most climbers would never carry a fifi hook on a free-climbing route, it is easy to improvise one with a quickdraw or just a couple of nonlocking carabiners: clip the quickdraw (or carabiners) between to your

Figure 7-9. Transitioning from rappelling to ascending on two strands of rope: **a**, *if you've passed the next rappel anchor, stop the rappel, tie a backup knot with a little bit of slack, and clip it to your harness belay loop;* **b**, *use a double-length sling or a cordelette to tie a friction hitch on the load strand above the belay device;* **c**, *clip the sling to your belay loop, tying an overhand knot to adjust the length so you are able to reach the friction hitch once you weight the sling;* **d**, *rappel until the belay device comes slack and the friction hitch takes your weight;* **(continued on next page)**

E

F

G

e, *remove the belay device;* **f**, *retie the third-hand friction-hitch backup that was below your belay device, using another sling to tie another friction hitch below the one connected to your belay loop;* **g**, *make the lower friction-hitched sling an appropriate length for a foot prusik.*

Figure 7-10. Stand in a sling to extend your reach, as well as pull on gear to assist you.

belay loop and a piece of protection (fig. 7-11). The goal is to pull upward against the "fifi" in opposition to whatever it is clipped to. This provides increased balance and reach, as well as the ability to step closer to the piece.

Figure 7-11. Clipping a quickdraw to connect protection to your belay loop provides an improvised fifi hook to pull upward against the piece it's clipped to.

Opposite: *Ian Nicholson climbs out the overlapping roofs on the final pitch of* Heaven's Gate, *Index Town Walls, Cascade Mountains, Washington.* (Photo by Jim Meyers)

CHAPTER 8

Leader Rescue

Depending on the terrain and the geometry of the pitch, leader rescue is usually either one of the easiest or the most complex forms of rescue. This is because everything hinges on the location and the leader's distance from the lower anchor.

If this distance is less than 50 percent of the rope, if the leader is conscious, and if the pitch is fairly straight up and down, the leader can simply be lowered (discussed in chapter 5) in a sequence typically as challenging as lowering someone at the rock gym. The techniques would be either the same or very nearly the same as for an uninjured person.

However, if the leader's distance from the lower anchor is greater than 50 percent of the rope that is out; if the leader is far off to one side of the previous anchor, having traversed off the fall line enough that it will be difficult for them to return to the belay; or if the leader is injured badly, was knocked unconscious and/or is unresponsive; all of the rescue options are complex and involve many steps.

LOWERING IF LESS THAN 50 PERCENT OF THE ROPE IS OUT

When there is less than 50 percent of the rope out and the leader is conscious, the belayer generally doesn't have to use any special techniques in order to lower the fallen climber. The belayer can lower them in a manner similar to how they would on any pitch that is less than half a rope length (see chapter 5). However, there are some things that the group needs to consider as they begin their journey downward.

AVOID LOWERING OFF A SINGLE PIECE OF PROTECTION

If someone takes a bad leader fall and becomes injured, avoid the temptation to lower off a single piece of protection, even if it's a bolt. It may seem tempting to lower off that single piece of gear, but don't do it. Sure, the highest piece of gear held the fall, but you have no way of knowing if it's been compromised or if changing the angle of tension during a lower will compromise it further. Leaving any sort of gear, be it cams, nuts, quickdraws, or other equipment, always seems like a big deal in the moment, but it is *never* worth it to cut corners when it comes to safety margins. Everyone's adrenaline is likely to be elevated, and no one likes to leave behind gear when they don't "need" to, but this is not the time; avoid bailing off a single piece of protection.

Obviously, in an ideal situation, an injured leader could build a small anchor or plug in a

LEADER RESCUE ON CUTTHROAT PEAK

BY IAN NICHOLSON

I was climbing as one of a group of three, with the leader roughly 70–80 feet out on the crux pitch of Cutthroat Peak's West Ridge, near Washington Pass in Washington's North Cascades. The crux pitch was well within the leader's abilities, but the rock was still a little slick from rain the previous day, and the weather remained unsettled, with swirling clouds and fog hanging over us all day. The crux pitch itself traverses 15–20 feet before going directly up some straight-in crack climbing.

The leader had reached easier terrain and was just about to plug in his fourth piece of the pitch, having placed three lower down but spread out on 5.6 terrain, which was easy for this strong leader. Just before the leader reached to place a cam, the worst happened: his foot slipped. The leader fell 20 feet, striking a 4-foot-wide ledge, which destroyed his helmet, before he tumbled off the ledge and fell another 20 feet until the rope came tight. The leader was knocked unconscious, moaning, hanging sideways on a steep slab around 30 feet to the right of the belay in vertical and possibly unclimbable terrain.

The third climber, Chris Ebeling, and I quickly tied off the belay device and transferred the load to the anchor using a munter-mule-overhand. I attached two friction hitches to the taut rope and climbed the rope for around 40 feet to the leader's final piece of protection. I reinforced this piece by putting in two more pieces of protection (a total of three), creating a "chain" or alpine anchor.

At this point, the fallen leader started to regain consciousness, and we began communicating about what had happened and what the plan was. Another group had climbed up and was roughly 50–60 feet directly below us on a large ledge. If this party hadn't come up to assist us, I would have started lowering or counterbalance rappelling, but with this second party on the scene, I was able to lower the fallen leader from the new anchor down to the ledge belay where the other party was.

We did a number of tandem rappels, but as the leader began to feel better, we let him rappel on his own. We moved slowly out to the car. After some initial resistance, the leader went to the hospital and we later learned that he was suffering from a hemopneumothorax—his lung was collapsing and filling with fluid—and he would likely have died had he not been seen that night. This experience illustrates how leader rescue has the potential to be either the easiest or one of the more complex forms of rescue, rarely falling in between.

The accident occurred on Cutthroat Peak, near Washington Pass, North Cascades, Washington.

Ian Nicholson leads on spaced bolts and tied-off knobs for protection at the Phantom Spires, South Lake Tahoe, California. (Photo by Rebecca Schroeder)

few pieces of protection in order to be lowered off, but in reality, if there is any question, just leave your last few pieces of gear and start lowering. Even though these pieces of protection are not "equalized," they are still backing each other up and significantly increasing the group's margin of safety, compared with lowering off a single protection point.

BE AWARE OF HORIZONTAL TRAVEL ON SEEMINGLY STRAIGHT-UP PITCHES

It is rare that a pitch is dead-vertical and straight up and down above the belay anchor; the majority of pitches wander horizontally to some extent. Some pitches obviously traverse, but others are trickier to assess. It is fair to say that most multipitch routes are not perfectly straight up and down.

If a leader falls on terrain that has some horizontal travel, it might be vertical enough for the leader to be lowered if they are relatively uninjured, but make an honest assessment of how much of a traverse is advisable relative to how hurt they are, knowing that the steeper the route, the more difficult it is to keep them from swinging back and forth during a lower.

To help keep the leader trending back toward the lower belay, have them clip a single-length (24-inch) sling from their belay loop to the strand of rope that travels down to the belayer. This way, even as the leader cleans protection, they will be "pulled" back in line toward the belay.

RESCUING IF MORE THAN 50 PERCENT OF THE ROPE IS OUT

Lowering an injured leader might not be an option because of a multitude of factors. The leader could be unconscious, they could have severely injured a lower limb, the route could traverse significantly enough that it is not possible to return to the anchor, or they could have led out a distance greater than 50 percent of the rope. You should have plan for when the leader is too far out of reach, whether that be due to the length or the traversing nature of the pitch.

The majority of the time, the belayer will need to tie off their belay device and ascend the rope to the injured person, then rappel. Under rare circumstances, when the leader is conscious and the terrain is fairly easy (can be climbed either entirely free or by pulling on gear), the belayer can tie off their device and climb, which will cause the leader to descend.

It can be daunting to contemplate: a yell, the rope comes tight as you catch the fall; the leader has well over 50 percent of the rope out, so you shout up to your partner, but . . . silence. Scott Bennett on the first ascent of the southwest ridge of K6 West in 2015. (Photo by Graham Zimmerman)

At the point where the two climbers meet, an anchor and a rappel station can be constructed for them to clip in to and rappel from. While this sounds like a much simpler option, in reality it is a lot less likely scenario than a counterbalanced ascension.

Using soft goods like slings to tie friction hitches for your waist and feet so you can ascend the rope in an improvised fashion is the most straightforward technique (see chapter 7). The belayer can start ascending directly after they have tied off their belay device and put a backup knot on, or they can transfer the load, get established with their ascension system (getting started is the hardest part), and then release the rope from the lower anchor or leave it attached as needed.

COUNTERBALANCED ROPE ASCENSION AND TANDEM RAPPEL WITH AN ABD

A leader rescue using counterbalanced rope ascension and tandem rappel gives the rescuer plenty of options and, assuming the gear the leader has placed is adequate, it is fairly safe for both the leader and the rescuer. If the leader has more than 50 percent of the rope out or is incapacitated, when even lowering for a short distance may do them further harm, and if you are belaying with an assisted-braking belay device (ABD), using a 3:1 mechanical advantage (see chapter 9)

Jonathon Spitzer is on a long pitch on Fish and Whistle, *on the north face of Vesper Peak in Washington's North Cascades.*

is likely the "easiest" of the leader rescues. An ABD is easier because you do not need to "escape the device" and you can use the device itself as a ratchet to ascend, which is far easier in counterbalance than using a traditional plate or tube-style belay device, which limits your ascension options (see the next section). Here are the steps:

1. Catch the fall and attempt to communicate with the leader. Tie a knot below the assisted-braking belay device so that there is no chance it could release as you ascend (fig. 8-1a).
2. Friction-hitch a sling onto the load strand coming from the belay device (fig. 8-1b). This will eventually be your foot prusik and also act as a redirect to allow you to ascend with a 3:1 mechanical advantage.
3. Clip the brake strand up through a separate carabiner on the friction hitch, and attach yourself to the rope if you haven't already (fig. 8-1c).
4. Start ascending in counterbalance and climb past the leader. Build a midstation anchor by equalizing midroute bolts or building a traditional anchor to be left behind (fig. 8-1d). It is okay to build an anchor incorporating the piece the leader fell onto, but inspect it if it is traditional protection. Never rappel off one piece of protection. Equalize pieces to create an EARNEST rappel anchor (see chapter 2).
5. Rappel back down to the leader so you are even with their position (fig. 8-1e).
6. Attach the free end of rope to the leader, then clip the long end coming off their harness up through the newly created master point. Next, build a munter-mule on your harness (fig. 8-1f and 8-1g) so that you are "counter balanced" with the leader through the new master point.

7. Pull the rope from the piece of protection the leader fell on and thread it through the new rappel that you just constructed (fig. 8-1h).
8. Build a rappel extension and rig it for rappel, then attach the leader to the same rappel extension or a new sling so you are both hanging off the same belay device (fig. 8-1i).
9. Release the munter-mule on the rope so both climbers' weight comes onto the rappel extension (fig. 8-1j).
10. Make tandem rappels (fig. 8-1k), keeping the injured leader slightly below the rescuer (fig. 8-1l), for as long as necessary.

COUNTERBALANCED ROPE ASCENSION AND COUNTERBALANCED RAPPEL WITH A TRADITIONAL BELAY DEVICE

If the leader has more than 50 percent of the rope out or is incapacitated, when even lowering for a short distance may do them further harm, and if you are belaying with a more traditional belay device, you must first escape the belay before ascending. The downside of this is mostly that it is physically harder, particularly getting off the ground and continuing to hold tension with the belay device clipped to your belay loop and pulling in opposition to the leader. Once you get established in ascending the rope, it generally isn't very hard, but getting started can take a little work. If you have an anchor nearby, you can temporarily escape the belay and transfer the load to the anchor before establishing the ascension system, then remove the anchor (if one was built) and take it with you. Here are the steps:

1. After catching the fall, attempt to communicate with the leader (fig. 8-2a).
2. Tie off your belay device with a mule hitch and overhand backup knot. Tie a backup knot in the rope underneath the belay device and clip it to your harness belay loop. This backup knot is imperative, both because you will soon be leaving the ground (or unclipping from the anchor, if you are on a multipitch route) and because severe consequences would likely result if your tied-off belay device were to come undone. Ensure that the rope remaining at the belay is stacked neatly so that it will pay out without becoming tangled, or coil it and take it with you.
3. Rig your "waist prusik" and "foot prusik" (see chapter 7) on the load strand above your tied-off belay device (fig. 8-2c). Getting off the ground is often the hardest part, as you need to maintain tension so that you don't unintentionally lower the injured climber. On a multipitch route, you can transfer the load to the anchor, get established with your ascension system (which requires the use of soft materials, not a belay device, as the rope will be taut), and then remove the anchor. If you have multiple pieces of material to use as third hands, rerig your belay device and a "long" third hand below it using cordelette for your foot prusik. If the terrain is steep, consider rigging your waist prusik on a load-releasable system (a munter-mule-overhand instead of a hard knot) where it connects to your harness, to make it easier to transition to rappelling later.
4. Start to ascend (fig. 8-2d). When there is enough slack, remove the belay device from the rope. As you go up, mind your clove-hitch backup knot, readjusting it every 3 feet or so (or tie a new backup knot every 6 feet or so), because if one friction hitch releases the other, both you and the leader will fall.

Figure 8-1. Counterbalanced ascension with an assisted-braking belay device (ABD) and tandem rappel: **a**, *tie a knot below the ABD so there's no chance it could release as you ascend;* **b**, *friction-hitch (1) a sling on the load strand coming (2) from the belay device;* **c**, *clip the brake strand (3) up through a carabiner on the friction hitch (4), and attach yourself to the rope if you haven't already;* **d**, *start ascending in counterbalance and climb past the leader, then build a midstation rappel anchor (5) to be left behind (here, the rescuer is equalizing midroute bolts with a red cordelette);* **e**, *if you haven't already done so in the process of creating the anchor, rappel back down to the leader so you are even with their position;* **(continued on next page)**

f *and* **g**, *attach the free end of rope to the leader (6) and create a counterbalanced clip-in with a munter-mule on your harness belay loop (7);* **h**, *pull the rope from the piece of protection the leader fell on and thread it through the rappel anchor that you just constructed;* **i**, *build a rappel extension (8) and rig it for rappel, then attach the leader to the same extension so that you are both hanging off the same belay device;* **j**, *release the munter-mule on the rope so that your combined weight comes onto the rappel extension;* **k**, *make tandem rappels as necessary;* **l**, *keep the injured climber slightly below the rescuer.*

Figure 8-2. Counterbalanced ascension and rappel with a traditional belay device: **a**, *try to clearly communicate with the fallen leader and describe the rescue plan;* **b**, *escape the belay and tie off your device with a mule hitch; then rig for a soft-goods-only improvised ascension;* **c**, *start to ascend—***d**, *as slack is created by ascending, remove the belay device and mind the clove-hitch backup knot, readjusting it every 3 feet or so; reach the fallen leader;* **e**, *ascend until you are even with the fallen leader;* **(continued on next page)**

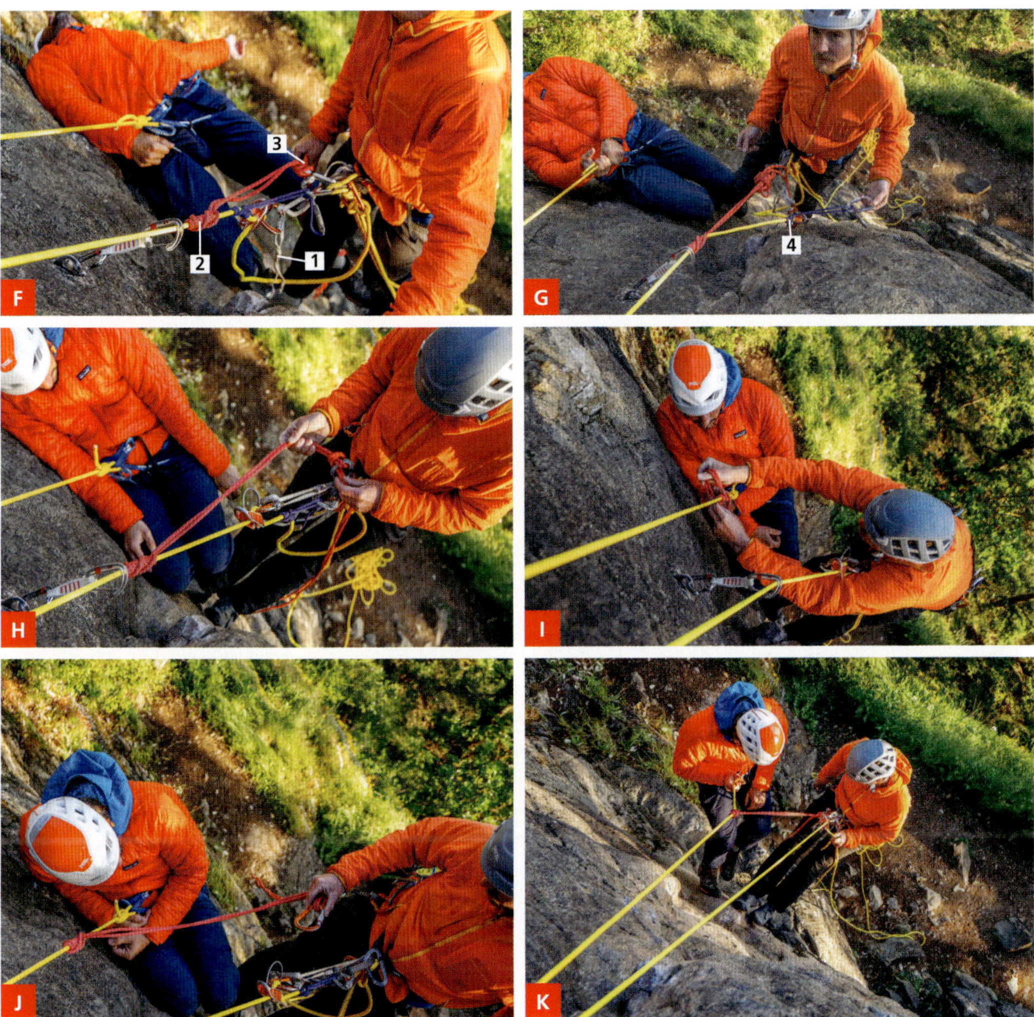

f, *put your rappel extension (1) on, along with your belay device, then tie your foot prusik (2) with a munter-mule-overhand (3) onto your belay loop, getting it as tight as you can (add another third-hand friction hitch below the belay device if necessary/possible);* **g**, *rock up on the foot prusik, getting it as tight as possible, to release your waist prusik, then remove the waist prusik (4) from your harness—place it underneath the belay device and lower yourself on the foot prusik's munter-mule until the belay device and friction hitch take tension;* **h**, *remove the foot prusik's friction hitch from the strand you are hanging on;* **i**, *put this friction hitch on the strand the injured leader is hanging on;* **j**, *clip the long end of this sling to your harness to set up a counterbalanced rappel;* **k**, *rappel counterbalanced together, with the friction hitch on the leader's harness "catching" so you move down at the same rate.*

5. Ascend until you are close enough to the injured climber to begin setting up a counterbalanced rappel (fig. 8-2e). It is a good idea to leave two or three pieces of protection between you and the leader because you might need to move upward by climbing and/or pulling on gear to lower the injured climber. If you need to, you can often just pull down on their strand as you push upward with your feet to "shift" or rock them downward, making it easier to leave more pieces of protection in without them getting in the way. Adjust your backup knot so that it is nearby.
6. Rig your rappel on an extension, with your waist prusik repurposed as a third-hand friction-hitch backup. This means you will need to remove that prusik from the rope; how to free it depends largely on the steepness of the terrain. If the terrain isn't too steep, just stand in your foot prusik and remove the waist prusik. If the terrain is steep, tie the free end of the foot prusik to a carabiner on your belay loop with a munter-mule-overhand and transfer your weight onto that (fig. 8-2f and g). Friction-hitch the waist prusik underneath the belay device as a third hand, then lower yourself out on the foot prusik's munter until the belay device and third hand take tension (fig. 8-2h).
7. If the terrain is just a little steep, you can likely push this knot up the rope until it takes your weight; if the terrain is too steep, attach an additional sling to the "eye" (the bight of the friction hitch where foot prusik attaches to the rope) in order to use it as a "handle" to assist in unweighting.
8. Move the foot prusik's friction hitch from your rope to the injured leader's rope (fig. 8-2i), then clip the long end of this friction hitch to your belay loop (fig. 8-2j).
9. Start the counterbalanced rappel (fig. 8-2k). As you let the friction hitch catch on the leader's strand of rope (and your harness), it "pulls" the leader down with you as you rappel (see Counterbalanced Rappels in chapter 4).

COUNTERBALANCED CLIMBING AND STANDARD RAPPEL

The "simplest" solution for rescuing a leader who is more than 50 percent of the rope away is counterbalanced climbing, but there are few circumstances in which this will actually work. This rescue technique requires that the leader be conscious and not horribly hurt and that the rescuer be able to climb and/or aid up the pitch. It also helps significantly if the pitch is fairly straight up and down. After you catch the fall and communicate with the leader, here are the steps:

1. Tie off your belay device with an overhand backup knot (fig. 8-3a).
2. Begin to climb, which causes the leader to descend (fig. 8-3b).
3. At the point where the leader is lowered to the same level that you have ascended to, construct a station to rappel from, then clip yourself and the leader in with separate rappel extensions (fig. 8-3c).
4. Pull the rope from the last piece of protection the leader was clipped to, and thread the rope through the new rappel anchor (fig. 8-3d).
5. If the leader is able, transfer the rappel ropes to their rappel extension so you can each rappel separately (fig. 8-3e).

Figure 8-3. Counterbalanced climbing and standard rappel: **a***, tie off your belay device with an overhand knot (1);* **b***, begin climbing, which causes the counterbalanced leader to descend;* **c***, when the leader descends to the point you've reached in your climb, build a rappel anchor and clip yourself and the leader in to it with separate rappel extensions (2 and 3);* **d***, pull the rope from the last piece of protection above and thread the rope into the new rappel anchor (4);* **e***, transfer the rope to the leader's extended belay device for a standard rappel.*

Silas Rossi climbs Square Meal *in the Shawangunks, New York* (Photo by Chris Vultaggio)

RESCUING IF LESS THAN 50 PERCENT OF THE ROPE IS OUT

Likely the most-involved leader-rescue situation is if the injured leader is less than 50 percent of the way out on the rope on a route that traverses significantly, has fairly horizontal pitches, or is on other terrain not conducive to ascending the rope.

ROPE-SOLOING SELF-BELAYED

The best option for fairly horizontal pitches or pitches that traverse significantly, where ascending via prusiks or counterbalanced climbing is not a reasonable option, could be the self-belay/rope-solo method. In these situations, a rescuer may need to self-belay to rope-solo up to the injured leader.

The idea behind self-belaying is to use one or two clove hitches as a self-belay as you climb. You find a stance or clip in to a piece of protection, pull out some slack (generally 5–10 feet, depending on the difficulty), and in the event that you fall, the rope comes tight to the anchor where it is tied off.

While this method is not necessarily speedy, it is faster than people think because in a rescue situation, the rescuer isn't aiming to truly "climb" the pitch but instead pulls on the rope or any protection to make upward progress as efficiently as possible.

Start by catching the fall and attempting to communicate with the leader, then follow these steps:

1. Build a multidirectional anchor, if necessary, then tie off your belay device with a mule hitch and overhand backup knot (see Figure 3-1) and transfer the load to the anchor (see Figures 3-4 and 3-5).
2. After escaping the belay and transferring the load, if necessary, tie a figure eight on a bight on the brake-side strand and clip it to the anchor with another figure-8 or a clove hitch (fig. 8-4a). This will be the knot that you work away from while self-belaying. It is not considered acceptable to self-belay yourself on the back side of a munter-mule-overhand.
3. Tie a clove hitch and clip it to your belay loop using one of the bigger locking carabiners you have (fig. 8-4b). Ensure the rope is stacked correctly so it pays out smoothly as you ascend.
4. As the self-belayer, you likely won't have much, if any, protection, so reclip all the

protection the leader has placed (fig. 8-4c). It is advisable to leave the leader's rope in all of the original protection (not shown in these photos, for clarity), which increases the margin of safety; the self-belaying climber will not feel any increase in rope drag from the additional rope.

5. Use whatever means you can to make upward progress safely and efficiently (fig. 8-4d), which could mean pulling on the leader's rope (see the Tip sidebox). Depending on the terrain, push 3–9 feet of rope at a time through your clove hitch as you climb; pushing more rope through

Figure 8-4. Self-belayed rope soloing: ***a****, build a multidirectional anchor and clip a figure eight on a bight to it with two locking carabiners opposite and opposed;* ***b****, attach a clove hitch to your harness belay loop with a large locking carabiner;* ***c****, clip the leader's protection as you ascend and regularly "milk" the clove hitch with both hands to give yourself more slack;* ***d****, use whatever means you can to make upward progress.*

means risking a bigger fall but is also more efficient.

6. Once you reach the leader, build an anchor and perform the tasks needed for whatever rappel seems the most appropriate for the situation.

Tip: Don't be afraid to "batman" by pulling on the rope to assist in upward progress regardless of climbing technique, but certainly do this if you are self-belaying up to a fallen leader. See "Tips for Basic Aid-Climbing Techniques" in chapter 7.

Opposite: *Wesley McCain is belayed with an ABD as he leads the classic fifth pitch of the* Northwest Corner *of North Early Winters Spire, North Cascades, Washington.* (Photo by Andrew Burr)

CHAPTER 9

Hauls, Raises, and Mechanical Advantage

As with so many techniques and concepts in this book, the ability to raise someone or something upward using friction hitches and carabiners to create bends in the rope and increase mechanical advantage is an invaluable skill in a number of situations. Whether you're helping a partner get through a crux or regain climbable terrain after taking a swinging fall off the route, or you're ascending big walls or difficult alpine routes that may require hauling a pack, knowing the basics of mechanical advantage is a good place to start.

MECHANICAL ADVANTAGE

This chapter's discussions about building systems to create and increase mechanical advantage—used to make it easier to pull a mass upward—take place in a frictionless world, which makes it far easier to calculate, explain, and understand this concept.

1:1 HAULING

Even though it has no mechanical advantage, 1:1 hauling provides a foundation for understanding how different types of mechanical advantage compare. To understand how 1:1 hauling works, imagine you want to raise an object 1 foot off the ground. You attach a rope to the top of the object and pull upward. To pull the object upward 1 foot, you must move the rope upward 1 foot, and you have to pull 100 percent of the object's weight the entire time.

This is basic, but it's worth pointing out before we dive into discussions of how to increase mechanical advantage, which reduces the amount of weight that needs to be lifted but requires pulling the rope a greater distance to achieve that weight reduction.

Tip: Keep the system closed! "Closing the system" is a term that many climbers use to mean that both ends of the rope have a hard knot clipped to the anchor (or other secure place) or that blocker knots are being used when appropriate. Closing the system like this prevents you from losing track of the end of the rope and possibly letting it pass through the system while you are lowering, rappelling, otherwise distracted. Serious injury or death can result when the system isn't closed. When climbers start a rescue, the system is usually closed as they are typically tied in to each end. However, as the rescue progresses, particularly more technical ones, you often untie people. Always pause and make sure the system gets closed before starting the next system.

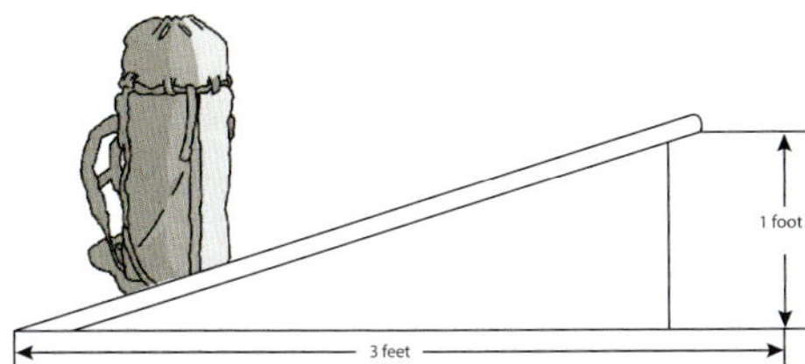

Figure 9-1. A ramp is a simple machine that increases mechanical advantage: here, you will have to move the pack 3 feet horizontally in order to raise it 1 foot vertically, but you will be pushing only about a third of the pack's weight.

SIMPLE MACHINES

Simple machines are devices that increase mechanical advantage by moving a mass farther but moving a smaller percentage of that mass's weight for the duration of the movement. Simple machines, which include things like ramps, levers, and pulleys, all work on this same principle.

One of the easiest simple machines to understand is a ramp (fig. 9-1). Say you want to lift a mass 1 foot off the ground. If you just lift it straight up with a rope, you pull the rope up 1 foot and the mass moves up 1 foot (1:1 mechanical advantage). However, if you use a 3-foot-long ramp to help raise the mass 1 foot of elevation, you have to move the object farther (3 feet of horizontal distance and 1 foot of vertical distance)—but you will be pushing only about a third of its weight up the ramp.

PRINCIPLES OF RAISES OR HAULS

Besides understanding mechanical advantage, two additional concepts are significant for raises or hauls: capturing upward progress and backing up the system. Another aspect to consider is that increasing the mechanical advantage of a system will *not* increase the load on the anchor.

CAPTURING UPWARD PROGRESS

Any system implemented to capture upward progress is termed a *ratchet*. Every time a hauler pulls up rope, the ratchet's job is to "capture" the slack and the progress made. If a hauling system doesn't have a ratchet, when the hauler releases the hauling strand of the rope, the system extends back out to its starting point.

Common ratchet options include a belay device in autoblocking mode, a third-hand friction hitch and carabiner (often called a *tractor*), an assisted-braking belay device (A.B.D.), or a mechanical ratchet like a Petzl Micro Traxion or Edelrid Spoc. Mechanical ratchets reduce more friction than a carabiner and capture progress far more efficiently than any sort of improvised system. They come in a range of sizes (fig. 9-2). This chapter helps you match the best ratchet to your desired hauling system.

BACKING UP THE SYSTEM

In any hauling system, you are no longer a focused and attentive belayer keeping a hand on the brake strand, so some sort of backup must be used. Always back up the raising or hauling system, to prevent catastrophe in the event that the ratchets fail to grab or the system fails because it was constructed incorrectly.

A clove hitch (see Figure 1-14) is a popular backup behind the hauling system. An advantage of a clove hitch over a "hard" knot like an overhand on a bight or a figure eight is that a clove hitch can be "milked"—the slack can be

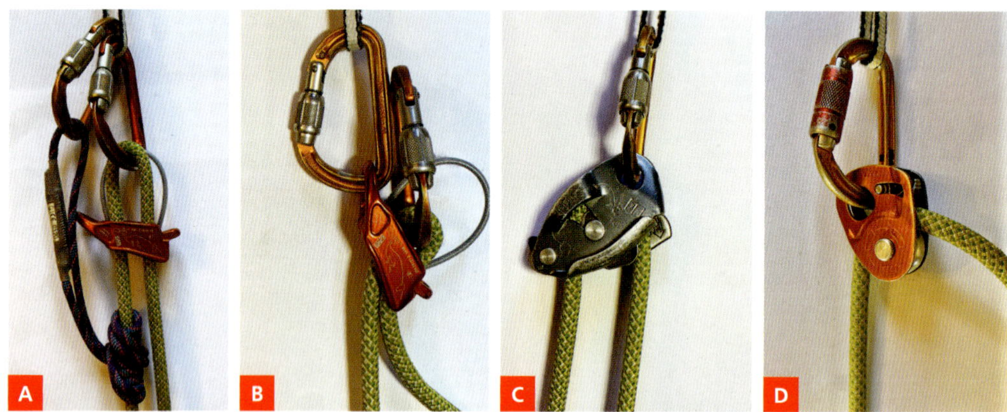

Figure 9-2. Different types of ratchets: **a**, *belay device in guide mode;* **b**, *third-hand friction hitch (here, a prusik hitch) and carabiner;* **c**, *an assisted-braking belay device (ABD—here, the Petzl GriGri);* **d**, *a mechanical ratchet (here, the. Petzl Micro Traxion).*

Tip: A general guideline is that no climber's life should ever rely on a single friction hitch. Their weight can safely hang on a single friction hitch, but it should be backed up with a stopper knot or a second friction hitch that has no chance to "mind" or "tend" (release) the first one. This well-established guideline is a good one to follow. If you practice enough with live loads, you will surely encounter a friction hitch that, for whatever reason—be it the material it's tied with or the number of wraps the hitch uses—won't effectively grab the rope. Conversely, if a bump in the terrain or rock "minds" the friction hitch, or if a person involved in a rescue "bumps" the friction hitch and accidentally "minds" it, the results could be disastrous if the climber is hanging by only a single friction hitch without a backup.

"pushed" through the hitch without retying it as slack builds up during hauling. A stopper knot (a.k.a. a "catastrophe" knot) is another backup option that will jam against the system should some aspect of it slip (see Figure 1-9).

INCREASING MECHANICAL ADVANTAGE DOESN'T INCREASE THE LOAD ON THE ANCHOR

It is widely thought that hauling with an increase in mechanical advantage puts an exponential load on the anchor, depending on the hauling system used. Likely due to the way that calculating mechanical advantage is taught, the thinking goes that the greater the mechanical advantage, the exponentially larger the load is on the anchor.

Luckily, this is a misconception: in a frictionless world (like all this chapter's calculations of mechanical advantage), the load on the anchor is always a percentage of the weight on the anchor. This is because the anchor cannot create mass; in fact, the weight is divided between the anchor and the hauler.

Say you pull directly up on a hauling system's rope to lift a 100-pound weight—you are hauling with a 1:1 mechanical advantage

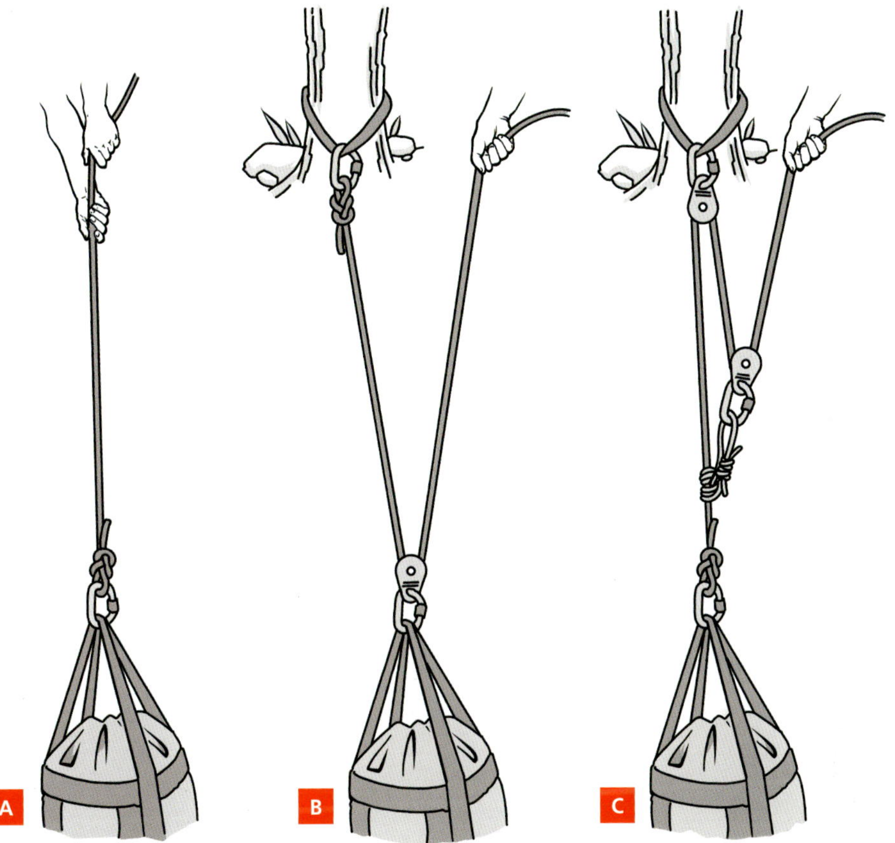

Figure 9-3. Comparing mechanical advantage: ***a****, in a 1:1 hauling system, either the anchor holds all of the load's weight or you haul all of the load's weight;* ***b****, in a hauling system with a 2:1 mechanical advantage, when you haul on the load, you pull half the load's weight and the anchor holds the other half of the weight;* ***c****, In a 3:1 hauling system, when you haul on the load you pull a third of the load's weight and the anchor holds the other two-thirds of the load's weight.*

(fig. 9-3a), raising 100 pounds; and when you are not hauling, the anchor is "pulling" 100 percent of the load's weight: 100 pounds. If you add a ratchet to the hauling system, you will be hauling with a 2:1 mechanical advantage (fig. 9-3b). When you start hauling, you are pulling half of the load's weight, which in this example is 50 pounds. That means the other half of the weight—50 pounds—is on the anchor. When the hauling system's ratchet takes the weight, it returns 100 percent of the weight (100 pounds in this example) back onto the anchor. In a 3:1 hauling system, created with the addition of a second ratchet (fig. 9-3c), you pull a third of the load's weight, with the anchor holding two-thirds

VERY SIMPLE HAULING TECHNIQUES

This section describes some basic raising or hauling methods that are less complex than hauling systems discussed later in this chapter.

VECTOR PULL

A vector pull is a great way to help a partner move up a very short distance (generally 6 inches or less) and to get through a crux section or possibly regain a critical hold that they can no longer reach. To vector pull, grab the loaded strand between the belay device and your partner and pull it up straight or to either side at a 90-degree angle from the load (fig. 9-4). This technique doesn't seem like it should be different from grabbing the rope and pulling it toward the anchor, but you have a great deal more leverage (mechanical advantage) due to how the force is distributed when your arm pulls at an angle perpendicular to the rope.

The advantages of the vector pull are that it is an ultrafast way to raise someone a few inches to help them get through a cruxy section, and no additional knots or friction hitches need to be added. It's also easy to do as the climber continues to move upward, letting you "assist" them through a challenging section. The downside is that you lose a lot of that leverage after you pull the rope just 1–2 feet out of line from where the load originally was, limiting how far you can raise the climber below.

DROP LINE 1:1 ASSIST

If the climber below needs help to get through a difficult section, particularly if they are in

Figure 9-4. The vector pull: simply grab the rope on the load side of the belay device and pull upward with your arm at a 90-degree angle from where the rope is traveling. (Photo by Jim Meyers)

Figure 9-5. The drop line 1:1 assist: drop the brake-side strand (1) coming out of the belay device (2) down to the lower climber and have them pull downward on it, which also pulls them upward. (Photo by Jim Meyers)

close proximity to the anchor, the drop line 1:1 assist is a simple and effective option. To perform the drop line 1:1 assist, drop the brake-side end of the rope coming out of the belay device, while maintaining control of the brake strand, to the lower climber (fig. 9-5). They can pull down on the brake strand while their primary (load) strand goes upward.

The drop line 1:1 assist is a fast, safe, easy way to help a partner climb up to the anchor if they are tired or the terrain is too difficult. The belay can assist a little in helping the lower climber make upward progress. A big advantage of the drop line 1:1 assist is that you can haul the lower climber relatively long distances compared to the vector pull. The disadvantage is that you need to be able to throw them a strand of rope in order to implement this technique.

DROP LOOP 3:1 ASSIST

A variation on the drop line 1:1 assist is the drop loop 3:1 assist. Instead of dropping the brake strand to the lower climber so they can pull up on it, the climber belaying from above drops a bight of rope (a V that opens upward). The lower climber clips the bottom of the V to their belay loop with any carabiner (it does not need to be a locker). This allows the belayer to haul with a 3:1 mechanical advantage, with the belay device acting as a ratchet to capture progress (fig. 9-6).

What makes this technique so efficient is that it's a 3:1 mechanical advantage, plus the hanging climber's ability to pull down on the brake strand greatly increases the hauling power of this very simple system. The disadvantage is that the hanging climber needs to be fairly close to the anchor, and while this is a major disadvantage,

Figure 9-6. Drop loop 3:1 assist: like the drop line 1:1 assist, the lower climber still needs to be close, but if the belayer can drop them a bight of rope from the brake-side strand (1) coming out of the belay device and they can clip that bight to their harness (2), the belayer can haul them up on that strand (3) with a 3:1 mechanical advantage. (Photo by Jim Meyers)

this system is so effective for these types of situations that it is worth remembering.

COMPOUND HAULING SYSTEMS

This section describes some compound hauling systems that are more complex to build and use than those discussed above.

3:1 DIRECT LINE HAUL FROM A BELAY

The most common of the compound hauling systems is the 3:1 direct line haul from a belay, as it is easy to set up, requires minimal gear, and offers an excellent balance of hauling power and efficiency. Say you are belaying a climber from above and they just can't get through a difficult section or they have fallen and swung out of line with the route. Here's how to set up the 3:1 direct line haul from a belay:

1. Ensure that you maintain control of the brake strand (fig. 9-7a) or tie a stopper knot on the brake strand roughly 3 feet below the belay device.

2. Use a third hand or short sling to tie a friction hitch—a prusik works great for this—on the load strand (fig. 9-7b), and clip the brake-side strand coming out of the belay device to the carabiner on the newly attached prusik.
3. Start hauling (fig. 9-7c).

You do not need any other backup on this haul system as long as you maintain control of the brake strand. Unlike the drop loop 3:1 assist, the lower climber doesn't have to be close to the belay for the belayer to be able to set this system up.

Tip: It is important to realize that, in the real world, a bend in the climbing rope introduces friction into the system—friction that increases exponentially with each new bend. Using carabiners and a rope that's 9.2 millimeters in diameter, a 3:1 hauling system actually works closer to a 2.3:1, and a 6:1 system pulls closer to a 4:1. Take these numbers with a large grain of salt, as they are affected by factors such as how much rope is in contact with the surface of the terrain, how extended the system is, and whether there are any large bends in the rope—such as a harsh change in direction, which is common over the lip of a crevasse or a large ledge above a steep rock face.

Figure 9-7. The 3:1 direct line haul from a belay: **a**, *be sure to* never *lose control of the brake strand, or tie a backup knot on the brake strand about 3 feet below the belay device;* **b**, *using a third hand or similar-sized piece of material, tie a friction hitch (1) on the load strand (2) and clip the brake-side strand (3) to the friction hitch's carabiner (4);* **c**, *start hauling, pulling on the brake strand (3).*

3:1 DIRECT LINE HAUL FROM BASELINE

For extended hauling situations, it is advantageous to haul with a ratchet other than a belay device because the belay device adds so much friction that it isn't useful for hauling over longer distances. Thus, it is worth being familiar with hauling from baseline, which is one of the trickier transitions discussed in this book. Here's how:

1. Check the klemheist hitch that you (potentially) used to transition into baseline—when the rope goes straight to the anchor, tied off with a munter-mule-overhand or other load-releasable system (see Baseline in chapter 3)—to make sure it still grabs well, as it must function as your ratchet unless you set up another system.
2. From baseline, use a third hand or short sling to tie a friction hitch (a prusik works great for this) on the load strand down-rope (toward the load, not the anchor) from the first friction hitch (fig. 9-8a). It is helpful if this hitch's material is smaller-diameter than that of the klemheist's.
3. Clip a carabiner to this prusik hitch and attach the brake-side strand of your munter-mule-overhand to the carabiner (fig. 9-8b).
4. Now build a backup for the system: clip a locking carabiner to the anchor (fig. 9-8c) and clove-hitch the long end of the rope that continues away from the prusik to this locker (fig. 9-8d). A good way to remember this clove hitch's location is that the backup goes "in back of" or "behind" the system.
5. This is the tricky and easy-to-forget part, with two options: The first is to untie the klemheist's munter-mule-overhand clipped to the anchor and open the locking carabiner it was attached to, ensuring that you remove only *one* strand of rope. The other option is to put a *new* locking carabiner behind the klemheist's munter-mule-overhand and clip it to the brake strand coming out of the munter-mule-overhand; once it is clipped, you can untie and remove the klemheist's original munter-mule-overhand (fig. 9-8e)—the order is key to avoid introducing unnecessary slack.
6. Start hauling, resetting both lower friction hitches (tractors) and ratcheting them as needed to capture progress (fig. 9-8f). Consider adjusting the clove hitch every time roughly 3 feet of slack develops.

Figure 9-8. The 3:1 direct line haul from baseline: **a**, *after checking that the klemheist (1) on the rope going straight to the anchor is tied with a munter-mule-overhand (or other load-releasable system that grabs well), tie another friction hitch, such as a prusik (2), on the load strand below the klemheist;* **b**, *clip a carabiner (3) to this prusik hitch and attach it to the brake-side strand of your rope's munter-mule-overhand;* **c**, *clip a locking carabiner (4) to the anchor;* **d**, *clove-hitch (5) the brake strand coming out of the prusik hitch to this carabiner to back up the system;* **e**, *then clip another locking carabiner (6) next to the rope's munter-mule-overhand (inside the system you just built)—and clip the brake strand of the munter-mule-overhand through this second carabiner;* **f**, *untie the rope's munter-mule-overhand; haul away.*

6:1 DIRECT LINE HAUL FROM A BELAY

If a 3:1 mechanical advantage isn't enough, converting a 3:1 system into a 6:1 makes the most sense, because it is far easier to increase the mechanical advantage of a 3:1 into a 6:1 rather than a 5:1. This technique takes only three steps. Its simplified name is

to load
1
2
A
to load
3
B
4
C
5
D
6
E
F

"C on a Z"—a very accurate descriptor, as you build a 2:1 system on top of a 3:1, essentially doubling its pulling power.

1. Starting from a 3:1 direct line haul as described above (fig. 9-9a), tie a clove hitch on the hauling strand of rope and clip it to a carabiner above your prusik hitch (fig. 9-9b); instead of the clove hitch, tying a second prusik is also okay.
2. Clip the back-side strand of the clove hitch to the clove hitch you just tied (fig. 9-9c).
3. Start hauling (fig. 9-9d), resetting both lower friction hitches (tractors) and ratcheting them as needed. Consider adjusting the clove hitch every time roughly 3 feet of slack develops, pushing slack through the clove hitch.

5:1 DIRECT LINE HAUL FROM A BELAY

A 5:1 mechanical advantage has a lot of pluses over a 6:1 mechanical advantage: it is more efficient for hauling and there is less friction; it also offers the distinct benefit of having only one friction hitch (tractor) that needs to be tended. This makes it an ideal hauling system when you need more mechanical advantage than a 3:1 system and are hauling over enough distance that the benefits of having to tend only one tractor outweigh the downsides of setting up this notably more complex system. A minus is that converting a 3:1 to a 5:1 is more difficult than converting a 3:1 to a 6:1.

1. Ensure that you maintain control of the brake strand or, if belaying from above, tie a stopper knot in the brake strand roughly 3 feet below the belay device so you can go hands-free. Use a third hand or short sling to tie a friction hitch on the load strand (fig. 9-10a); a prusik works great for this.
2. Girth-hitch a double-length (48-inch) runner or other longer piece of material to the anchor (fig. 9-10b).
3. Now clip the double-length runner to the prusik hitch you just tied (fig. 9-10c) and pull it upward, tensioning the system.
4. Next, with another carabiner, clip the brake strand below the belay device to the free end (the end not connected to the anchor) of the double-length runner (fig. 9-10d).
5. Clip the brake-side strand coming out of the belay to the double-length runner (9-10e). Adjust the friction hitch (tractor) as needed. If you didn't tie a backup clove hitch, make sure to maintain control of the brake strand.

CONVERTING A 3:1 SYSTEM TO A 5:1

Converting a 3:1 into a 5:1 has one critical step that must be done in a specific order to avoid exposing the hanging person or load. These steps assume that you have a sufficient ratchet and that you already have a clove hitch backing up your system.

1. From a 3:1 system, girth-hitch a double-length (48-inch) runner or other long piece of material to the anchor.
2. Now clip the runner to the carabiner attached to the prusik hitch (tractor) on the load strand.
3. Clip a carabiner to the free (non-anchor) end of the runner, then clip this carabiner to the brake strand—this is the critical step.
4. Now unclip the brake strand from the prusik-hitch carabiner.
5. Start hauling, resetting the friction hitch (tractor) and ratcheting as needed. Consider adjusting the clove-hitch backup every time roughly 3 feet of slack develops.

Figure 9-9. The 6:1 direct line haul from a belay: **a**, *start from a 3:1 direct line haul with a backup clove hitch;* **b**, *tie a clove hitch on the hauling strand and clip it to a carabiner just above the lower friction hitch (prusik);* **c**, *clip the back-side strand of the clove hitch that backs up the system to the clove hitch you just tied;* **d**, *start hauling.*

Figure 9-10. The 5:1 direct line haul from a belay: **a**, *use a third hand or fairly short piece of material to tie a friction hitch (here, a prusik [1]); on the load strand coming out of the belay device;* **b**, *girth-hitch a long runner (2) to the anchor;* **c**, *clip the runner through a carabiner (3) on the friction hitch;* **d**, *clip another carabiner (4) to the runner's free (non-anchor) end;* **e**, *clip the brake strand (5) to this new carabiner and start hauling.*

Figure 9-11. The 5:1 haul from baseline: **a**, *check that the klemheist hitch on the load strand still grabs well;* **b**, *use a third hand or short sling to tie a friction hitch (here, an autoblock) on the load strand, and clip a carabiner to this hitch;* **c**, *girth-hitch a double-length runner to the anchor, and clip the runner through the carabiner on the autoblock hitch;* **d**, *clip a carabiner to the runner's free (non-anchor) end, then clip the brake strand of the rope's munter-mule-overhand to this carabiner—and then back up the brake strand to the anchor with a clove hitch on a locking carabiner;* **e**, *clip another locking carabiner to the anchor—behind the rope's munter-mule-overhand—and clip the brake strand coming out of the munter-mule-overhand through this carabiner;* **f**, *untie the rope's munter-mule-overhand;* **g**, *start hauling.*

5:1 HAUL FROM BASELINE

If you are in the middle of a complex rescue and are operating from baseline or if you are hauling a load over an extended distance, hauling with a ratchet rather than the belay device is much more efficient, because the belay device adds so much friction that it isn't useful for longer hauls. Being familiar with hauling from baseline, which is one of the trickier transitions in this book, is worth it for the right circumstances:

1. Check the klemheist hitch that you (potentially) used to transition into baseline—when the rope goes straight to the anchor, tied off with a munter-mule-overhand or other load-releasable system (see chapter 3)—to make sure it still grabs well (fig. 9-11a), as it must function as your ratchet unless you set up another system.
2. From baseline, use a third hand or short sling to tie a friction hitch—an autoblock hitch in Figure 9-11b, though a prusik also works great—on the load strand down-rope (toward the load, not the anchor) from the klemheist; clip a carabiner to this hitch.
3. Clip or girth-hitch a double-length (48-inch) runner or other long piece of material to the anchor. Now clip the double-length runner through the carabiner on the hitch you just tied (fig. 9-11c) and pull the runner upward, tensioning the system.
4. Next, with another carabiner, clip the brake strand of the rope's munter-mule-overhand to the free end (the one not connected to the anchor) of the double-length runner.
5. Now build a backup for the system: On the long end of the rope that continues away from the runner, tie a clove hitch on a locking carabiner and clip it to the anchor (fig. 9-11d). A good way to remember the location of this clove hitch is that the backup goes "in back of" or "behind" the system.
6. Next is the tricky and easy-to-forget part: removing the rope's munter-mule-overhand that is an integral part of baseline. There are two options for doing this. The first is to untie the munter-mule-overhand and open the locking carabiner it was attached to, ensuring that you remove only one strand of rope. The other option is to put a new locking carabiner behind the munter-mule-overhand and clip the brake strand coming out of the munter-mule-overhand to this carabiner (fig. 9-11e); once it is clipped, you can untie and remove the original munter-mule-overhand (fig. 9-11f).
7. Start hauling (fig. 9-11g), resetting the lower friction hitch (tractor) and ratcheting it as needed. Make an effort to adjust the clove-hitch backup every time roughly 3 feet of slack develops.

PROBLEM-SOLVING WITH A BLOCK AND TACKLE

In the most basic sense, a block and tackle is a quick and simple hauling system that is very easy to set up. The name is a maritime term that is well over a thousand years old—*block* refers to a pulley, and *tackle* is a rope system with a number of bends. A block and tackle certainly isn't the most efficient technique for moving large loads any significant distance, but if you need to unweight something, create slack in a tensioned system, or haul a person or load a short distance, it could certainly be the ticket. A block and tackle is well known as a good technique for getting out of a jam.

To set up a block and tackle, clip a carabiner to each of the two points you wish to bring together by hauling. The top carabiner will most likely be on the anchor, but the lower one can vary from being on an object, a person, or a friction hitch on the rope, as in Figure 9-12. These redirected carabiners acting as pulleys are the "block" of the block and tackle. While you don't "need" the carabiners, the larger the carabiner, the less friction there is and, thus, the more efficient the hauling is:

1. Clip a carabiner to each of the objects or systems you are going to bring together by hauling. It should be noted that using larger carabiners to reduce friction will make it easier. (In Figure 9-12, the lower carabiner is clipped to a friction hitch on the rope and the upper carabiner is clipped to the anchor).
2. Take a longer piece of material like a cordelette (fig. 9-12a) or a double- (48-inch) or triple-length (72-inch) sling and clip it to the lower carabiner on the friction hitch and then through the upper carabiner on the anchor (fig. 9-12b). (To reduce friction, you could start by clipping the cordelette or sling to a separate carabiner on the anchor.)
3. Clip both redirected carabiners (a.k.a. pulleys) in a circular fashion, "wrapping" the sling's material back and forth between them as you alternate clipping one carabiner then the other (fig. 9-12 c and d), avoiding Xs, which can increase friction and reduce the mechanical advantage.
4. Start hauling (fig. 9-12e). Note that you can haul only as far as the two "blocks" (redirected carabiners) are apart, but you will lose a significant amount of leverage as they get close together.
5. If needed, it is possible and perfectly acceptable to tie off a block and tackle, locking it in place and allowing you to go hands-free. Tie a mule hitch by folding over a bight of the brake strand to make a loop, then pass the loop around all the strands in the hauling system, and pass the brake strand through the loop you just made (fig. 9-12f). Tie the mule hitch close to one end of the hauling system, as it will get "pulled" against one end or the other. Finish by tying an overhand backup knot in the exact same fashion as you would a munter-mule-overhand (fig. 9-12g). Release as necessary.

USING PULLEYS

In a block and tackle, you can use pulleys instead of carabiners. Pulleys reduce friction, which in a sense makes the system easier to use and requires less force to move a given mass. Climbers don't usually carry a lot of pulleys, even in the world of glacier travel and crevasse rescue, and if climbers do have pulleys it is frequently only one. Pulleys range in size, weight, and complexity (fig. 9-13).

If you are going to add only one pulley to your block-and-tackle system, it should be closest to the person doing the hauling, because in this position the energy it saves is compounded throughout the system. Let's say you save 15 percent efficiency when you place the pulley on the friction hitch (tractor) on your first bend in a 3:1 system. That 15 percent "harder pull" is then passed through the whole system, effectively giving you 15 percent more mechanical advantage. If you put the pulley farther down in the system, its ability to save energy will be reduced.

THE OTHER SIDE OF THE ROPE

BY ANGELA HAWSE

Over the past several decades, I've been a first responder and rescuer for the mishaps of others on numerous occasions. In 2020, I was the one on the other side of the rope, the "victim" for the first time. Thanks to the rapid response by competent, skilled friends, I've been able to get back on my feet.

My training partner Brad and I met on an early morning in December for one of our typical uphill training hikes with weight. An escarpment on the edge of town had become our quick go-to for a steep 1,000 feet of elevation gain in a short distance, one we often did together. I can see it from my kitchen window and had eyed another line that might make a good loop. When we got to the top, I suggested we give the loop a go.

We traversed below the mesa rim on extremely loose terrain and, once we found the line, descended. In no time, we got into a few short cliff bands that we easily negotiated. A third of the way down, a larger cliff band sent us both looking in different directions for viable options through it. I found a ledge-ramp system, concerningly loose but doable, and worked my way to the bottom.

At the bottom, still on loose but less consequential terrain, I let my guard down. My footing gave way at the same time my weighted pack threw my top-heavy center down the fall line. I reacted quickly, outstretching the other foot, but unfortunately it landed on more unstable terrain. As I was hurled forward, I looked down to see my outstretched foot twist 90 degrees out from under my knee, and before I tumbled to a stop, I knew my ankle was broken.

I yelled out to Brad to get down to me. In a short time, he was by my side, evaluating what to do next. He came up with all kinds of possibilities for carrying me out, which I quickly vetoed!

Neither of us—both longtime guides—had a first-aid kit or any splinting material. Brad was carrying his climbing gear, and I had shoved a weight vest in my pack, which was absolutely useless. Brad's harness ended up being an asset later, but we both felt like idiots for not carrying anything useful for the situation.

I remembered that my neighbor Nick might be home working on his house so I speed-dialed his number. Luckily for me, he was there. Even more fortunate, Nick is on the Black Canyon of the Gunnison National Park's search and rescue team and as competent as anyone I know. He quickly sprang into action and recruited two more skilled neighbors to help. Within 10 minutes, Nick was in his car at the bottom of the escarpment trying to locate us with binoculars. Fortunately, I had a red jacket that Brad was able to wave, and Nick found us as tiny dots on the immense landscape. In another 20 minutes, he'd driven to the top and scrambled down to my side with painkillers and splinting material! Although it sure didn't seem like my lucky day, it was turning out to be, given the circumstances.

By the time Nick had me splinted up, our other two friends had arrived above, ready to assist. Nick scrambled back up to meet them, assessing the way out, and hatched a plan in short order. It would take two rope lengths with 5:1 systems to get me up and out. Fortunately, well-placed sturdy pines made solid anchors for rigging on the appallingly loose, steep slope. My location was out of the fall line and well sheltered by the cliff band from a plethora of loose rocks they dislodged as they cleared our route through the cliff bands. The concern once the rope was weighted was the many other rocks that could possibly dislodge from above. I don't know how many laps up and down Nick made getting the anchors set, loose rock cleared, and two 5:1 systems prerigged for my friends to pull us up on. It all happened quite fast, and in no time Nick was down again with a harness for me, one for him, and the end of a rope in hand.

Nick explained it would go as follows. He would tie in to the end of the rope, with me on a 7-millimeter Purcell prusik girth-hitched through my harness, rigged on the rope above his tie-in. Brad would then help me onto Nick's back, and once my prusik was adjusted up the rope to take most of my weight, Nick would climb up with me on his back, keeping me off the rocks and the ground with the assistance of the 5:1 pulled by our friends above.

It sounded sketchy, and looking up at our route through the first cliff band, it surely was, but it worked. Nick is a big, strong guy and has done this in the vertical many times in the Black Canyon of the Gunnison. Here, the off-vertical terrain was much more challenging, but he powered through and somehow managed to stay on his feet, keeping mine out of harm's way. Looking down at my limp, splinted ankle coming close to contacting the cliff bands was terrifying. Nick's calm reassurance despite his grunts of effort and the tugs on the rope from above got me through it. And with one transition to the top anchor and the last 5:1, they had me on top, quickly into the car, and ushered to the ER. Sure enough, the diagnosis was three broken bones in my lower left leg.

The takeaways were many, with the number one being immense gratitude for my competent friends and the fact that they were all home and jumped quickly on the call to rescue. A few smaller takeaways have stuck with me: (1) Have a pack ready for action for the times when I'm on the other end of the call. (2) Ditch the weight vest and put useful items in my pack, such as a first-aid kit with painkillers, when I'm not guiding. (3) When reconning unexplored terrain, go up it first instead of down, especially if it's loose. (4) Don't let my guard down when finally out of consequential terrain (cliff bands), as it's all potentially consequential in a fall. (5) Technical solutions in steep terrain are often much more challenging than in the vertical and require creative problem-solving and strong backs!

Angela Hawse, who has been guiding for more than 25 years, is an International Federation of Mountain Guides Associations–certified guide and current president of the American Mountain Guides Association.

Angela Hawse being carried during her rescue after breaking her ankle (Photo by Eric Ming)

1
2
A
3
B
4
C
D
E
5
F
6
G

Figure 9-12. Block and tackle: **a**, *put a friction hitch (1) on the load strand on the other side of where you need to create slack and clip a carabiner (2) to this friction hitch, then take a cordelette (3) or a double- or triple-length sling and clip it to the friction hitch's carabiner—this will be used to create the mechanical advantage;* **b**, *run the long end of the sling through a carabiner on the anchor (4);* **c**, *clip the sling back down through the carabiner on the lower friction hitch;* **d**, *then, in a circular fashion, clip the sling back up through the anchor's carabiner—repeat this as many times as necessary, clipping one carabiner and then the other;* **e**, *start hauling;* **f**, *tie off the block and tackle with a mule hitch (5);* **g**, *back up the mule hitch with an overhand knot (6), and release the overhand and mule as necessary.*

Figure 9-13. Not all pulleys are created equal: compare how "efficient" the pulley is, generally displayed in a percentage, as well as how easy it is to load the rope into. (Photo by Truc Allen)

OVERCOMING FEAR OF THE BLOCK AND TACKLE

BY EMILIE DRINKWATER

Let me preface this story by saying that I fear many things in the mountains—avalanches, snakes, lightning, to name a few. But of all these things, perhaps the one I fear most is having to perform some kind of technical rescue. Don't get me wrong; technical skills are super fun, especially when practicing them in the comfort of your backyard or at the base of a crag on a sunny day. But in real life? No thanks.

Back in the day as a new guide, I recall learning a little about the block and tackle, a problem-solving tool for when you inevitably botch something. This block-and-tackle thing had been described as a series of pulleys with the rope looped between them that, when pulled on, would magically lift a heavy load, thereby fixing the problems that occur when a rope is weighted and not able to be easily unweighted. It sounded utterly confusing, and I vowed never to need it.

That worked pretty well for a long time, but all good things must come to an end, and when they do, it is sure to be at an inopportune time. At the time of this story, I'd been through a few guide trainings, but the idea of using the block and tackle in real life was still terrifying.

My climbing partner and I were supposed to walk off a climb on a nice, simple trail. Yet there we were, retreating down complex terrain. My partner started down first, gingerly weighting the single strand of rope, then tiptoeing over the edge into a cavernous free-hanging rappel. This part of the adventure wasn't supposed to happen. Then an unexpected storm began to hammer us with gusty winds and painful needles of ice and sleet.

The unplanned descent was moving along well enough, but things changed in an instant as my partner's long braid blew straight into her belay device, bringing her to an immediate and painful halt. She tried, to no avail, to muscle her way out of the situation with one-armed pull-ups and leg flailing, but any movement only pulled her hair in deeper. She was only 20 feet below me, and I thought maybe I could lower my knife down and she could just chop off the hair and continue the descent. . . . Though I was young and inexperienced, I did have enough forethought to recognize that a knife near a tensioned rope might not be the best solution.

If only she could unweight the rope, even for a second, the situation would be amended. And then I remembered, "If you botch something, the block and tackle is a problem-solving tool." If there was ever a time to employ such a magical problem-solving resource, it was now. Our tagline was unweighted and dangling in the wind, so I pulled it back up, fixed the end to our anchor, and lowered my partner a loop. Then another and another. With three loops of tagline running up and down from our anchor to her harness, I started to pull, and voilà, her weight lifted off the climbing rope and belay device, and her hair was free.

I've learned a lot over the years, primarily from mistakes and being forced to find ways to fix them. The block and tackle is no longer shrouded in mystery for me; I still prefer to avoid such technical solutions in the

Emilie Drinkwater climbing near her home in Little Cottonwood Canyon, Utah (Photo by Erin Tribe)

first place, but this simple mechanical-advantage system has come in handy on a number of occasions, from climbing rescues to hauling my car out of a ditch.

Now if only there were a solution for snakes and lightning too.

Emilie Drinkwater is an AMGA/IFMGA mountain guide based in Salt Lake City, Utah, but she travels far and wide for work and adventure.

Opposite: *Keith Sidle rappels off the second gendarme on the east ridge of Forbidden Peak in Washington's North Cascades.*

CHAPTER 10

Improvised Carries and Harnesses

This chapter focuses on some very useful techniques for carrying an injured climber and improvising harnesses—invaluable skills due to their simplicity and the wide range of possible situations in which they could be implemented.

IMPROVISED CARRYING DEVICES AND LITTERS

Lower-leg injuries resulting from a fall on the route or the approach are common, and it isn't out of the question that a climber's foot, ankle, leg, or knee could be injured enough that they aren't able to walk out under their own power. Depending on the number in the party, the size of the injured person, and the distance and terrain that need to be covered, self-rescuing might involve a few short, albeit arduous, carries to the car—say, if it's a quarter mile away—or that might simply not even be an option. While a number of the techniques in this section can make it possible for just one or two people to carry an injured climber a short distance, moving them a long distance requires a lot more people.

SPLIT MOUNTAINEERS-COIL ROPE CARRY

A quick and simple way for a single rescuer to carry their partner is with a split mountaineers-coil rope carry. Carrying someone with a split mountaineers coil is great for patients who are stable but have lower-leg injuries that they might not be able to walk on. Obviously, carrying a full-size human being is not an easy task; the weight of the injured climber and the relative strength of the rescuer, as well as the terrain that needs to be traveled through, play a huge role. Even for the best rescuer-to-injured-person weight and strength ratios, this rope-carry technique won't work for ultrarugged terrain or long distances. But on decent trails and with some rest breaks, it is possible to carry an injured climber a few miles if they weigh about the same as or less than the rescuer.

1. The first task is to tie a slightly oversized mountaineers coil, a technique commonly used to carry a rope on glaciers.
2. Split the slightly oversized mountaineers coil in half so that it makes a horizontal figure eight (fig. 10-1a).
3. Unfortunately for the rescuer, it is often "easiest" for the injured person to get into the rope loops first, as it can be tricky for someone with a lower-leg injury to "slide" into the loops after they have gotten on to the rescuer's back. Have the injured person sit on a rock or a log that ideally is around the height of the rescuer's waist,

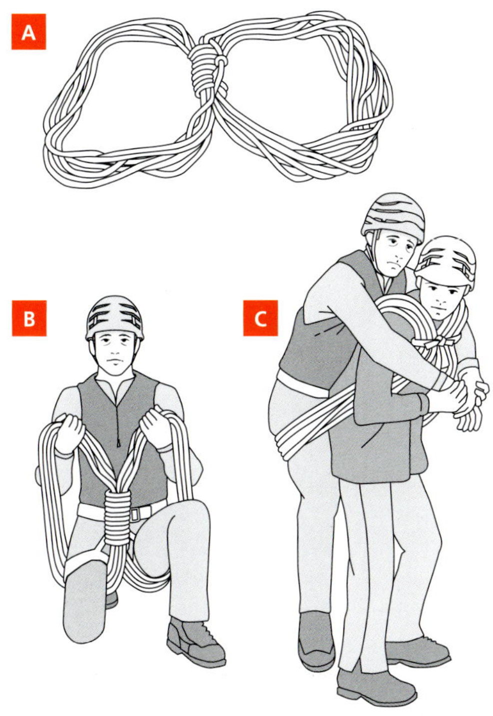

Figure 10-1. Split mountaineers-coil rope carry: **a**, *coil the rope, sizing the loops to fit from the injured person's armpits to their crotch, then separate the coil in half to form a pair of loops;* **b**, *have the injured person place their legs—or help them or do it for them—through the loops;* **c**, *if possible, have the injured person help you put an arm through each loop, then lift the injured person onto your back.*

then have them put one leg through each of the circles of the split mountaineers coil (fig. 10-1b). If there is nothing around for them to sit on and they still have one good leg, they can "stand" to put their legs into the coils, but it still isn't as easy as getting into the coils while sitting.

4. Once the injured person has a leg through each loop, the rescuer backs up to the injured person, who—if possible—helps the rescuer slide one arm through each loop (fig. 10-1c).
5. Standing up is the hardest part, so the injured person should do everything they can to assist their rescuer in this maneuver, maybe by pushing down on trekking poles or grabbing a nearby tree.
6. The rescuer starts walking.

Tip: The rescuer no doubt will experience fatigue and pain in their shoulders and back once they are carrying the injured person. Improvising a chest strap with a sling or other material as in Figure 10-1 can help. The rescuer can even grasp the injured person's legs under the rescuer's arms and hold a sling or other material between both hands to help take a bit of the load off their shoulders. It can also help to have the injured person wrap their arms around the rescuer's shoulders, as does having them lean their torso into the rescuer's back to create a little friction.

BACKPACK CARRY

To some, the backpack carry is the obvious solution, while it might never occur to others. There are few times when we are traveling in the backcountry that we don't have some form of backpack. Of course, backpacks are built for carrying "things." While few if any backpacks that most backcountry enthusiasts wear are intended to carry a human being, many have useful features like a zippered sleeping-bag compartment, which can be unzipped to allow a person's legs to stick through. Or, in dire circumstances, leg holes can be cut in the pack with a knife to facilitate carrying someone

CARRYING SOMEONE OUT OF THE LIBERTY BELL GROUP

BY IAN NICHOLSON

The thought of carrying another human being any kind of significant distance seems impossible . . . until you need to. The year was 2007, early in my guiding career, and I was with a group of four people after having just climbed the *Beckey Route* on Liberty Bell in Washington's North Cascades. We were on the way down later in the afternoon and, having just gotten off the very steep, rocky, tricky section of climbers' trail, had reached the junction with the Blue Lake Trail around two or three hours before dark. Within 100 feet of hitting this main trail, ironically, one person in the group rolled their ankle on a small rock.

We would later find out they had broken their ankle, but in the moment all we knew was that it was impossible for this person to bear weight on that leg and that it had become very swollen very quickly. Luckily, it was only two miles on a well-traveled, easy trail back to the car. We had no cell coverage, and this was in the days before inReaches, SPOTs, or similar satellite communication devices.

Our options were to have one of us run two miles out to the car and then either drive 16 miles to the closest town (which still had no cell coverage but did have a pay phone, though no businesses would be open at that hour) or drive 25 miles to the closest cell coverage (which was nearly all the way to Winthrop). Doing the math, it seemed like there was no way to get outside assistance before dark, and while we had some puffy coats and would likely survive a night out, there was no question it would be miserable, especially for the injured climber.

I decided that we should try to carry the injured person. They weighed 155 pounds and I weighed 175 pounds, but I had a whole summer of walking uphill under my belt and it seemed like a doable, though daunting, option. Instead of just doing a rope carry, I opted to use a mix of carrying techniques ranging from a rope-backpack carry to a pure piggyback carry. Without question, all of these techniques made my shoulders and back hurt, but they did so in different ways, and that was the key for the rest of the afternoon.

I could go around 15 minutes at a time before needing a five-minute or so break. During the break, I would change the technique to vary the location of pain. After what seemed like a very reasonable two hours, we were back at the car just as it was getting dark.

While carrying someone might seem impossible, sometimes you never know until you actually put them on your back and start walking—which in this instance turned out to be far better than someone running out for help or waiting for rescue.

The Liberty Bell Group near Washington Pass, North Cascades Washington

fairly long distances far more "comfortably" than a rope carry can.

A majority of the time, most people are not carrying a pack big enough to fit their climbing partner in, even if they are willing to cut some leg holes in it. Another option is to loosen the shoulder straps all the way and tuck the injured person's legs inside the shoulder straps (and above the waist belt). Due to the often thin nature of the webbing lower on the shoulder straps, this method can be uncomfortable for the injured person, but it's probably not much worse than other options, and it will likely feel like a welcome change for a few 15-minute pushes after a rescuer has been carrying someone using other methods.

ROPE STRETCHERS

If a climber sustains an injury severe enough that it is impractical to carry them with a split mountaineers coil or in a backpack, one great option is creating a stretcher to move them. While building a rope stretcher is not super complicated, ideally the first time you build one is not when you actually need to use it. Take 30 minutes on a rainy day to practice setting one up in your home with your climbing partners.

The ability to move even a very hurt patient is invaluable, but under most circumstances moving someone any significant distance is not really an option. That is okay, because it is an additional skill to consider using in conjunction with the split mountaineers coil rather than an either-or decision. A rope stretcher is a better option for moving potentially very injured patients short distances—say, from the base of a cliff to a nearby field that will be used as a landing zone for a helicopter.

Two people can move a single patient, but it's *hard* work, as roughly 50 percent of that person's body weight is supported by just your arms. If there are any other people nearby, recruit them to help move the injured person. Having two or three people on each end of the stretcher is ideal, and if more people are available to help, frequently rotating carriers helps speed things up and reduces rescuer fatigue significantly.

There are two main ways to build a rope stretcher: the first uses solely the rope, and the second uses the rope and carabiners.

Rope-Only Stretcher

The rope-only stretcher takes a while to set up because each loop must be threaded by the entire remaining rope. If you have even only a few carabiners, using them is recommended (see the next section), and you can thread the bights that you don't have carabiners for. Here's how to build one with only rope:

1. Starting from the middle of the rope, lay it down in an S or zigzagging pattern roughly 1 foot wider than the patient (fig. 10-2a). Use half of the rope to zigzag up to the head of the stretcher and the other half to zigzag down to the foot of the stretcher, with the stretcher's entire length around 1 foot longer than the patient is tall.
2. Using the long ends of rope that extend from each end of the zigzagging pattern, tie a clove hitch around each bight created by the angles in each S or zigzag (fig. 10-2b). Make sure the rope that ends at the foot creates clove hitches all the way up one side and that the rope that ends at the head creates clove hitches all the way down the other side.
3. Pull the entire remaining rope through each of the holes created by the clove

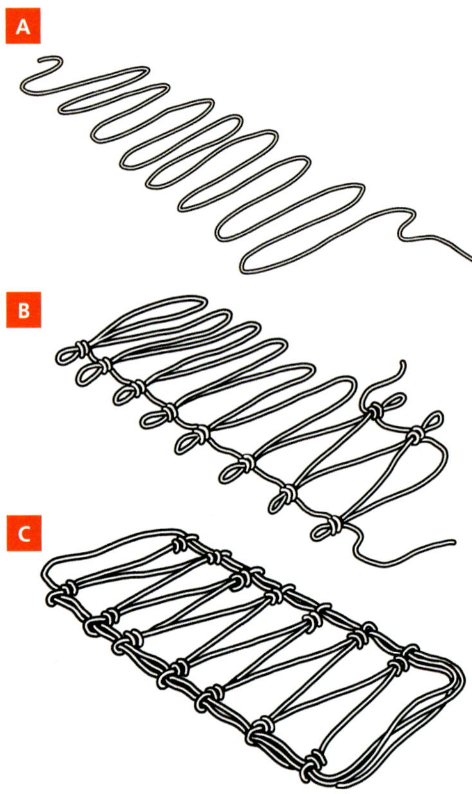

Figure 10-2. Rope-only stretcher: **a**, *starting from the middle of the rope, lay down an S or zigzagging pattern a foot longer and wider than the patient;* **b**, *bring the long end of rope that extends from the top of the zigzagging pattern up one side and tie a clove hitch around each bight created by the angle in each zigzag, then repeat with the long end of rope that extends from the bottom of the zigzagging pattern, tying clove hitches up the other side;* **c**, *circle the long ends of rope around the sides, through the clove hitches, until all the rope is used—around three to five passes encircling the zigzag pattern—then tie a hard knot at each end and attach it to one of the clove hitches.*

hitch–bight combinations. Continue to circle the entire rope around the litter, threading it through each clove-hitched bight each time the rope goes around. Depending on the length of your rope and the size of your litter, this will generally require three to five passes (fig. 10-2c).

4. When you run out of rope, tie a hard knot like a rewoven overhand or a rewoven figure eight at each end and attach it to one of the clove hitches. You do not need a load-releasable knot since the system is easy to "unload" every time you put the patient down, which will likely happen frequently.

Rope Stretcher Using Carabiners

The rope-and-carabiners setup works the same way as the one using just the rope, except it is much faster to build if you have around 15–25 carabiners—any load-bearing type, locking or nonlocking. If you are rock climbing, be it sport or traditional climbing, it is pretty easy to come up with 25 carabiners between three people. In a scrambling situation, it's a real possibility that you won't have enough. However, assuming you do, here's how to build a rope stretcher using carabiners:

1. Just as for the rope-only stretcher above, start from the middle of the climbing rope and lay it down in an S or zigzagging pattern that is around 1 foot wider than the patient. Use half of the rope to zigzag up to the head of the stretcher and the other to zigzag down to the foot of the stretcher, with the stretcher's entire length around 1 foot longer than the patient is tall.
2. Just as for the rope-only stretcher, use the long ends of rope that extend from each end of the zigzagging pattern to tie a clove hitch around each bight created by the

angle in each S or zigzag. Make sure the rope that ends at the foot of the stretcher creates clove hitches all the way up one side and that the rope that ends at the head of the stretcher creates clove hitches all the way down the other side.

3. If you have enough carabiners, clip one to each loop that is clove-hitched.
4. Circle the remaining rope around the entire litter, clipping it to each carabiner each time the rope goes around. Depending on the length of your rope and the size of your litter, this will generally require three to five passes.
5. When you run out of rope, tie a hard knot like a rewoven overhand or a rewoven figure eight at each end and clip each knot into one of the carabiners. You do not need a load-releasable knot since the system is easy to "unload" every time you put the patient down, which will likely happen frequently.

Figure 10-3. While sticks can be great, they're often not available. This rope stretcher, which was reinforced with trekking poles and cordelette, was used to carry someone several miles. (Photo by Rachel Spitzer)

Tip: Trekking or ski poles can work, if they are sturdy enough, to augment either of the above rope-stretcher designs. Dowels or appropriately shaped sticks work even better than trekking or ski poles. While you may not always have such items available, making the sides of the rope stretcher rigid helps it to be less fatiguing for the carriers and more comfortable for the patient. Sticks also make the litter more maneuverable. To integrate the sticks, simply make the loops created by the clove hitches big enough, and slide the sticks through the bights (fig. 10-3). You still need to run or clip the rope through all the bights to support the stretcher.

IMPROVISED HARNESSES

The thought of tying in to the rope directly without the use of a harness doesn't even cross most modern climbers' radar. Yet it is worth noting that climbers of yore used improvised methods as the sole means of attaching themselves to the rope for more than a hundred years, which is longer than the modern seat harness has been in use. This section describes a few tried-and-true methods that should still be in every climber's tool kit, though they certainly aren't techniques that you will use all the time.

BOWLINE ON A COIL

While a bowline on a coil is nowhere near as comfortable as a modern seat harness,

AN IMPROVISED CARRY IN SOUTHERN PATAGONIA

BY RACHEL SPITZER

It was January 23, 2008, and my two climbing partners, Anna Pfaff and Jean Riddle, and I were on our way to the base of Aguja Saint-Exupéry in southern Patagonia in Argentina. Due to a variety of circumstances, I had ended up in Patagonia alone for my first trip to the area. Despite that and due to amazing weather, I'd met some incredible individuals, attempted some of the big climbs, and even got to the summit of Aguja Poincenot. I was super excited when Anna and Jean invited me to attempt the uberclassic *Chiaro di Luna* on Saint-Exupéry with them.

Armed with a paper topo, a bunch of cams, and a small bivy kit, we made our way out of Nippininos base camp. We were about 45 minutes into our approach when the adventure began. As we traveled up the loose talus field, we spaced ourselves out some distance from one another to try to avoid falling rocks triggered by another person. I had my head down, looking for the proper rock to step on—the one that looked the most stable. Thousands and thousands of times I had done this before: walked up loose talus slopes or moraines on the way to a climb. I wasn't thinking about stepping on the wrong rock. I was thinking about how excited and lucky I felt to be attempting this beautiful granite spire with two other female climbers.

And then it happened. The rock I stepped on gave way, causing several large boulders to fall on me. Although it seemed like it went on forever, I'm sure it was less than a second of actual time. I did manage to let out two very loud and distinct screams of pain and fear. When the rocks stopped, I found myself in immense pain, hyperventilating and hunched over, trying not to vomit from the pain. Jean quickly took my pack off. I yelled that something was broken, probably my ankle because one of my feet didn't look like my other foot.

I was scared. Jean reminded me that Anna is a nurse, then handed me some ibuprofen and some Vicodin. I started to relax. Jean and Anna quickly built a splint out of a foam pad, ski poles, and athletic tape, and we decided that Jean would go back for help and Anna would help support my leg as I "crab-walked" down the boulder field.

We made it down about 100 feet before two other Americans showed up. They had heard my screams and the rockfall all the way back at Nippininos and figured something was wrong. Within the next hour or so, about 10 other people

Jean Riddle splints Rachel Spitzer's broken leg below Saint-Exupéry in southern Patagonia, Argentina. (Photo by Anna Pfaff)

showed up—people of all nationalities and backgrounds, all willing to help get me to more definitive care.

One person was sent back to town to let the El Chaltén rescue team know what had happened. The Colombians grabbed the rope and started making a hammock of sorts to carry me. The Slovenians told jokes. Since my leg was swelling so much, Anna and another person took off my boot. I remember I hid my eyes when they removed my sock and boot in case there was a major deformity or a bone sticking out of my skin. Fortunately or unfortunately, we noticed only a significant deep, open wound that suggested an open fracture on my lower leg. The girls bandaged it as best they could.

When the hammock was complete, all the guys took turns carrying me down the rugged terrain. It was very difficult because there were lots of loose rocks and ice, so they had quite a challenge. I knew the guys were trying their best, but at times I was afraid they would drop me or the hammock would give way. But the energy level was high, and everyone seemed to come together to help me out.

The person sent to town quickly returned and announced that on the way he had run into a man on the El Chaltén rescue team who had a radio and was able to radio to town to send more people to help carry me down. The man on the El Chaltén rescue team also started working on getting a helicopter to the valley but thought there was little chance of that happening, since one helicopter was broken and the pilot was on vacation.

It took a very long time to get me back to Nippininos due to the difficult task of carrying me over very rough terrain. At that point, the hammock had unraveled and become worthless. Fortunately, one of the Slovenian climbers had a lot of search and rescue experience and built an even better stretcher using the rope and ski poles. It was very comfortable! It was decided that as many people as possible would try to carry me out through the night, and when they met the group coming up from town, they could return to Nippininos. It was starting to get dark, and it was time to bundle up for the long carry out: 12 miles of very rough terrain back to El Chaltén.

The selfless individuals who gave up their climbing goals to help me had carried me for only about an hour when word came that a helicopter was going to come! I was very happy because I didn't want to hold people back, especially people I had never met before. I also was scared because I didn't know what was going to happen next or where I was going to go. As the sun was setting, a military helicopter landed on the glacier. Anna unhesitatingly volunteered to come with me. We landed in El Chaltén briefly, and after some discussion it was decided we would continue on to El Calafate, where there was a slightly bigger hospital.

Anna and I arrived at the El Calafate hospital at about midnight. The doctor was called in, and the work began to assess the damage. X-rays were taken, and the physician put me under general anesthesia while he sutured up my wound and put me in a traction splint that involved a pin through my ankle and weights (cans of paint) attached to that pin. Very little communication occurred since my Spanish is poor and the doctor spoke no English.

While this was an unlucky event, I feel so lucky that I had so many people—good friends and new friends—help me during this time. The camaraderie I witnessed in the Torre Valley was really amazing and helps me realize how special the climbing community is. I'll never forget this trip and these vivid memories, and while my climbing ambitions didn't exactly wane after my accident, my life goals shifted toward a more stable life and career. I am a different person because of these events and I am 100 percent okay with that.

Rachel Spitzer is an all-around crusher and former mountain guide turned cancer nurse based in North Bend, Washington.

Figure 10-4. Bowline on a coil: **a**, *pass one end of the rope around your back;* **b**, *make three complete wraps around your waist;* **c**, *with the long end of the rope, make a loop that coils upward toward you;* **d**, *pass the loop through your waist wraps from the bottom up, so if the loop were to open it would face downward;* **e**, *fold the loop over the wraps, then pass a bight from the long end of the rope into the loop you just created;* **(continued on next page)**

f, *pass the short end of the rope (hanging from your wraps) through the bight coming up through the loop that encircles the wraps;* **g**, *pull the long end of rope—you should see the loop holding the shorter end invert, pivot, and tighten;* **h**, *tie a half fisherman's (barrel) backup knot with the short end;* **i**, *the finished bowline on a coil.*

climbers long used this method to attach themselves to the rope for everything from hard routes in the Alps to the first decade of ascents of El Capitan in Yosemite National Park. While climbers have survived gigantic falls with the bowline on a coil, the risk of damaging your ribs or organs is unquestionably higher for lengthy falls, than with a modern harness. Despite its downsides, the bowline on a coil remains a simple technique that is great for belaying skiers on steep terrain (because the bowline can pivot freely as you turn, reducing the odds for an awkward twist if the skier were to fall) or for belaying someone who doesn't have easy access to a seat harness or a harness in general.

1. Pass one end of the rope behind your back (fig. 10-4a), then wrap it around your waist three times (fig. 10-4b). You can use more wraps, but when belaying, three wraps are considered a minimum. Keep roughly 2 feet of slack on the short end, which will be used to tie the coils off.
2. Create a loop with the long strand. The way you create this loop is key to the success of this knot. The loop should spiral upward from the long end toward you, and the loop should point inward, toward you (fig. 10-4c). This is a very natural way to create this loop, but it is also easy to mess it up.
3. Pass the loop up from the bottom of the wraps to go behind them so a few inches of loop come out of the wraps (fig. 10-4d). The loop should open downward at this point.
4. Now pass a bight from the long end of the rope through the loop you just created that is poking out from the top of the wraps (fig. 10-4e).
5. Next, push the free/short end of the rope through the bight coming up through the loop that encircles the wraps (fig. 10-4f).
6. Pull the long end to tighten, which should invert the knot, making the bowline become apparent (fig. 10-4g). Give the long end a pull test: if any individual wrap cinches, you messed up and need to tie it again. When you pull on the long end, you should see it pull on all the wraps (coils) simultaneously.
7. Lastly, tie a half fisherman's (barrel) knot backup with the short end (fig. 10-4h). The bowline *does* require a backup (fig. 10-4i).

SWISS SEAT

Another improvised harness is the Swiss seat. While it was traditionally built out of webbing, not that many people carry the 18–24 feet of webbing required to make this harness. Luckily, it works just as well with 6- to 7-millimeter cord, something many climbers have an 18- to 24-foot section of in the form of a cordelette. While this improvised harness is strong, taking any sort of fall in it could lead to serious injury or death. However, it is useful if your party needs to make a rappel or be belayed up lower-angle (but possibly consequential) terrain.

1. Leaving around 10–12 inches of a tail in the cordelette, tie an overhand knot to create a loop just barely big enough to be pulled all the way from your foot to your

Figure 10-5. The Swiss seat: **a**, *tie 2 overhand knots in a cordelette to create 2 leg loops approximately 4 inches apart;* **b**, *step into the leg loops;* **c**, *wrap the cordelette around your waist at least 3 times (4 would be better);* **d**, *tie the ends of the cordelette together with a square knot;* **e**, *finish the ends with a barrel knot to ensure that the square knot stays closed;* **f**, *the tie-in points for a Swiss seat.*

A
B
C
D
E
F

upper thigh—to location similar to where the leg loop of a traditional rock-climbing harness would sit. Be sure to test the fit; this loop should be snug.

2. Move 3.5 or 4 inches along the cordelette from the first knot and tie a second overhand knot that mirrors the first exactly, to create your second leg loop (fig. 10-5a).
3. Slide both leg loops on (fig. 10-5b), then wrap the cordelette around your body, wrapping the cordelette around at least three complete times (fig. 10-5c).
4. Take the end that you just wrapped around your waist and the end coming out of the first leg loop and tie them together with a square knot (fig. 10-5d); finish with a barrel knot (half fisherman's) backup (fig. 10-5e).
5. When you tie in or clip in, make sure to capture both of the "hard points" traveling between the two leg-loop knots and *all* of the strands that make up the waist belt (fig. 10-5f).

Tip: A Swiss seat is fine for rappelling or following on low-angle terrain, but it should not be used on lead.

DULFERSITZ RAPPEL

The dulfersitz, named after its inventor, Hans Dülfer, is a technique in which you use your body to create friction to slide down the rope. At one point, the dulfersitz was the default technique for rappelling, but it fell out of favor as harnesses became more prevalent. Given the choice between using a dulfersitz or a double-locking-carabiner rappel on a harness (see chapter 4), you should certainly default to the double-locking carabiner rappel, as it provides far more friction and security while letting you rappel in a familiar fashion. As is the case with the bowline on a coil, the dulfersitz isn't a technique most climbers will find themselves suddenly using regularly, but it can be a great way to increase security. However, unlike the bowline on a coil, the dulfersitz takes more skill to use (assuming it's tied correctly) and it will "feel" less secure, and rightly so.

1. Pass the rappel rope(s) that are coming down from the anchor through your legs from front to back. If you are right-handed, bring the rappel rope(s) up behind you from between your legs and cross the rope over your right butt cheek (take care to not put the rope in your butt crack). If you are left-handed, cross the rappel rope(s) over your left butt cheek. The brake strand will eventually be on the same side as where the rope crosses your butt. Wrap the rappel rope(s) in front of you up across your chest and over the shoulder opposite from where the rappel rope(s) wrapped your butt and hip (fig. 10-6a).
2. Now wrap the rappel rope(s) back down behind you across your back, so your brake hand is on the opposite side from where the rappel rope(s) crossed your shoulder (fig. 10-6b).
3. With your other hand, grasp the uphill end of the rappel rope(s) going from between your legs to the anchor (fig. 10-6c). Having your body in a well-balanced "L" shape helps significantly, with control and comfort.

Figure 10-6. The dulfersitz rappel: **a**, *pass the rappel rope(s) from the anchor through your legs from front to back, then up behind you and over the butt cheek of your dominant side, and then back across your torso to the opposite shoulder;* **b**, *wrap the rappel rope(s) back down behind you across your back so your brake hand is on the opposite side from where the rappel rope(s) cross your shoulder;* **c**, *grasp the uphill end of the rappel rope(s) with your other (nondominant) hand.*

Tip: The dulfersitz is an effective method of rappelling but is less secure and less safe than most modern methods. The dulfersitz is also less intuitive than modern rappelling, and it is far easier to lose control of the rappel with a dulfersitz. Thus, if you have a harness, consider other methods in steeper terrain—lowering, lowering with a bowline on a coil, or rappelling with double locking carabiners—unless you have practiced the dulfersitz previously.

Opposite: *IFMGA Mountain Guide Jonathon Spitzer guides in a helicopter during a rescue on Ama Dablam in the central Himalaya, Nepal.* (Photo by Jonathon Spitzer)

CHAPTER 11

When You Need Help

Sometimes you can't self-rescue and you need to call for outside help. Maybe you or a member of your group are injured enough that self-extrication is an impossibility due to the terrain, the extent of the injury, or the remoteness of your location. Help may come in a variety of ways, but most commonly it will come from a ground-based search and rescue (SAR) effort or via a helicopter. Once the call is made, at least in North America, that help is in most cases two to four hours away, if not longer. But you can take steps to optimize the rescuers' ability to help you in whatever form that might be.

CALLING FOR HELP? THE EARLIER THE BETTER

If there is an incident, it is *far* better to get help coming sooner rather than later. While the exact amount of time required for a team of rescuers to arrive on the scene varies widely in wilderness and nonroadside settings, in North America it will generally take more than two hours. This is because there isn't usually a SAR team just hanging out next to a helicopter, close to all of their gear, ready to jump up and go like a traditional ambulance or firefighter might be hanging out at the fire station. Generally, SAR groups need some

Graham McDowell tries to radio out from Rainy Knob to White Saddle Air, Waddington Range, British Columbia.

WHEN TO CALL FOR HELP

BY CHERI HIGMAN

As a rule, if your situation is such that you are considering whether to call for a rescue, you should probably call in the cavalry. When an accident occurs, a series of decisions, either bad or good, has led a team or person to the situation they are in. An accident may be a good indicator that you should question the decisions made thus far and reach out for some help.

Generally, SAR organizations classify missions into two categories: search (a person is lost) and rescue (a person needs support to get out of the backcountry). If you are questioning whether to call for help, here are some guidelines:

- **Do you have an injury that poses a risk of life or limb?** This includes head and neck/spine injuries, illnesses, cardiac issues, abdominal issues, and trauma resulting in angulation of or reduced blood flow to an extremity.
- **Do you have an injury that prevents you from being able to self-extricate?** For example, this could be a broken, sprained, or strained lower extremity, a painful upper extremity, or damage to the face or sensory system.
- **Are you stranded somewhere?** This could include being cliffed out, slipping down a gully, or being trapped by creeks rising unexpectedly or tides coming in. If so, do you have the time and resources to wait things out for the conditions to change? Are the conditions going to change? Do you have the right equipment to safely self-extricate? Can you keep yourself warm, fed, and hydrated?
- **Are you lost?** If yes, immediately call for help and stay put. Too often, rescuers and the lost person circle each other because the person does not stay in one place. With technology today, SAR operations can create very sophisticated search patterns, and your call for help has likely triangulated your position.

Often, if a loved one is expected to return and is overdue either at a check-in location or back at home, it is the folks sitting at home wondering if they should call SAR who set the wheels in motion. First, do you have the ability to get into contact with the party in the field? If so, reach out to them and see if you can get a status update. If you can't reach them, ask yourself whether their outing could result in their coming out later than expected—perhaps they underestimated the duration of a climb or a multiday backpack? If so, allow them 24 hours past the time they are due before calling for help. If it's a short half-day or one-day trip and they have missed their return time and evening has set in, call for SAR support.

Ultimately, if you are out in the backcountry wondering whether you should call for help from outside resources, push that SOS button and get the system in motion. If you have the ability to text with your SOS, let someone at home know what the situation is and also have them reach out to 911 on your behalf. This ensures that emergency medical services have your message, and it lets us know what the challenge is so that we can more hastily get the right resources into the field.

Cheri Higman was the first female chairperson in Seattle Mountain Rescue's history and continues to serve on its board as well as acting as its education chair. She is an active field member and joined the unit in 2016.

time to alert and assemble their team members, who aren't always in a central location, and it will take some time for that team to travel to the helicopter launch or the trailhead. Standby SAR teams are available in only a few specific places or very lucky instances in North America. This means that you should generally call for help *earlier* in your rescue rather than later. Once your team decides that you will need outside help, immediately make the call in whatever fashion you can.

Ian Nicholson uses a satellite phone in the Alaska Range more than 60 miles from the nearest road. (Photo by Graham Zimmerman)

WHAT TO KNOW ABOUT DIALING 911

In most cases, it is better to call 911 rather than a search and rescue operation. Maybe the operator doesn't personally know what you need, but they will know who to talk to in order to get you what you need. Depending on the situation, help from a helicopter or land-based SAR team can take many forms, from the military to volunteer groups, which are often managed by the sheriff's department. Let 911 figure out which group will give you the best chance for help rather than trying to cut them out of the equation, as it often isn't in your best interest.

In most areas of the United States, if you call 911 because you are in need of a rescue in technical terrain or in the wilderness, your call will be routed to the local sheriff's department rather than an ambulance or local hospital. The sheriff's department will then decide which resources the rescue is likely to need.

Another major advantage of dialing 911 is that the operator and center that you called will slowly try to "ping" or locate you via your phone signal. The weaker your phone signal is, the more difficult it will be for them to geolocate you, and the longer it will take, but the second you make a connection, the 911 center will start trying to pinpoint your location.

Let the 911 operator know where you are (be as precise as possible), the status of the injured person, any immediate threats or concerns (are you moving?), and what you need. If you know how, convey latitude and longitude coordinates or UTM coordinates. There are countless navigation apps, and even common ones like Google Maps can give you coordinates in longitude and latitude or UTM, even if you don't have cell

An in-flight medic crew assists with a rescue. (Photo Tom by Healy)

coverage. So take a few minutes to familiarize yourself with how to pinpoint your location using any one of a number of applications on your phone.

INFORMATION TO GIVE TO THE 911 OPERATOR

- **Where you are**—ideally UTM coordinates or latitude and longitude in conjunction with a place name or aspect of a mountain feature
- **Status of the injured person**—primary problem or injury, level of mobility, et cetera
- **Immediate threats or concerns**—are you in a safe location and will you stay put? Or do you need to move to a safer location and where will that be?
- **What you need**

EMERGENCY COMMUNICATION OPTIONS

There is no perfect emergency communication device, but being familiar with the areas you like to frequent and the specific options available to you in those regions will set you up for success.

CELL PHONES

The majority of people nowadays own and carry a cell phone of some kind. We all know that if we have cell coverage, a cell phone is a fantastic tool if we need to call for help. But then the question becomes, what do we do when we don't have cell coverage?

While your phone shouldn't be your only emergency communication option in more-remote areas, it's worth using it to dial 911, even if it doesn't display any bars. Doing

WHAT A TWO-WAY SATELLITE COMMUNICATION DEVICE DOES AND DOES NOT DO

BY SETH WATERFALL

Once, when working inside the ranger station at Camp Muir at 10,000 feet on Mount Rainier, I was approached by a man named Michael. I asked how I could help him, and he informed me that he had just activated his SPOT device by accident. I thanked him for letting me know and took down his name, but he stayed put at the door to the ranger station. I asked if there was anything else I could help him with, and he looked confused and said, "Well, you might want to come outside because there will be a helicopter coming any minute!"

I didn't know how to react at first, but I informed him that the emergency locator beacon he purchased did not come with a helicopter orbiting his location 24/7. Michael seemed unsatisfied with that answer but went back to setting up his tent.

The park dispatcher called me moments later and reported a SPOT activation near my location. I gave the dispatcher Michael's information, and we closed out the incident. Five minutes after that, the dispatcher called again and said that Michael's wife was calling and wanted to talk to him. The dispatcher said they'd patch her through to the ranger station and asked if I'd go get Michael.

I found Michael out by his tent and told him that his wife was about to call on my radio so she could speak with him. He looked at me and said, "Can you just tell her that I'm okay?" I said, "No, because I've been married longer than 10 seconds, and I know that's a conversation between you and your partner."

Needless to say, the conversation with his wife didn't go great for Michael. But it did get me thinking about what people expect when they call for help and/or activate a device such as a SPOT or inReach.

Ideally, what would happen is that your information would be given to a 911 operator in your area who would then mobilize the appropriate local resources. However, this is generally not the case. Depending on the device, your distress signal will go to an organization such as the International Emergency Response Coordination Center, Focus Point International, or the Air Force Rescue Coordination Center. These organizations then act according to their own protocols and procedures to activate the rescue response. They are all reliable and effective, but it is important to understand how the lines of communication work for your particular device.

If your device simply sends an SOS alert with your location, this is the equivalent of calling 911 and hanging up. Someone will respond to your location, but they will be tasked primarily with locating you, assessing the situation, and stabilizing any life-threatening conditions. They will have to report back to their incident-management team and request resources for your extraction.

Ideally, you should be able to communicate two-way with your rescuers. The messenger devices are good for this. Better yet is a satellite phone, and the best is a cell phone. A cell phone will put you in direct contact with a 911 dispatcher, then an incident-management team.

A National Park Service ranger "tagging in the line" after a short-haul mission in Olympic National Park, Washington (Photo by Seth Waterfall)

When first calling for help, get the important facts out first. Here's a prioritized list:

1. Who you are and who is injured or in need of assistance
2. Your callback number
3. The nature of the incident; for example, is someone injured or lost?
4. The location of the incident or the last known location of the lost person
5. The number of injured or lost
6. An injury or illness report giving the mechanism of injury or nature of the illness
7. Any safety concerns, such as avalanche danger, rockfall, aerial hazard for helicopters, et cetera
8. Weather at the scene

This information can be used by an incident manager to assign appropriate resources to travel to your location and begin to transport you to definitive care.

Seth Waterfall is a former mountain guide and lead climbing ranger for Mount Rainier National Park in Washington.

so opens several little-known avenues that may enable you to complete the call.

First off, all cell phone carriers are mandated to carry each other's emergency calls. That means that even if your cell phone service provider doesn't offer coverage in a given area, you may be able to make a connection via another service's coverage (which you won't be able to see until you dial 911).

Additionally, calling 911 eliminates your phone's preference for minimum call quality. Many outdoor enthusiasts have experienced the "ghost bar," in which they see bars but can't make a call or send a text. This is generally because the cell tower is too far away and your phone decides for you that the quality of the call won't be very good, so it won't connect you. However, when you dial 911, your phone throws that minimum-call-quality preference out the window and will try to put you through, even if it's a poor connection.

Lastly, your phone will work "harder" to connect to those faraway towers when you dial 911. This means your battery will drain faster, but any modern phone knows that when its user dials 911, it is an emergency and it will boost its signal search to try to make a connection.

Obviously, none of these factors is a guarantee that you will make a connection, but it is always worth trying, as there are countless stories of people whose phones displayed no bars but they were still able to get through when they dialed 911.

TWO-WAY COMMUNICATION DEVICES

Relying on a cell phone in areas with very little or no coverage isn't necessarily a good idea. Instead, if you frequent more-remote areas, consider investing in a two-way satellite communication device, such as the Garmin inReach, SPOT X, or ACR Bivy. These and similar devices have exploded in popularity in recent years because they are easy to use, are relatively inexpensive, and will more or less work the world over. Sure, you might not have coverage for as long as 20 minutes at a time, but as soon as a satellite rolls back overhead, you will be able to send and receive messages.

The key with the inReach and its two-way messaging ability is that you can actively ask for help and answer questions about what is going on. You should certainly hit the SOS button, but you should also message a friend to have them call 911 on your behalf. This is because National Park Service rangers have estimated that roughly 75 percent of total inReach SOS buttons are false alarms. This means that when you hit the SOS button, many rescue organizations frequently take a wait-and-watch approach. It isn't that help won't come if you press the SOS button, but SAR groups will often watch your movement patterns. Are you continuing along at a normal pace on a trail? Or does it look like something is wrong?

Messaging a friend with some details about what you need lets them actively tell the 911 operator or the SAR team what is going on and will help get your rescue initiated immediately, rather than in a few hours.

Satellite Phones

Unquestionably the best tool if you truly have to deal with an emergency is a satellite phone. No other device offers reliable and easy-to-use two-way communication regardless of where you are in the world. You can call 911 yourself or have a doctor call you; it's literally as simple as using a cell phone. The downside of sat phones is the cost of both the purchase and the "minutes" used. They are also heavier and bulkier than their satellite texting counterparts.

This combination of cost and bulk keeps them from being common on less remote trips, but if you are planning a trip to a more remote corner of the globe for an extended period, at least consider renting one. Renting one is easy, as many of the businesses that rent them plan to mail them, and it keeps the price of bringing one along far more reasonable. Sat phones might be on the more expensive side and suffer from regularly dropping calls, but it's tough to beat their general reliability and ease of use, plus the fact that you can essentially use them anywhere in the world.

Radios

VHF/UHF radios are excellent two-way-communication tools, but they don't work everywhere and require a higher level of knowledge to use than a sat phone or a two-way satellite communication device, which offer far more familiar interfaces. Radios are far cheaper than most of their satellite communication counterparts, with handheld VHF/UHF radios starting around $40 and many solid options in the $100–$250 range.

Radios work best in locations where there are a number of repeaters already in place—which, luckily for most climbers, is the majority of mountainous national parks, Forest Service land, and crown land found in the western United States and Canada. Most of these frequencies are public information and can be found via a quick internet search; however, a major caveat is that they are only to be used in the event of an emergency. This means that you are not to speak on these frequencies for any reason other than an emergency.

It takes a fair amount of skill to program radios and to properly take advantage of their features, but they are a very functional tool, even in remote areas. While radios do work quite well, you must also learn how to plug in all the information, such as the correct frequencies for a given area, as well as the nuances of the frequencies (which may include different transmitting and receiving channels), repeater information, and their possible tones/codes.

If radios are a good resource in your area but programming one seems like an overwhelming option, it is possible to take a class or even hire someone familiar with

Ian Nicholson communicates via a radio near Rogers Pass, Glacier National Park, Canadian Rockies, British Columbia. (Photo by Chip Daly)

THE *ONE* ESSENTIAL

BY DALE REMSBERG

We all know that we need to be prepared for our adventures, and the classic principle of the Ten Essentials is a great tool as a checklist. I have found that what is in my essentials kit varies by the activity and location where I'm guiding, so I try not to get dogmatic about my packing list.

But . . . there is one thing I *always* have with me: communication to the outside world! For me, this is a hard "must." Depending on the zone I'm working in, it may be as simple as my cell phone, but that's often backed up by a small two-way satellite communication device, and in areas where radios work I usually carry a small VHF radio.

All the planning and training finally paid off for me when I fell on a remote ice climb in Canada. When my fall came to a stop, my client was able to reach me; I asked him to pull my VHF radio out of my pack, and I quickly turned it on and radioed via a repeater to Parks Canada: "Mayday Mayday Mayday, this is mountain guide Dale Remsberg and I have fallen and I'm injured. Does anyone copy?"

To my amazement but not surprise, a dispatcher responded immediately and asked for my location and the nature of the injury. They put me in direct contact with an IFMGA Parks Canada rescue technician who was familiar with the climb I was on. There was a helicopter en route within 15 minutes, and one hour after the fall I was being packed in a vacuum litter and helicoptered to a waiting ambulance for transport to the hospital.

I did not know it at the time, but it turned out I had a broken back and a cracked pelvis. The feeling of being connected to a rescue team and knowing someone was on the way is a feeling I will never forget, and the communication devices helped speed up my rescue. To this day, I put considerable energy into packing the correct communication. Do your homework, write down the local rescue numbers, and practice sending messages in a controlled setting so you know how your devices work. The proper emergency communication tool for your location is the most important thing you can bring in your pack; it can literally be the difference between life and death.

Dale Remsberg is an IFMGA mountain guide and the technical director for the AMGA.

Dale Remsberg had a properly programmed radio to communicate with Parks Canada after a ground fall on Curtain Call, *in Banff National Park, caused a number of severe and life-threatening injuries.* (Photo by Lindsay Fixmer)

A group waits for the helicopter to evacuate a climber with an unstable lower-leg injury in Washington's Central Cascades. (Photo by Kurt Hicks)

researching different frequencies and repeater information and inputting it into a multitude of radios to set up your radio for you.

ONE-WAY COMMUNICATION DEVICES

It's far better than nothing to use a one-way satellite communication device like the traditional SPOT, but these devices are a lot more limited than two-way models. Most of these devices have a few preset messages, which is nice, but if you really need help fast, all this model offers is the SOS button. As mentioned above, the SOS button will help get you a rescue, but unlike a two-way model, it won't allow you to actively message someone or give the rescuers a way to contact you.

HELICOPTERS 101

The organization or agency that might send a helicopter varies widely with the area, ranging from National Park Service or US Navy helicopters in some national parks to US Air Force or medevac helicopters in other places, especially at lower elevations. Helicopters aren't plentiful, but most mountainous areas have a few different sources that might provide a helicopter rescue. In the United States, unlike Europe, only a handful of the biggest SAR operations have a dedicated helicopter.

WEATHER CONDITIONS

Visual flight reference (VFR) is the minimum of unobstructed air that a pilot needs to see in order to fly. Generally speaking, helicopters require at least a half mile of visibility (possibly under a higher cloud layer) and a mile of visibility during nighttime. These guidelines are sometimes disregarded for civilian SAR missions where life and limb are at risk and more frequently so with military aircraft, as they may have more sophisticated and precise navigation equipment on board. The rescue team will certainly ask you about

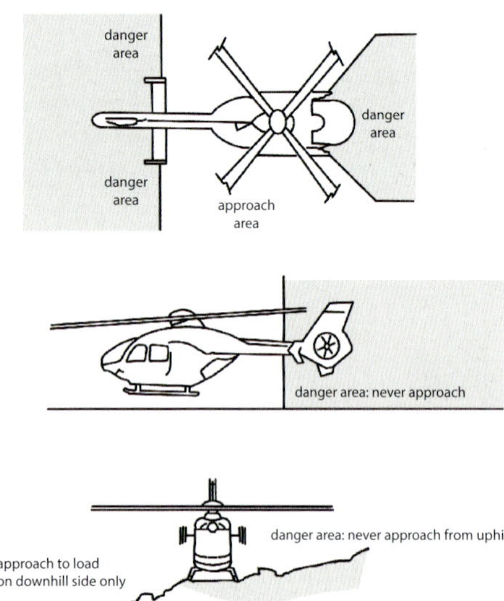

Figure 11-1. Be aware of the helicopter's location and its orientation to the hillside. (Source: Eurocopter)

sky coverage and visibility before sending a helicopter out. Think about cloud levels (as they relate to peaks), fog, and wind, and be as accurate as you can.

When it comes to wind, flying and landing a helicopter is generally not possible in wind speeds of more than 50 miles per hour, even with fairly clear skies. Helicopters normally don't have issues in rain or snow, which do not affect the thrust created by the rotors. In most cases it's the poor visibility associated with snow and rain that keeps the helicopters from flying more than the precipitation itself.

IDEAL LANDING SITES

Knowing what to look for when it comes to a helicopter's ideal landing area is extremely helpful in the event of a rescue:

Size: at least 100 feet by 100 feet
Shape: square, circular, or rectangular
Slope: relatively flat (less than 10-degree slope)
Surface: free of debris and equipment

APPROACHING A HELICOPTER

Never approach a helicopter until the pilot is aware of your location and gives you a signal to approach. This is usually some type of thumbs-up or wave. The pilot will do their best to set you up for the safest approach, but the terrain might dictate that they land in a specific orientation.

Stay low around the helicopter, particularly if the ground is uneven, and *never* walk around the tail of the machine (fig. 11-1). Walk bent at the waist to lower your head height, and avoid carrying anything that sticks up above you.

If there is any degree of slope, approach the helicopter from downhill. Ideally, approach the helicopter diagonally, heading straight to one of its two front windows from the nine o'clock or three o'clock position. *Never* approach or walk around near the rear of the aircraft, as the tail rotor is essentially invisible and could kill you if you happen to walk into it.

WINCHES

If a helicopter does not have all of the terrain prerequisites described above in which to land, a winch can be used to raise and lower rescuers or hoist the injured person. In areas where weather or terrain conditions prohibit the helicopter from actually setting down, many rescue helicopters have the ability to "long-line" or raise an injured person from the ground using a winch. The winch is a crane-like feature that lowers a steel cable from the helicopter to the ground.

TIPS FOR A HELICOPTER RESCUE

BY TINO VILLANUEVA

Need a helicopter rescue? Where you are and the type of terrain you are in will dictate the procedure. Here are some general tips:

- **Provide your location when calling for a rescue.** Refer to a well-known landmark "12 miles southeast of X Peak in Y Basin" and/or latitude and longitude coordinates. Also report critical weather and location conditions—wind speed and direction, clouds and visibility, landing-zone obstacles or hazards.
- **Look for a very flat area.** Slope angles of less than 10 degrees are ideal. In areas flat enough to land, clear the area where the helicopter will land. A 100-foot by 100-foot area is a good minimum area to clear. Make sure all loose items are secured and cannot blow away.
- **Anticipate how wind direction affects landing.** The helicopter will most likely land with the nose into the wind and the tail facing downhill. When setting up your pickup site, if at all possible, especially in soft snow, build in tail-rotor clearance by either siting near a knob that drops away or on downhill slopes, to keep the tail rotor out of the snow when the helicopter settles in.
- **Provide visibility clues.** In flat light, stomp tracks into the snow to provide contrast or choose a landing zone near rocks, brush, or something other than snow. It can be beneficial to rig a wind sock out of bright fabric. To protect the pilot's vision, avoid signaling with bright flashing white lights, especially as it gets darker.
- **Be aware of the rotor.** When the helicopter lands, be aware of rising terrain. The main rotor will be closer to rising terrain, as will you if you are in terrain rising up around the helicopter. The tail rotor is the most dangerous area—stay away!
- **Prepare the patient.** Provide them (and your team) with warm clothes, wraps, goggles, gloves, et cetera to protect from rotor wash. In technical terrain or areas not flat enough for landing, which will necessitate a haul from the helicopter, having a harness already on the patient can be beneficial.
- **Don't approach until signaled or approached.** The helicopter may land right next to you; keep your eyes on the helicopter and provide simple hand signals if appropriate. Always approach from the front, making sure the pilot has eyes on you and signals the okay. Be prepared to follow directions provided.

Tino Villanueva is an International Federation of Mountain Guides Associations mountain guide and longtime heli-ski guide.

Tino Villanueva helps guide a helicopter as it approaches for a landing in the Chugach Mountains, Alaska.

A YOSAR helicopter short hauls a rescuer to a ledge where a landing was not possible in Yosemite National Park, California. (Photo by Jack Cramer)

The team on the ground should be prepared to move quickly, because hovering uses a lot of fuel and is a difficult maneuver for both the helicopter and the pilot. A crew member will always accompany a stretcher when it is both lowered and raised. It is likely that two people at a time will be winched—a rescuer and a member of the team being rescued—but in certain circumstances, an uninjured member of the team being rescued may need to be winched alone. While the helicopter team would always prefer to winch anyone with an accompanying crew member, the situation might require that a person be winched alone.

A trained crew member will always be sent down first and will instruct the group on the ground about what the plan is. The rescuer will be equipped with a single strop or similar fast-attaching harness. That said, most rescuers using a long line will incorporate a climbing harness if you have one, so put it on or keep it on if you are able. While it is possible the rescuers might incorporate a climbing harness if the injured person happens to have one on, the rescuers also might rely solely on the single strop harness because of its speed in the mountain environment—especially in changing or adverse weather conditions.

A single strop harness is incredibly common in mountainous winch operations. It simply slips over the person's head and is pulled up into their armpits. As the person is being raised, it is essential that their arms remain down, or they run the very real risk of sliding out of the strop harness and falling to the ground. Likewise, when the injured person arrives at the helicopter, they should not attempt to climb in or assist the operator in any way, as their arms may become dislodged.

SEARCH AND RESCUE OPERATIONS

While there are dozens of professional and volunteer rescue organizations, most of the time in North America there isn't a rescue team waiting around a hangar, even in good weather. In some national parks where significant amounts of climbing takes place, there is often a group of professional and highly trained rescuers or climbing rangers. These groups will know the terrain once they know the location of the incident and will decide

A Yosemite Search and Rescue team member is lowered down to two stranded climbers after an unexpected storm in Yosemite National Park, California. (Photo by Jack Cramer)

what the most efficient way to respond will be—overland or by helicopter. Areas not in national parks, which unquestionably account for the greatest amount of terrain that climbers frequent, do not have a professional rescue team. In these areas, when a rescue is initiated the rescue is often organized through the local sheriff's department, which may have the ability to call on a given area's volunteer SAR team to assist in a rescue.

Once a SAR team is assembled, there is generally a planning and briefing period during which the team assesses the situation and potential risks to figure out the best course of action before heading into the field. It is difficult to estimate an actual average time for rescuers to reach climbers in remote settings (more than an hour's hike from definitive care). However, over more than a hundred rescues in Washington's North Cascades and Mount Rainier National Parks, California's Yosemite National Park, Wyoming's Grand Teton National Park, and Colorado's Rocky Mountain National Park, the average helicopter rescue response time was between two and four hours—from the moment the team was alerted to when they arrived on the scene, under optimal conditions. Obviously, the weather, the team's exact location, and countless other factors can affect the amount of time it takes for rescuers to arrive on the scene.

The volunteers in most of these SAR organizations are exactly that—volunteers who dedicate their own free time to be on call and assist with rescues should a situation arise. While SAR teams are volunteers, they receive significant training, and the SAR organizations

Seattle Mountain Rescue loads up for a training run in the Snoqualmie Valley, Washington. (Photo by Seattle Mountain Rescue)

frequently have requirements for minimum levels of experience and training in order to participate. If you are interested in volunteering with your local mountain-rescue group, look into SAR organizations in your area. Consider volunteering with your area's local SAR team. Not only is it a great way to help people and give back to the community, but you are also bound to learn new skills and create meaningful life experiences.

Opposite: *A climber traverses the summit ridge of Aiguille de Mermoz with Fitzroy in the background, Argentinian Patagonia.* (Photo by Mikey Schaefer)

CHAPTER 12

Scenarios and Solutions

This chapter includes 10 stories that were selected because they represent a number of the most common problems that climbers face in the real world. In the majority of these cases, knowing a few simple techniques can easily avert a forced night out or a full-blown epic. For the more severe scenarios, knowledge of these techniques could easily mean the difference between life and death.

Each scenario also provides a solution, but any medical care is omitted, as it is outside the scope of this book. These solutions also omit calling for help, as any life-threatening situation should be coupled with calling for help—although the "if" and "how" you reach out for help will depend very specifically on your location and proximity to advanced care.

The photos included with each scenario are not from the events themselves but represent similar terrain in which they happened, to help give context. Lastly, a number of these stories were slightly altered to fill in unknown information and facilitate a better learning experience. However, all of the problems themselves remain the same as they were actually experienced.

SCENARIO 1: FOLLOWER STRUGGLES AT A CRUX

You led up the crux third pitch of a five-pitch route. It was not only the most difficult of the route, but it was also slightly run-out and protected by a mix of bolts and traditional placements. The placements were solid but a little spaced, and the pitch featured several devious friction moves.

At the belay you set up the anchor, pull up the rope, and holler down that the lower climber is on belay and can start up. They start climbing; around halfway up the pitch (and still at least 50 feet from you), they get to the hardest of the pitch's three cruxes. They try nearly a dozen times, but every time their feet just skitter off the dime-sized edges. You remember that section involved tricky friction with poor handholds. Luckily, it was protected by a bolt around 3 feet below where the climber is now. The next piece is around 15–20 feet above them, where the climbing eases.

They have taken more than 30 minutes and still have not gotten through this section; not only are they frustrated, but you are both wasting daylight and the descent is

Bob "The Bobster" O'Rourke following on Cascade Kronenbourg *in the Canadian Rockies* (Photo by Dale Remsberg)

notoriously tricky. There is no hope for them to reach the next piece of protection some 15–20 feet above them, and the bolt below offers no help for upward progress.

SOLUTION

First, remember to stay calm and encourage your partner. You wouldn't want someone yelling at you if you couldn't figure out tricky friction moves, so exercise understanding and compassion. If they've tried a dozen times, though, you both know it is time to do something.

Given that they're 50 feet from you, it is generally not advisable to drop them a strand of rope to pull on. The easiest way to get them through the difficult section is by hauling them, and because it's a slab—meaning at least a little bit of weight is on their feet—a 3:1 haul will likely be enough (see chapter 9).

Place your third hand below the belay device on the load strand and tie a friction hitch; next, clip that friction hitch with the brake strand coming out of your belay device—assuming you are belaying with an autoblocking belay device (like a Petzl Reverso or Black Diamond ATC Guide) or an assisted-braking belay device (like a Petzl GriGri or an Edelrid Eddy). As you haul them, have them push up with their feet and hands to make hauling easier. Tell them not to pull up on the rope, because that creates slack that you as the belayer are not able to take in.

CONSIDERATIONS

While you might consider having the second climber go into ascension mode, this creates problems similar to them just trying to "batman" up the rope. As they ascend, they will create slack, and unless they want to ascend all the way to the anchor, they will need to clip in to an intermediate anchor so that you can pull the slack out. Or they will need to create a new clip-in point by tying a figure eight on a bight and clipping it to their harness, and then just let the slack hang as they climb. Ascending the rope can be done safely but will be less fun and very likely a lot more time-consuming.

SCENARIO 2: BELAY DEVICE DROPPED MIDROUTE

You and your partner are four pitches up a six-pitch route, both enjoying the beautiful day and marveling that by sheer chance there is no one else on this popular route today. As you both stand clipped in to the anchor, you transition gear to your partner who is going to lead the next pitch. While doing so, you mistakenly unclip your belay device and watch in dread as it bounces a few times down the side of the cliff before dropping into a canopy of trees some 400 feet below you.

This route is within your and your partner's abilities and there is plenty of daylight remaining, but neither you nor your partner has ever climbed this route before. Both of you will need to be belayed on the remaining pitches above, and both of you will need to make the six single-rope-length rappels back to the ground. The majority of the rappels are off chain anchors.

SOLUTION

First, consider your abilities to perform the techniques discussed below. If you have these skills, your experience will be nearly the same as with two belay devices; without these skills, your odds of some sort of epic rise significantly.

To climb the final two pitches, the leader should be belayed with a traditional belay device and should build a munter hitch to belay the second (see chapter 1). The reason is that most people are far more experienced in belaying with a traditional belay device, and as the falls can be more severe catching a leader compared to holding a follower, the person belaying the leader should take the device and the person who leads the pitch should use a munter hitch to belay the second.

Once both climbers are at the top of the route, the better option is to use a double-locker rappel or the double-carabiner-brake rappel (see chapter 4). The double-locker rappel is much faster to set up and break down but requires at least two locking carabiners (which you can likely spare) and either a third locker or two more nonlocking carabiners opposite and opposed to clip in to your harness.

CONSIDERATIONS

While it is possible that you could rappel with a munter hitch, attempting to make six raps down even a fairly vertical wall will create twists so bad they will border on impossible to deal with. Even with the best technique, you will turn your rope into an utter rat's nest after just one or two raps.

SCENARIO 3: ONLY ONE ROPE FOR A TWO-ROPE RAPPEL

You and your partner climb a four-pitch route to the freestanding summit and walk across the top to the other side of the formation, where you'll need to make two rappels to get down. While eating lunch on the summit, you decide to read the descent description one more time, only to realize that it says you need *two* ropes to get down—but you brought only *one* 60-meter rope with you.

You quickly scour the internet, and it validates the guidebook's description: you do need two ropes to get down. You and your partner agonize over your poor planning. This is your third day out together, and all the other routes you have done needed only a single rope to get down, but this one has two rappels, both around 40–45 meters long.

SOLUTION

The best option to get down is a Reepschnur rappel (see chapter 4). In this situation, you likely should prerig the location of the knot and lower one person on a single strand down to the next set of anchors (see chapter 5). The climber not being lowered should take all available soft pieces of technical goods, especially longer slings and a cordelette if you have one. While lowering, make sure to close the system—tie a knot in the end of the rope—so you don't mistakenly lower your partner off the rope.

Once they are at the lower anchor, thread the chains (if you haven't already) with a little bit of slack on the strand leading to the lower climber. Tie an alpine butterfly knot (see chapter 1) on the side of the rope that isn't going directly down to the lower climber, and attach this end of the rope to your harness

Ian Nicholson leads up the third pitch of Promised Land *on the Goat Wall, Mazama, Washington.* (Photo by Andrew Burr)

so that you don't lose it. Rappel down on the single strand of rope going to the lower climber. Before committing to the system, ensure that when you load the long strand of rope, the knot blocks against the chains and is captured by the carabiner clipped between the two strands.

Once the short end of the rope comes tight, start attaching things to it. This "short end" will be only a "pull" end. Use your long pieces of soft material first, but anything

Tracey Bernstein follows the infamous chimney pitch on the Kor-Ingalls *on Castleton Tower, Castle Valley, Utah.*

works—cams, nuts, slings, quickdraws, you name it. Do this until you reach your partner at the lower rappel station. Pull down on the chain of items you have attached to the short strand of rope until you are able to retrieve it.

CONSIDERATIONS

While a Reepschnur rappel is a great technique for getting out of a jam,there is a higher likelihood of the rope getting stuck, due to both the bigger knot and all the items you have to attach to the short end in order to pull the rope. Because of this, it is generally better to bring the appropriate amount of rope. However, if you ever need to cut your rope, if a section of rope was damaged, or if the rappels require a longer rope or even two ropes, as was the case in this incident, the Reepschnur is likely your best option.

SCENARIO 4: LEADER STRUGGLES AT A CRUX

You and your partner are road-tripping to a new zone that is packed full of long traditional routes. Excited to be there, you and your buddy hop on a route you have been dreaming about for months. The grades are generally proving to be stiffer than at your local crag, and on a number of occasions you and your partner are forced to "take" (the belayer holds the lead climber's weight while they hang on a piece of protection).

While you are leading the last pitch, the route proves too difficult. The crack has only shallow, spaced finger pods, and poor footholds make it tricky to place protection. You eventually get a good piece of gear in, but you have tried six, seven, eight times to do the moves and are forced to take every time. You can't muster the muscle or the mental commitment to punch through the steep crack.

SOLUTION

A lot of people place gear while simply hanging on the rope, but unless it's a splitter crack, a little bit of aid-climbing technique will go a long way and will be *much* faster (see chapter 7). Besides being faster, it will also allow for much better placements because you can reach farther and it allows you to cover a lot more ground between placements.

Start by clipping a quickdraw in to the piece and hang off that rather than just

While we all love free climbing, don't be afraid of a little improvised aid if the situation demands it. If a section of rock is too hard to free climb, make upward progress by pulling on or clipping directly in to gear or by stepping in slings. Here, Ian Nicholson aids on South Early Winters Spire's Northeast Buttress, North Cascades, Washington. (Photo by Andrew Burr)

hanging on the rope. This will help improve your reach, and your belayer will thank you. Then clip a single-length sling in to the piece. It might take some effort, but try to step up into the sling. If you need to clip a second single-length sling to establish yourself before stepping into the higher sling, that is okay. Ideally, every time you place the next piece of gear, your last piece is below your waist. Pull in opposition to the weight of your feet rather than hanging from your harness on the piece. This will notably increase speed and the distance between placements.

CONSIDERATIONS

You can clip the rope to the higher piece (if it's bomber) to use it as an adjustable daisy chain, but if the piece is anything but bomber, then just stand in slings attached to the piece and avoid the temptation to clip the protection until it is at waist level.

SCENARIO 5: POWERFUL WIND DURING A RAPPEL

You and your partner are experienced alpine climbers and you just topped out on a long route in the mountains. You high-five on the summit and cruise over to the rappels just a few hours before dark.

The descent requires four single-rope rappels, and your rope must be sufficiently long. The wind, however, is ultrastrong—strong enough that the first bundle of rope your partner tosses blows nearly straight sideways and ends up in a twisted mess. You can see a party far below you battling with their ropes. While the rappels are steep, you should have a good line of sight between the rappel anchors.

SOLUTIONS

There are two primary solutions, depending on the ability of the team members to communicate and/or see each other.

The simplest solution is to lower one climber (see chapter 5) to the lower set of anchors with both ends of the rope. This ensures the rope gets where you want it to go and avoids having it be blown around by the wind.

If you can't communicate very well and there is no chance of visual contact (generally having just one of these conditions is fine), saddlebags are a good option (see chapter 4). Contrary to popular belief, saddlebags don't take that much time. Take in butterfly coils starting from the ends of the rope, as if you were going to throw them. But *don't* throw them; instead, place them inside tripled-up slings or quickdraws and do several sets. You can stack the two strands of rope together or keep them separate—it really comes down to whatever is more efficient for what you are doing—but generally 60 meters of rope (assuming you pay a little of it down the cliff face) will require three or four saddlebags that you drop as you descend.

CONSIDERATIONS

The advantage of saddlebagging over lowering is that there is no chance of miscommunication—of the lower climber passing the anchors without being able to communicate with the higher climber to stop lowering or of being put down on a ledge only to have a lot of slack accumulate. Sure, you could stack the rope to the point where it perfectly pays out, but that is generally more time-consuming than it's worth.

SCENARIO 6: ROPE GETS STUCK MIDRAPPEL

You just finished a steep and challenging long route, and you and your partner start down the rappels. They are all single-rope rappels, and your rope is sufficiently long. After completing the fourth of the route's six rappels, you pull the rope for what feels like only a foot or two and it won't budge; you try rocking it back and forth, but nothing: it won't move in either direction. You try using all your and your partner's weight to pull down on it, but the rope still won't budge in the slightest. . . .

SOLUTION

You still have access to both strands of rope, which means you know they are still threaded through the rappel anchor, so ascend the rope to retrieve it (see chapter 7). The route is steep, so using two slings is preferable to using a belay device in autoblocking mode, because a belay device will be more difficult to pull slack through. Tie each sling in a friction hitch, one of which you attach to your harness belay loop (your "waist" prusik) and the other fashioned as your "foot" prusik, with a loop for your foot. Before starting, tie a backup (in both strands of rope) in the form of a hard knot like

Andy Dahlen ascends the Freeblast *while climbing El Capitan's* Salathé Wall, *Yosemite National Park, California.*

a figure eight on a bight and clip it in to your belay loop with a locking carabiner.

To ascend, weight the waist friction hitch and slide the foot friction hitch up the rope. Then stand up to weight the foot friction hitch and slide the unweighted waist friction hitch up the rope. This technique allows you to make upward progress a foot or two at a time. Repeat until you reach the spot where the rope is stuck, free it, and rappel back down.

CONSIDERATIONS

It should be noted that if you don't have access to both strands, you would need to lead back up to the rappel anchor. You should never ascend a single strand of rope attached with unknown integrity and/or around an unknown anchor. You are literally gambling your life without knowing the odds.

SCENARIO 7: FOLLOWER KNOCKED OUT BY ROCKFALL

You have led the third pitch of a four-pitch route; now you are belaying the second climber directly off the anchor, and they are just below you. You cheer them on through the final section of the pitch as they climb

Ryan Davdistel on the East Face of Lexington Tower, North Cascades, Washington (Photo by Andrew Burr)

to around 15 feet below the belay. All of a sudden a rock flies by, seemingly out of nowhere. You shout, *"Rock, rock, rock, rock!"* and close your eyes as it barely misses you when it flies by. A millisecond later, you hear the horrible sound of it striking your partner and feel the vibrations through the rope. The rope goes taut. You look down and shout to your friend, and there's no response. . . . They appear to be breathing but are slumped over in their harness, hanging unconscious against the wall. Their helmet is pulverized but at least, at this point, it has likely saved your partner's life.

SOLUTION

There is a lot you need to do, but the first is to stay calm and take a deep breath. While time is important, doing things correctly is more important than hurrying for speed's sake; remember the saying "Slow is smooth but smooth is fast." In this situation, you can see the injured climber; later you figure out that your friend took a direct hit to the helmet with a baseball-sized rock (medical care is intentionally omitted, as it is outside the scope of this book).

It is a good idea to first put a stopper knot behind the belay device to act as a "catastrophe" knot in the event that something goes awry. In this situation, it is easier to transition into baseline (see chapter 3) before setting up a counterbalanced rappel. Once you get on a counterbalanced rappel (see chapter 4), tend the friction hitch so that it doesn't grab the rope, keeping the injured climber at a steady elevation. Once you and the injured climber are side by side (or at the desired distance), let the friction hitch grab so you both descend at the same rate.

At the anchor, you will need to perform a weighted transition (also in chapter 4) using the rope or other long piece of material to attach both of you to the anchor in a counterbalanced fashion. This is a tricky maneuver that should be practiced at home before you need it in the field. With this technique, you are able to shift the injured climber slightly by "counterbalancing" them with their own body weight.

Once you are both attached via a counterbalanced system, attach both of you to a double-length sling and rig a tandem rappel (also in chapter 4). Rappel as many times as necessary.

CONSIDERATIONS

If the injured climber is not in visual contact, it might be worth rappelling down to check on them and provide medical care if needed. Transitioning to baseline is not necessary if you have two belay devices or if you have only a very short distance to go, in which case you could consider a munter hitch.

SCENARIO 8: LEADER INJURED IN A SHORT FALL

You are belaying the leader on the last pitch of a three-pitch route. Around halfway up the pitch and 50 feet or so out from the belay, your partner gets to one of the more difficult sections of the route. They place a #5 Camalot and inch up an off-width crack in the corner. Around 5 feet above the #5, while trying to stem out to a distant foothold, their foot pops off and they take a very awkward fall with their arms deep in the crack. You catch the relatively short fall and shout a few words of encouragement and ask if they are okay.

The lead climber shouts down that their arm got stuck briefly in the crack when they fell and now they can't move their arm. After some discussion about the state of their injury, you and your partner determine that their shoulder is dislocated and still out of the socket—a very painful injury that in most circumstances leaves the injured arm useless and unable to bear weight.

SOLUTION

Since the leader has less than half the rope out, you first need to lower them to the anchor (see chapter 5). Generally, it's a good idea to leave at least two or three pieces of protection, but because of the severity of the injury, you just leave everything in to focus on getting them down more quickly. Once they are at the anchor, you and your partner need to make two more rappels to get down.

In this case, you think it will be difficult to hear and/or see your partner, so you opt to tandem rappel (see chapter 4) instead of lowering. You thread the ropes to the middle mark, tie knots in the ends, and toss them down the steep cliff below. You girth-hitch a double-length sling to your harness, tie an overhand knot in the sling at around one-third of the distance across it (with the shorter length closer to your girth hitch), and clip the other end of the sling to your partner's belay loop; this way your partner will hang just below you during the rappel (side by side would be quite uncomfortable for their shoulder).

You clip your belay device in to the loops on either side of the knot in the sling, then you thread the ropes through your device. You attach your third-hand friction-hitch backup, putting an extra wrap in the hitch so it has enough friction to handle the weight of both you and your partner.

You do not need to do any complex attachment systems at the subsequent anchors

Andrew Lamb leads the tricky overhang on the second pitch of Solar Flare, *Red Rock, Nevada.*

because, while your partner is in pain, they are conscious and able to clip and unclip themself at the anchors.

CONSIDERATIONS

Don't underestimate how difficult it can be to try to remove cams or nuts with only one good arm and the other arm in a lot of pain. Meanwhile, if there is any question about the injured person's ability to control the brake strand while rappelling, you can choose between either a tandem rappel or a lower.

SCENARIO 9: LEADER INJURED IN A LONG FALL

You are belaying the leader, who is 150 feet out on the first pitch of a long multipitch sport climb. After clipping a quickdraw to the final lead bolt of the pitch, your friend reaches down to pull up slack to clip it. Moments before they clip, the worst happens: their foot pops and they take a long, awkward fall. The last bolt was only 8–10 feet down, but with the rope stretch and the additional rope brought into play from the blown clip, they easily fall

25-plus feet. Unfortunately, in the middle of their fall, their feet land squarely on a small 8-inch-wide ledge before the momentum of their body pulls them off. They plummet a few more body lengths before the rope comes tight.

You shout up to see if they are okay. The leader sounds a little shaken up, to say the least, but mentally with it; they say that they didn't hit their head but they are afraid that both of their ankles are broken, and attempting to put any weight on them is excruciating.

SOLUTION

Even if you had another rope, you can't get this person down by lowering because the knot would jam into any protection they have clipped on the pitch. You need to escape the belay and ascend to them.

First, tie off your belay device (see chapter 3). You are belaying on the ground, but, like a lot of routes that start on the ground, there is no anchor and the first and second bolts are around 8–12 feet off the ground, a fairly common distance.

Once your belay device is tied off, you ascend the rope, backing yourself up every 6 feet or so (see chapter 7).You ascend nearly all the way up to the leader, leaving two or three pieces of protection in place. You then lower them a short distance (see chapter 5), build a new anchor, attach the team to it, and rappel down, using whatever rappel method suits the terrain and injuries.

CONSIDERATIONS

When belaying on the ground, you may or may not have the ability to transfer the load to an anchor. Any time you can transfer the load to an anchor, that is generally preferable, as the hanging climber won't creep slowly downward or get bounced around as much.

Once your belay device is tied off, you can either ascend the rope or climb counterbalanced, which causes the leader to slowly descend. However, counterbalancing has some serious downsides if the person is hurt (see chapter 8).

SCENARIO 10: LEADER INJURED AND ROPE DAMAGED IN A SHORT FALL

You and your partner are on a newer route with some seriously suspicious rock. The plan to get down after the climb is to just rappel the route using single 60-meter-rope rappels. On the third pitch of the five-pitch route, you belay your partner as they navigate a section of particularly bad rock. They have less than 50 percent of the rope out, but they aren't that close to you, maybe 60–70 feet. They shout down for you to watch them, as they have gotten to a particularly rotten section. "These holds are terrible," they shout. Around 8 or so feet out from their last bolt, they suddenly shout, "*Faaaallllllling!*" You hear the blasting sounds of several large rocks bouncing down the wall just out to your left and feel the rope come tight. You know this isn't good.

You shout up to your partner to see if they are okay. They respond that they pulled out several rocks, some of which ricocheted into both their forearm and their upper arm, and they are worried their arm might be broken. You both decide to forget about the gear clipped to the wall and just get down. As the belayer, you lower them down to the anchor and pull the rope. As you pull it, you now see there is a significantly damaged section of rope, on which your partner was just lowered. To get to the ground, you need to make two 29.5-meter rope-stretching rappels.

SOLUTION

There are two problems here, both of which contribute to the solution you choose. One problem is that you have a damaged section of rope, but the rappels are long enough that you can't just not use it. The other is that you have a partner with a painful and significant arm injury.

The best solution to this situation is to lower the injured climber (see chapter 5) using an in-line knot pass (see chapter 6) to get them to the ground, at which point they can untie. You then pull the rope up and perform two Reepschnur rappels by yourself to get to the ground.

CONSIDERATIONS

Without the partner with the injured arm, you could just rig a Reepschnur rappel by tying an alpine butterfly at the midpoint of the rope and clipping it back to the other side of the rope once it has been threaded through the rappel chains (see chapter 4). Doing this would mean you wouldn't even need to isolate the damaged section of rope with an overhand knot, as that entire side would just be a "pull cord."

If you were worried about your partner, you could consider a tandem rappel, but while this would work from a technical perspective, it might be pretty uncomfortable for your partner, depending on the extent of their injuries. Any knot pass can be implemented for most sustained vertical lowers, but in the above situation an in-line knot pass is likely to be the best because it will get the injured person down in a timely manner without them having to rappel with a potentially damaged arm. They will also not be subjected to their injured arm potentially (and almost certainly painfully) bumping against you during a tandem rappel.

Stephen Williams searches for pro on the Northwest Rib *of Mount Shuksan, North Cascades, Washington.*

Opposite: *A climber ascends the* West Arête *of the Bastille, Eldorado Canyon State Park, Rocky Mountains, Colorado.* (Photo by Dale Remsberg)

CHAPTER 13

Preparation and Practice

Not only does this book provide a number of self-rescue techniques for the most common situations climbers are faced with—techniques that can be used in a range of applications—but it also presents them in ways that are replicable in the field. While it helps to read about various skills and strategies, it is far more important to run through them in a low-stakes environment, either at home or at the crag. Practice ascending the rope, rappelling counterbalanced, setting up a 3:1 haul—repetition is essential to being able to perform any of these maneuvers in a sticky situation or, worse yet, during a stress-filled real-life rescue. To increase your odds of success, practice, practice, and practice some more.

WHAT SHOULD YOU BRING?

The goal of this book is not to encourage you to bring a lot of "extra" gear but to teach you how to effectively use the gear you are most likely to already have with you. Obviously, every route will require a unique set of equipment, but this section covers some of the soft goods and tools that you would be wise to carry on nearly every technical multipitch rock or alpine route—even on fast-and-light ascents. Each item has a multitude of applications. (For information on the following specific items of gear, see the relevant chapters: headlamps, in the introduction; the Beal Escaper, chapter 4; mechanical prusiks, chapter 7; mechanical ratchets and pulleys, chapter 9; communication devices, chapter 11.)

DOUBLE-LENGTH SLINGS

Two double-length (48-inch) slings are very useful tools you can have on a multipitch route, and they weigh almost nothing. When used with a third hand (see below), they can take the place of a cordelette.

THIRD HAND

A short piece of 5- to 6-millimeter cord—used primarily as a third-hand rappel backup, tied in a friction hitch such as a prusik—has a near-infinite number of additional applications, from ascending a rope to hauling (where it acts as a tractor) to transferring a load (where it can be used with the back side of the belayer's clove-hitch tie-in to the anchor to assist in weighted transfers).

CORDELETTE

While it is possible with some creativity to rig most anchors with a double-length sling, a 15- to 21-foot piece of 6- to 7-millimeter cord—a.k.a. a cordelette—makes building

There is no "perfect kit" or single piece of gear that works for all situations; instead, bring not only the gear you need for a given climb but also the knowledge and skills for performing a wide range of tasks with that gear. Here, Ian Nicholson carries a heavy rack on an attempt of an unclimbed face in the Kichatna Mountains of the Alaska Range. (Photo by Graham Zimmerman)

complex anchors *super* fast, particularly if you are running low on gear. The low cost of 6- to 7-millimeter cord also means you hopefully won't think twice about cutting it up to beef up older rappel anchors or to facilitate building your own anchors in an emergency. Also, while you don't need a cordelette for self-rescue, it certainly makes most rescue techniques far easier.

LOCKING CARABINERS

Climbers attempting a multipitch route should strongly consider bringing at least three locking carabiners (a.k.a. lockers) each: two for an auto-blocking belay device and one for the climber's clove-hitch attachment to the anchor. Having one extra locker beyond that helps. Note: you might see "HMS" on some locking carabiners, which stands for *halbmastwurf sicherung*, a German phrase that means "half clove-hitch belay."

BELAY DEVICE

As discussed in chapter 2, using either an assisted-braking belay device (ABD) or an autoblocking belay device is a worthwhile option and as subtle an increase in gear weight as it gets. Play with using an ABD in a multi-

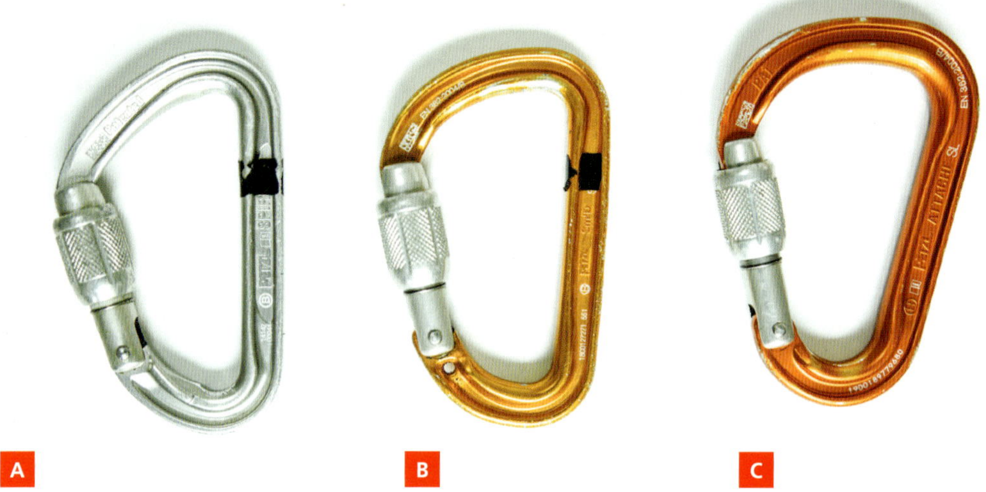

Figure 13-1. A variety of locking carabiners: **a**, *lighter-weight;* **b**, *midsized that can still be used to adjust a clove hitch;* **c**, *full-sized HMS or pear-shaped.*

pitch environment; it might seem like "one more thing," but the level of security these devices provide makes them worth it. They are also the lowest-friction and easiest-to-pull device for belaying a second climber so long as you are climbing in a group of only two. They just add a tremendous amount of security and facilitate better belaying while also opening the door to using a much greater number of techniques, from simple fixes to get out of a jam to complex rescues. See chapter 2 for a detailed discussion of belay devices.

KNIFE

Having at least one knife in the group on multipitch routes is invaluable: it facilitates retreat from any point, and it is the one tool that can modify any piece of load-bearing soft goods you have with you (fig. 13-2). While a lot of climbers like to joke about "cutting the rope," the ability to do just that if the rope gets stuck or you have to build a new rappel

Figure 13-2. A knife clipped to a climbing harness: this extremely light yet extremely versatile tool is a worthwhile addition to the team gear. (Photo by Brian Muller)

anchor(s) or clean up an old or dangerous rappel anchor makes having a knife worthwhile. Even on routes with bolted anchors, the rope can get stuck to the point where it cannot be retrieved, or it can blow sideways off the route you climbed up. A knife also lets you cut up your soft goods to reinforce anchors.

QUICK LINKS

Be a steward: on popular routes, consider bringing a rated quick link or two and material to improve existing anchors and replace old webbing that you cut away. Climbing quick links—oval plated- or stainless-steel rings closed with a screw gate that come in diverse diameters, materials, and shapes—are perfect for creating an anchor point. Quick links are what attach chains to bolt hangers at rappel anchors and are what you leave on cord or webbing on rappel anchors on trees, blocks, or gear tied together. While webbing is initially stronger than the 6- to 7-millimeter cord that cordelette is made of, it is significantly less durable and will degrade and lose strength considerably faster. As a result, it is preferable to use a 6- to 7-millimeter cord instead of webbing on your rappel anchor.

WHAT SHOULD YOU PRACTICE?

In climbing, there seems to be a near-infinite number of not only problems but also techniques to solve them. The truth is, while there are a lot of possible situations and solutions for them, if you learn just a handful of techniques, you can solve a very large number of problems. To that end, this book is arranged around broader themes, presenting skills that have a wide range of applications. For further practice, consider signing up for a course or hiring an AMGA-certified guide in your local area for a day of instruction in rescue skills. Even the most experienced climbers will likely get a lot out of it.

Andy Dahlen is happy that his belayer is using an assisted-braking belay device (ABD) on Davis-Holland/Lovin' Arms *on the Upper Town Wall, Index, Washington.* (Photo by Jim Meyers)

HOW TO PRACTICE

The US military has done dozens of studies on human performance under stress, particularly in situations that deal with a significant injury or the chance of death. Nearly all of these

A group of guides practices hauling systems during an AMGA Advanced Alpine Guide Course, North Cascades, Washington. (Photo by Jason Antin)

studies found that while the vast majority of people perform poorly in stressful situations with which they are less familiar, after training and practice, people perform much better in the same scenarios.

This means a little bit of training can go a long way. Maybe practicing some of the techniques described in this book will simply help you get that rope free or get down before dark, or it might just help you save yourself, your partner, or someone you don't even know. I would never have guessed I would use any of these techniques to save someone, but over my 23-year climbing career I have been involved in six situations where inaction would very likely have resulted in death. And there have been countless other instances where these skills helped me to get out of a jam. Practicing skills on the ground is an excellent way to stay fresh, and going over systems for a few hours at the start of every season will go a long way toward setting you up for success.

The Example of Avalanche Beacon Drills

If you are a backcountry skier, snowboarder, or snowmobiler, you likely wear an avalanche beacon when you go into the backcountry—and you probably practice with your beacon a minimum of once a year. You probably know that this is important, because time is crucial when it comes to locating people who are buried in an avalanche and digging them out. The longer someone is trapped underneath the snow, the lower their odds of survival, which drop significantly after the first 15 minutes.

While the relevance of avalanche beacons to climbing self-rescue isn't immediately apparent, the through line is the importance of practice. Say a group of backcountry skiers are suddenly forced to find two partners who have just disappeared under an avalanche: the rescuers are faced with an immediately stressful and potentially life-threatening situation. People who haven't practiced with their beacons have little chance of locating a buried beacon, let alone two, but people who train and practice have a much better likelihood of success. The idea of practice is not to enable you to rush through the necessary steps more quickly; it's to make you more proficient, and faster as a result—and the same is true with technical climbing rescues. Practice being proficient so that when you are faced with a stressful situation, you can safely and efficiently resolve it.

SKILLS TO PRACTICE FOR MULTIPITCH ROCK CLIMBING

Escaping the belay and transferring the load to the anchor (see chapter 3) is a cornerstone of technical rescue: if you can't get out of the system, it is pretty tough to do anything else. The other skills described below begin with what you are most likely to need and/or what is easier to perform, with chapter references to help you find the information for your practice session.

Passing a Knot

Having to pass a knot isn't among the more common problems that climbers need to deal with, but the technical concept of transferring a load from one strand of rope to another *is* a cornerstone of technical rescue and a basis for close to half the techniques described in this book. Practice passing a knot using a few different techniques (see chapter 6), because the skills you learn and become familiar with will be foundational to all technical rescue techniques and will easily give you a greater understanding of technical systems. Practice an improvised knot pass, an in-line knot pass, and rappelling past a knot. While these are nice skills to have, the concepts learned in knot passing are transferable across all rescue systems.

Hauling

Setting up a simple 3:1 hauling system is easy, takes only a tiny bit of gear, and has countless applications (see chapter 9). It's a good technique to have wired into your skill set in order to help a friend get through a crux move, to pull up a heavier pack, or to deal with more serious situations such as unweighting some sort of load that is clipped to the anchor. This skill is super easy, and you may have a climbing partner who will be eternally grateful to you if they end up on a route too challenging for them and need the assist of a simple 3:1 haul.

Ascending

Having the skills to ascend either a single or a double rope is invaluable. It is also a technique worth practicing on a cliff, a tree, or some other steep feature to learn what it feels like. Ascend a rope using the gear you will likely have on your harness, practicing single- and double-strand improvised ascension methods (see chapter 7). However, always be wary of ascending a single strand of rope that failed to come down when you pulled the ropes after a rappel, as you have next to no ability to assess its strength or integrity.

Tino Villanueva practices an improvised knot pass. (Photo by Jim Meyers)

Lowering Off the Anchor

Make sure you know how to lower your partner directly off an anchor (fig. 13-3). This is a simple concept—you might not necessarily need to practice it all the time if you are proficient with it—but it's still a super valuable skill that a lot of climbers aren't familiar with, often using less efficient work-arounds instead. The ability to lower someone or something directly off the anchor using a few different methods based on the tools you are likely to have with you is invaluable (see chapter 5).

Double-Locker Rappel

At some point, you will forget or drop your belay device, so being able to set up a double-locker rappel using just carabiners (fig. 13-4) is a skill that most climbers will find themselves using. Knowing how to rappel without a belay device, while not the most common of techniques, helps you avoid doing something sketchy. Whether it's for a single rappel or many consecutive ones, being able to efficiently construct a double-locker rappel (see chapter 4) lets you descend safely, smoothly, and in a timely manner.

Munter Hitch for Belaying

Similar to knowing how to rig a double-locker rappel, knowing how to construct a munter hitch for belaying a leader or a second climber (see chapter 1) is an invaluable skill that most climbers will use at some point in their

Employing a 3:1 hauling system while belaying off the anchor (Photo by Jim Meyers)

Kristin Arnold works on transitioning from a rappel to an ascent.

Figure 13-3. A climber is lowered using a belay device with the brake strand redirected. (Photo by Dale Remsberg)

careers. The munter can also be used for lowering (see chapter 5). A reminder: while the munter is an excellent tool for belaying, it is a poor option for steeper consecutive rappels.

Tandem Rappel

A tandem rappel is when two people—or one person and a haul bag or other larger load—rappel off a single device. This technique could be used when there is one competent climber and another climber is scared, injured, or otherwise unable to rappel because they are incapacitated, are at risk of slipping into an unconscious state, or are nervous. The other reason to rig a tandem rappel is for descending with a haul bag, as this gives the rappeller both better control of the haul bag and the ability to "escape" should the situation require it. Tandem rappels aren't versatile in their application, but if you need them, then generally the situation is dire, so at least familiarize yourself with the setup (see chapter 4).

Figure 13-4. A double-locker rappel setup uses two locking carabiners to create friction for the rappel, plus two nonlocking carabiners opposite but not opposed as a backup. (Photo by Jim Meyers)

Counterbalanced Rappel

A counterbalanced rappel, like the tandem rappel, is not as versatile as other techniques discussed in chapter 4, but the process of transitioning from a belay from above into a counterbalanced rappel is an excellent mental exercise that will test a number of skills. A complex skill that involves numerous steps (see chapter 4), the counterbalanced rappel is undoubtedly one of the less commonly used techniques discussed in this book, but if the second climber is injured, it is extremely likely that the counterbalanced rappel will be the technique you'll need. Practicing it also reinforces several other techniques, thus sharpening your skills and your ability to critically think through a given situation.

TOO FAST, TOO FURIOUS

BY ZACK "BONES" SMITH

In June 1999 at 21 years old, Aaron Martin and I ventured to the Ruth Gorge, Alaska, to see what the real mountains were like. We were both working in a warehouse for minimum wage and routinely sold our blood plasma to finance our first big trip. When the plane dropped us onto the Ruth Glacier for three weeks, I realized I had never actually snow camped. The pilot told us that when we wanted to leave, we should stamp out a runway and write a message in the snow. This would be our only communication with the outside world. He warned us to ration our food in case he couldn't pick us up for "a while."

We were the sole humans in the entire gorge, and the only hint of civilization was the occasional plane buzzing far above us. All we could see was white snow, gray rock, and blue sky. The never-ending silence was interrupted only by the cacophonous collapse of a serac or an avalanche. Several times our camp was sprayed by powder snow shedded from a peak miles away.

I had been scared before, but this was a new, deeper fear. Climbers with a lot more experience than me had died here.

We cautiously explored up and down the glacier on snowshoes and made several attempts at climbing something. Every time we tried a route, it would deteriorate into absolute kitty-litter choss and we would flee back to our snow prison. The snowshoes were a terrible mode of transportation compared to skis, so roped crevasse falls were an almost daily occurrence. We endured large stretches of bad weather and learned what the term "Ping Pong World" meant: the glacier would get so socked in with clouds that we couldn't differentiate between the ground and the sky—it was like being trapped inside a giant ping-pong ball.

Despite our numerous failures on other peaks, we decided to attempt our main goal. The west face of the Eye Tooth shoots out of the glacier for 2,800 feet of nearly vertical granite. The line is obvious, a straight shot on a protruding prow leading to a spiked summit. When we penguin-waddled to the base on our snowshoes, we knew we had found what we were looking for. Both of us had learned how to climb in Yosemite Valley, and this route felt like the alpine version of El Capitan.

That spring in Yosemite National Park, the speed-climbing craze was in full effect. There was a major mental shift happening on the bigger climbs. If you didn't bother bringing extraneous equipment like food, water, or shelter, you could rocket up a route in a morning that had traditionally taken several days. Icons like Dean Potter, Timmy O'Neill, Sean Leary, Rolando Garibotti, Jose Pereyra, Miles Smart, Hans Florine, Steve Schneider, and Russ Mitrovich were reinventing big wall climbing every week. Techniques like short-fixing and simul-climbing were shrinking the massive routes into mere outings. The aggressive, ballistic, and all-out style had its dangers. All the normal safety margins were shaved away to gain another minute. Close calls and huge whippers were always being discussed around campfires and picnic tables. Much like car racing, to be the fastest you had to be the closest to crashing.

Zack "Bones" Smith leading on an attempt of the Citadel in the Kichatna Mountains, Alaska Range (Photo by Josh Wharton)

Aaron and I were way too shy to actually discuss these techniques with our heroes, but we listened to the stories and scribbled notes on napkins when no one was looking. Slowly and quietly, we ticked off all the major features in the Valley in this new style. The freedom of moving up huge swaths of difficult terrain was like hard alcohol to us, and we gulped it down with little restraint.

So we had packed our bags full of gear and the confidence of youth and headed north to Alaska.

Three-quarters of the way into the 23-pitch route, everything was coming together. All the bad memories, terror, and struggle were washed away by pitch after pitch of perfect alpine granite. By using the techniques we had practiced in Yosemite, we were cruising up the peak.

Until the storm hit.

We either didn't see it coming or ignored it. Within minutes, the rock was covered in verglas and the wind was ripping open the sky. It was clearly time to bail. On our first rappel, the rope got stuck and we didn't have the technical skills yet to attempt to retrieve it. Instead of reascending the pitch, we panicked and cut the rope. No problem; we had two ropes. Just a rappel or two later, the second rope got stuck. This time we tried to go up and retrieve it, but we didn't know a good system for it and quickly bailed on that possibility.

We were forced to cut the second rope. We stared down 2,000 feet of vertical, snow-covered granite and began rappelling with two 25-meter pieces of rope. The route is set up with rappel stations every 60 meters so we knew we would come up short every time.

Ahhhh, hindsight: if only we had known then what we know now . . . if only someone had told us what a Reepschnur rappel was, that would have made our lives a lot easier. . . .

As we continued down, the buildup of snow made us miss existing anchors on the moderate terrain on the lower-angled bottom of the face. The ropes snarled as we rappelled and got hung up every time. Saddlebagging? Not something that was on our minds.

We started changing our tactics: One of us would lower the other who would then set gear on the way down. Then the first person would belay the top person down, with that person cleaning the anchor and gear, essentially down-climbing on lead without leaving anything behind—we needed every piece. Our tiny rack dwindled. We used our ice hammer to smash Stoppers into cracks, a technique we called "Stopper heading." We committed to several one-piece anchors in this way after the heavier person went first with a backup. At one point, the only option was to sling a horn for an anchor, but we were out of slings, so we chopped a section off the end of one of our ropes to leave behind.

The speed-climbing concoction that we had enjoyed on the sunny walls of California was tasting very bitter in the cold of Alaska. While the two areas might both feature large granite walls, this was a very different arena. It might sound "cool" to epic, but it wasn't—it was just cold. Every rappel down, we just wanted to survive our experience. We wished we had known more options in order to ascend to retrieve a stuck rope; we wished we had known more efficient ways to lower; and we *really* wished we'd known about the Reepschnur rappel to deal with having chopped the rope. Even saddlebagging on the lower, snow-covered rock face would have made our situation far easier to deal with.

The bottom line is, as you get strong and attempt bolder and more committing routes, make sure your ability to deal with unforeseen issues increases at an equal rate.

Zack "Bones" Smith learned how to climb in Yosemite with his dad using hip belays and swami belts. Single-push technical terrain in alpine environments like Alaska and Patagonia is his forte, but he also enjoys casual afternoon bouldering sessions with friends.

Acknowledgments

Thank you to my two sons, Henry and Hayden, and my wife, Rebecca Schroeder, for their support in this project. I'd like to thank everyone I have ever been lucky enough to share a rope with, but particularly my longtime climbing partners Ryan O'Connell, Graham Zimmerman, Graham McDowell, Tino Villanueva, and Andy Dahlen.

I want to thank Larry Goldie, Jeff Ward, Dale Remsberg, and Chris McNamara for their endless mentorship and inspiration. I want to thank Tino Villanueva, Rachel Spitzer, Chris Marshall, Neil Satterfield, Matt Schonwald, Adam Butterfield, and Brian Muller for being willing to pose for photos and Jim Meyers and Truc Allen for being willing to take photos. Additional huge thanks to Mikey Schaefer, Aaron Burr, Tom Evans, Kurt Hicks, Chip Daly, Jonathon Spitzer, Jason Antin, Josh Wharton, Lindsay Fixmer, Anna Pfaff, Sarah Janin, and Dustin Portzline for the use of their spectacular photos throughout the book.

And I must thank Graham Zimmerman, Angela Hawse, Mikey Schaefer, Seth Waterfall, Ron Funderburke, Chantel Astorga, Ron Funderburk,Larry Goldie, Tino Villanueva, Emilie Drinkwater, Alan Rousseau, Dale Remsberg, Rachel Spitzer, Robert Smith (a.k.a. Uncle Rob), Mike Soucy, Silas Rossi, Jonathan Spitzer, Cheri Higman, and Zack "Bones" Smith for writing excerpts, sharing their opinions, and helping this book provide additional insight while also taking it to another level.

Additional thanks to my family and friends Mackenzie Nicholson, Jussi Tahtinen, Jonathan Nicholson, Detmar and Susan Schroeder, Josh Brewer, Alex Chew, and Debbie Black and to my Aunt Sue and Uncle Bob (Nicholson) and Aunt Ago (Agnes) Sykers. Also to my mom, Megan Nicholson (may she rest in peace). Additional big thanks to other life influencers Greg and Paula Shaw, Steve Swenson, Matt Schonwald, Jaime Pollitte, Paul McKinley, John Race, Oliva Cussen, and Mark Gunlogson.

Thank you to Yosemite Search and Rescue (YOSAR), Seattle Mountain Rescue, and Jack Cramer for the use of their photos.

I would like to personally thank each and every person I have ever shared a rope with, while teaching courses or while guiding. There are too many to name, but don't think that I don't feel extreme gratitude, for you have helped to shape me as a person and build me up to who I am today.

Lastly, sincere thanks to all those associated with Mountaineers Books for helping me to produce the best book I possibly could on the subject: Kate Rogers for trusting I could do it; Mary Metz for guiding me through the process; Kris Fulsaas, Matt Samet, and Laura Case Larson for helping me to express myself coherently; and Laura Shaw and McKenzie Long for putting it all together with design and production skills.

Suggested Reading

Chauvin, Marc, and Rob Coppolillo. *The Mountain Guide Manual: The Comprehensive Reference—From Belaying to Rope Systems and Self-Rescue*. Guilford, CT: Globe Pequot/Falcon, 2017.

Donahue, Topher, and Craig Luebben. *Rock Climbing Anchors: A Comprehensive Guide. 2nd ed.* Seattle: Mountaineers Books, 2019.

Fasulo, David. *Self-Rescue.* 2nd ed. Guilford, CT: Globe Pequot/Falcon, 2011.

Fitch, Nate, and Ron Funderburke. *Climbing: Knots*. Guilford, CT: Globe Pequot/Falcon, 2015.

Forgey, William W. *Wilderness Medicine: Beyond First Aid*. 7th ed. Guilford, CT: Globe Pequot/Falcon, 2017.

Kirkpatrick, Andy. *Down: The Complete Descent Manual for Climbers, Alpinists and Mountaineers.* Hull, UK: Andrew Kirkpatrick Ltd., 2020.

Lentz, Martha J., Steven C. Macdonald, and Jan D. Carline. *Mountaineering First Aid.* 5th ed. Seattle: Mountaineers Books, 2004.

Linxweiler, Eric, and Mike Maude, eds. *Mountaineering: The Freedom of the Hills*. 10th ed. Seattle: Mountaineers Books, 2024.

Lipke, Rick. *Technical Rescue Riggers Guide.* 2nd ed. Bellingham, WA: Conterra, 2009.

Long, John, and Bob Gaines. *Climbing Anchors.* 3rd ed. Guilford, CT: Globe Pequot/Falcon, 2013.

———. *Climbing Anchors Field Guide.* 2nd ed. Guilford, CT: Globe Pequot/Falcon, 2014.

Luebben, Craig. *Knots for Climbers.* 3rd ed., revised and updated by Clyde Soles. Guilford, CT: Globe Pequot/Falcon, 2011.

National Ski Patrol. *Mountain Travel and Rescue: National Ski Patrol's Manual for Mountain Rescue*. 2nd ed. Seattle: Mountaineers Books, 2012.

Olliffe, Neville, and Madeleine Rowles-Olliffe. *Knots: The Step-by-Step Guide to Tying the Perfect Knot for Every Situation*. Seattle: Skipstone, 2010.

Owen, Peter. *The Ultimate Book of Knots.* Guilford, CT: Globe Pequot/Lyons Press, 2003.

Phillips, Kens with James Thompson. *Technical Rescue Handbook.* 11th ed. Washington, DC: US Department of the Interior, National Park Service, Emergency Services, 2014.

Prattley, Grant. *Rope Rescue and Rigging: Field Guide*. 3rd ed. Christchurch, NZ: Over the Edge Rescue, 2020.

Soles, Clyde. *The Outdoor Knots Book.* Seattle: Mountaineers Books, 2004.

Wilkerson, James A., Ernest C. Moore, and Ken Zafren, eds. *Medicine for Mountaineering and Other Wilderness Activities*. 6th ed. Seattle: Mountaineers Books, 2010.

Index

Page numbers in *italics* denote figures.

Photo by Chad Thatcher

An internationally licensed IFMGA/UIAGM mountain guide, **Ian Nicholson** has been guiding for nearly two decades and climbing for more than 25 years. He has climbed all over the world with over a dozen first ascents to his credit.

In addition to working as a full-time mountain guide, Ian instructs and examines as part of the American Mountain Guides Association's (AMGA) National Instructor team, serves on the AMGA's technical committee, and works for the American Institute for Avalanche Research and Education (AIARE) as both an instructor trainer and a pro instructor. In these roles he is directly involved in training the next generation of mountain guides and avalanche professionals. Ian has also participated in six highly consequential technical rescues, using many of the techniques outlined in this book. He is the recipient of two Denali Pro Pin Awards for assisting other climbers in dire need in the Alaska Range.

Ian's writing credits include the guidebook *SUPERTOPO: Washington Pass Climbing*, and he is a contributor to *Climbing* magazine, OutdoorGearLab.com, and WildSnow.com. He lives in Seattle with his wife, Rebecca, and two sons, Henry and Hayden.

recreation • lifestyle • conservation

MOUNTAINEERS BOOKS including its two imprints, Skipstone and Braided River, is a leading publisher of quality outdoor recreation, sustainability, and conservation titles. As a 501(c)(3) nonprofit, we are committed to supporting the environmental and educational goals of our organization by providing expert information on human-powered adventure, sustainable practices at home and on the trail, and preservation of wilderness.

Our publications are made possible through the generosity of donors, and through sales of 700 titles on outdoor recreation, sustainable lifestyle, and conservation. To donate, purchase books, or learn more, visit us online:

MOUNTAINEERS BOOKS
1001 SW Klickitat Way, Suite 201 • Seattle, WA 98134
800-553-4453 • mbooks@mountaineersbooks.org • www.mountaineersbooks.org

An independent nonprofit publisher since 1960

OTHER TITLES YOU MIGHT ENJOY FROM MOUNTAINEERS BOOKS

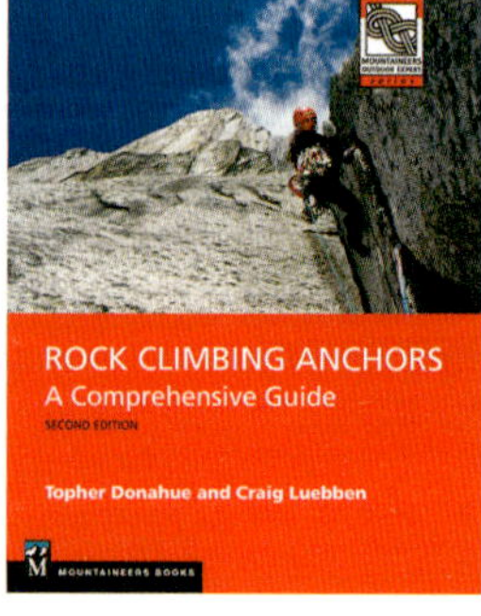